A CAPTAIN'S MANDATE

By the same author

Ensign in Italy

A CAPTAIN'S MANDATE

Palestine: 1946–48

by

Philip Brutton

LEO COOPER
LONDON

TO THE WELSH GUARDS
AND TO
THE VICTIMS OF TERRORISM
OF ALL NATIONALITIES AND RELIGIONS

First Published in Great Britain in 1996
by
LEO COOPER
190 Shaftesbury Avenue, London WC2H 8JL
an imprint of
Pen & Sword Books Ltd,
47 Church Street,
Barnsley, South Yorkshire S70 2AS

A CIP record for this book is available from the British Library

ISBN 0 85052 497 0

Typeset in Monotype Plantin by
Phoenix Typesetting, Ilkley, West Yorkshire

Printed in Great Britain by Redwood Books, Trowbridge, Wilts

Contents

Abbreviations

A	The A side of AA & QMG i.e. administration and law.
AA & QMG	Assistant Adjutant & Quartermaster General.
ADC	Aide-de-Camp.
Adj.	Adjutant.
Air O.P.	Air Observation Point/Post.
ALA	Arab Liberation Army.
AMWD	Air Ministry Works Department.
BEME	Brigade Electrical & Mechanical Engineer.
Bde.	Brigade.
BIO	Brigade Intelligence Officer.
Bn.	Battalion.
C.in C.	Commander-in-Chief.
CMO	Chief Medical Officer.
CRE	Commander Royal Engineers.
CREME	Commander Royal Electrical & Mechanical Engineers.
Cwt.	Hundredweight, (15 cwts ¾ ton).
DAA & QMG	Deputy Assistant Adjutant & Quartermaster General.
DCLI	Duke of Cornwall's Light Infantry.
Div.	Division.
E.P.I.P.	Standard Military Tent.
GI GII GIII	GSO I etc. i.e. General Staff Officer Grade I, II, III.
GHQ	General Headquarters.
GOC	General Officer Commanding.
HMS	His Majesty's Ship.
HMSO	His Majesty's Stationery Office.
HQ	Headquarters.
Hrs.	Hours. i.e. 1400 hrs = 2 pm.
IZL	Irgun Zvai Leumi (National Military Organization).
KDG	King's Dragoon Guards.
KRRC	King's Royal Rifle Corps.
Lehi	Lehame Herut Israel (Fighters for the Freedom of Israel i.e. the Stern gang, named after its founder, Abraham

	Stern shot by Palestine Police).
LO	Liaison Officer.
L.of C.	Lines of Communication.
LST	Landing Ship Tank.
MELF	Middle East Land Forces.
METC	Middle East Transit Camp.
Mons	Mons Barracks, Aldershot. The Infantry Wing of the Royal Military College, Sandhurst in World War II.
NAAFI	Navy, Army and Air Force Institutes, providing canteens, shops and provisions.
NCO	Non Commissioned Officer.
OC	Officer Commanding.
O2E	Senior officers' staff college.
Para.	Parachute (Regiment/Battalion).
P.T.	Physical Training.
Q	The Q side of AA & QMG i.e. administration and supply.
RAF	Royal Air Force.
RAOC	Royal Army Ordnance Corps.
RASC	Royal Army Service Corps.
RDG	Royal Dragoon Guards.
RN	Royal Navy.
RNVR	Royal Navy Volunteer Reserve.
RQMS	Regimental Quartermaster Sergeant.
RSM	Regimental Sergeant Major.
SOE	Special Operations Executive.
TJFF	Transjordan Frontier Force.
VE	Victory in Europe (VE Day=8 May, 1945).
WO1	Warrant Officer Grade One.
YWCA	Young Women's Christian Association.

Acknowledgements

My thanks are due to many for help, encouragement and advice concerning this book, among whom Leo Cooper, Tom Hartman and Georgina Harris have been my most loyal and patient supporters.

Essential background has been provided by Miss Alex Ward, Head of Army Historical Research, and General Sir David Fraser. Miss Sarah Pepin, House of Commons Public Information Office, kindly researched and sent me relevant extracts from *Hansard* and the HMSO publication: *Palestine: Statement of Information Relating to Acts of Violence*.

I am particularly appreciative of the background provided by Dan Kurzman's *Genesis 1948, The Politics of Dispossession* by Edward W. Said, *Water and Power* by Miriam R. Lowe, and *The Palestine Triangle* by Nicholas Bethell, with whom I corresponded, as I did with John Grigg and Kenneth Rose, all of whose comments were most helpful. General Sir William Jackson's *Withdrawal from Empire* and his letter provided important points. *The British Empire in the Middle East 1945–1951* by William Roger Louis gave an accurate and unbiased American assessment.

In writing half a century afterwards, memories fade in some details, and I was especially pleased to re-read H. V. Morton's *In the Steps of the Master*, written originally only nine years before 1945, during which time little had changed. On a different aspect, *KGB* by Christopher Andrew and Oleg Gordievsky provided a convincing historical record of Stalin's plans to control the new State of Israel.

The History of the Haganah and other books by Israeli authors have also provided background information. More particularly, I would like to thank Brigadier Haim Yifrah, Israeli Military Attaché in Paris, Dr Elhanan-Oren of the Israeli Defence Force's Department of History, and Dimona Bastia for their generous help.

At Regimental Headquarters, Welsh Guards, I am most grateful for the assistance of Lieutenant and Quartermaster A. J. Powell, formerly Superintending Clerk, Regimental Sergeant Major K.W. Stacey,

Superintending Clerk Meirion Ellis, ex Welsh Guards, and Sergeant T. M. Carson, Welsh Guards, whose help with both the Regiment and the other six Household Regiments, as well as with the Parachute Regiment, has been exemplary, and to all of whom I also extend my thanks.

I would, too, like to thank M. T. Harrington of the British Library, and B. Carter of the Public Records Office, Kew, Barry and Maureen Brokaw, Major G. D. Cooper, Captain J.F. L. Denny, Julia Draper, Major N. S. Kearsley, Major-General P.R. Leuchars, Earl Lloyd George of Dwyfor, Lieutenant-Commander Peter Lucy RN, Jane Mitchell, Colonel Sir Julian Paget Bt, Brigadier J. F. Rickett and Fanny Rickett, Colonel E. I. Windsor Clive and my Canadian cousins, Lillian Bingham and Ted Taylor, for their great help.

Finally my gratitude must be expressed to my mother for keeping my letters, and to my daughter, Amanda, for finding and filing them; and to Captain Andrew Gibson-Watt, and Pammie, who provided an invaluable commentary, allowing me, also, to use facts gleaned from operational military orders of the era, which had, it seemed, been inadvertently but fortuitously retained.

Philip Brutton
Paris, 4 March, 1996

Author's Note

It took the indigenous Celtic British four hundred years to abandon the idea of reconquering land seized and occupied by the Anglo-Saxons in what was to become Angle-land or England. It is hoped it will not take as long for the Arabs to acknowledge their loss in Palestine and for Jewish zealots to forego their militancy. This is the crux of the question: it is not about justice, religion, politics or Welsh original sin, categorized as such, but collectively about facts on the ground and their acceptance.

The Balfour Declaration, sponsored and promoted by the British Prime Minister, David Lloyd George, in 1917, opened the way to Jewish immigration. This could not be implemented until the British Army had conquered Palestine in 1918. In less than eighteen years, in 1936, the Jews owned 13½% of cultivable land with 28% of the population at 385,000. It is now five and a half million. This book tries to deal objectively with the facts.

On 1 March, 1922 - Saint David's Day in the Christian calender - Yitzhak Rabin was born in Palestine. He died as Prime Minister of Israel on 4 November, 1995, when an apparently sane but rabid Jewish assassin, Yigal Amir, aged 25, pumped three dumdum bullets into his upper body after he had addressed a peace rally in Tel Aviv. The assassination revealed, if anyone doubted it, that both extremist Jews and Arabs fervently wished to reverse the due process of non-belligerency.

The British Mandatory power, in the twenty-eight years of its existence, experienced the same phenomenon. Jewish terrorism was, however, more refined in its extremes of cruelty than that of the Arab. In covering the last years of the Mandate, this book describes some of the details.

Brief reflection, and some research, could conceivably disclose the Balfour Declaration as being ascribed to a form of political persuasion, nowadays termed a slush fund: the legal funding of political parties being overt in Great Britian. The Zionists contributed liberally to both political parties in 1917. They also entertained liberally (without an intended pun) and Lloyd George's reputation for hawking honours does little to diminish the idea that the Declaration itself was a matter of political business. Certainly, his later admiration for Adolf Hitler somewhat dispelled the impression that he was a Zionist by inclination.

Abba (Aubrey) Eban, a former Israeli Foreign Minister, wrote after the assassination of Yitzhak Rabin: "There is reason to believe and hope the shock suffered by our nation will be translated into a more lucid understanding of Israel's real choices: our founders understood that our land is the home of two nations, two faiths, two tongues and two historic experiences. The Palestine people suffered irreversible loss of territorial oppportunities by pretending that their rights totally transcended ours. Yitzhak Rabin was resolute in his refusal to let his beloved homeland commit a similar error."

There was, of course, no *pretence* about Arab rights transcending those of the Jews. In Arab eyes, in 1948, both right and might were theirs to exercise. It was to prove otherwise; and whereas it was the British who renegued on previous undertakings to the Arabs which promised independence after War's end, it was the Arabs who sold land to the Jews during the early years of the Mandate. In 1918 there were few Jews in Palestine - 10,000 in all - to acquire anything.

"That Yitzhak Rabin was not allowed," Abba Eban continued, "to witness the full fruits of his realism is a human tragedy of heartrending scale." Rabin's realism was related to the facts as he found them. Arab extremists fight for a return to a wholly Arab-dominated Palestine, free of Jews, whose zealots demand a return of *their* land which they lost irretrievably in AD 70. "Killers," as Shimon Peres described them, "invoking the name of God, while they are really the devil's emissaries."

Conflict is not limited, consequently, to that across the divide of Arab and Jew: assassinations have occurred within Arab ranks - King Abdullah of Jordan and Anwar Sadat of Egypt are the most prominent among scores - while Yitzhak Rabin's murder may have been the most prominent, it was certainly not the first. As early as 1924, only four years after the beginning of the Mandate, Jacob Israel de Haan, the spokesman for an ultra-Orthodox party, was shot while leaving a synagogue in Jaffa Street, Jerusalem. He opposed the Zionist movement and was thought to have been killed by Haganah. Nine years later, two men shot Chaim Arlosoroff, leader of the Labour Party, on a Tel Aviv beach. His killers were right-wing Jews.

Ten years after this assassination, in 1943, Eliahu Giladi began plotting the death of David Ben-Gurion, leader of the later Mapai or Labour Party, and other moderate Zionist leaders. He was a member of the terrorist Stern Gang. Giladi was shot in the back, also on a beach, this time south of Tel Aviv. The assassination was initiated by his close friend, Yitzhak

Shamir - acknowledged in his memoirs - who has denied pulling the trigger.

Yitzhak Shamir became Prime Minister of Israel after Menachem Begin, whose gang had fought Ben-Gurion's government in 1948, when the IZL unloaded arms from the LST *Altalena,* refusing to submit to their government's authority. Many Jews were killed when this hooliganism was suppressed. In 1983 a peace activist, Emil Grunsweig, was killed when a grenade was thrown into a crowd which was demonstrating against Israel's invasion of Lebanon. The government pulled back from this ill-conceived operation, initiated by Menachem Begin as Prime Minister and implemented by Ariel Sharon. Thus, beginning with the Prophets, Jew killing Jew is not new.

At the funeral of Yitzhak Rabin, King Hussein of Jordan described the dead man as "a brother, a colleague, a friend, a man, a soldier. Let our voices rise high to speak of our commitment to peace for all times to come." This moving testament, however, expresses the viewpoint of politico-economics, however genuine the personal feeling. It is certainly the voice of reason which underlines the symbiotic necessity of interdependence between Palestine, Jordan and Israel, and the need to curb emotion which excites the extremists.

Rabin's assassination, in effect, was the result of transforming warped religious ideas into political action. This Jewish *jihad* predates and mirrors its Moslem equivalent and has now led to an examination of the Law of Return, whereby all Jews have the right, should they wish to claim it, of Israeli citizenship. Many of the extremists originate from the United States and are now seriously considered returnable.

Yitzhak Rabin was a member of the Haganah when I was in Palestine. He was soon to go to England and undergo British military training which stood him well when he became the Israeli Chief of Staff and architect of victory. His cabinet colleague, and twice his successor, Shimon Peres (Persky) who arrived in Palestine in 1934, aged eleven, was put in charge of weapons procurement by David Ben-Gurion in 1948. He did a magnificient job. He saved Israel from extinction. It is likely Yasser Arafat has achieved the same goal for the remaining half of his homeland. This, however, depends upon whether violent rhetoric - "verbal gallows" - and subsequent actions on both sides can be eradicated, how much land is retained, requisitioned or relinquished under Israeli plans for defence, the continuance or abandonment of Israeli settlements, the status of Jerusalem, the return of refugees and, in terms of Syria, the question of the Golan Heights. It is an awesome catalogue, compared to which the running, or ruining, of the British Mandate was a simple matter.

Prologue

Saint David's Day in Palestine, on 1 March, 1947, was traditional. The adjunct of the bomb was exceptional. The 1st Battalion, Welsh Guards, had marched past the Mandate's High Commissioner, General Sir Alan Cunningham, who had conquered the Italian armies in Somaliland and Abyssinia six years earlier. Instead, however, of pontificating with his peers in the Lords as Viscount Cunningham of Addis Ababa – the whims of awarding honours being unpredictable – he had been proffered the poisoned cup of ruling Palestine on behalf of His Majesty's Government. Fleetingly this thought had passed through my mind as I saluted him and received my leek – the traditional co-emblem, with the daffodil and the dragon, of the Principality.

The bomb was reserved for Andrew Gibson-Watt, our escort and myself: we were returning to Brigade Headquarters, whence, as staff officers and members of the Regiment, we had been invited, making the five-mile journey by jeep. In practice our bomb was unflatteringly futile and incomparably ineffective to the one which had blown up the Jerusalem officers' club on the same day, killing in its barbarous fashion thirteen and injuring sixteen. The terrorist gang responsible – Irgun Zvai Leumi – had also simultaneously perpetrated sixteen other acts of mayhem and violence.

Although we were unaware of these incidents, the fact Brigade had sent two vehicles to escort us indicated an alert. It was early evening. The moon was in its first quarter. The night sky was clear. I was sitting next to the driver with a loaded and cocked Tommy gun on my lap: a most effective automatic weapon in its day. A 15-cwt truck was ahead and another jeep behind.

I was aware, as we approached Headquarters and a particularly notorious stretch of road, that there was nothing to be done but to wait, first to see if an attack materialized, and secondly to judge the form after the event, if we were alive. Meanwhile, I reflected, as the origin of words interested me, that David was derived from the Hebrew and meant beloved.

There was, however, nothing beloved about the roadside bomb – or mine – which we later learnt was unique among such incidents in that it failed to kill or maim. Either greed, in this case a desire to kill the occupants of two vehicles instead of one, saved us, or the would-be murderer, relying upon his dexterity to thrust down the plunger of a manually operated bomb – or, if electrical, creating a circuit – mistimed. There might, too, have been other factors.

This meant that his inhospitable device exploded just in front of the jeep carrying my companions and myself, and barely behind the escort vehicle ahead. I immediately gave orders to extinguish lights, take cover and fire into the orange grove. As a fire order this was imprecise, but it had a purpose: a demoralizing tactic, after the failure of the attack, before pursuit. The Headquarters searchlight, however, was beamed upon us, and this put paid to any action on our part. We returned to camp.

No one, of course, in a war or in a terrorist-inspired insurrection such as we were experiencing in Palestine, was free from danger. In this case, not for the first time, death had come fairly close. In its way, this was life. I reflected unemotionally and dispassionately upon the past few years, and how often there had been close calls during air raids, common to millions, and in particular the narrow miss while Ensign of the Guard at Saint James's Palace, early in 1944, when a bomb cluster straddled the building, killing many outside, but none in.

There then followed Italy, described in *Ensign in Italy*, beginning with night patrols in Cassino, not without danger, accompanied by my runner and soldier servant, the gallant Guardsman Lewis 35, who had himself been blown off the jetty at Boulogne in 1940. I recalled the officers' dinner in the upper room of the peasant house, after the place had fallen, and sitting between Hugh Arbuthnot, the Carrier Platoon commander, and Kemmis Buckley, in charge of 3" mortars. Both survived the War, but several of those present did not, and many more were wounded. This was particularly the case only a few days later when 6th Armoured Division, in which 1st Guards Brigade was serving, was held up before Arce in a battle which lasted more than three days. The Brigade suffered 300 casualties, of which 112 were Welsh Guardsmen. Twice those at my side were killed.

After this there were more casualties north of Rome and a considerable battle just beyond Perugia where the Parachute Regiment again dug in, as they had at Cassino and Arce. We pushed them back, but my signaller, Jones 62, a young married man was killed next to me. Without any sense of settling accounts I killed at least two of the enemy: emotions in battle are dangerous. They affect judgement.

The pursuit up the Arno Valley was without me, as I was in hospital with malaria and jaundice. There were more casualties and I rejoined the 3rd Battalion beyond Florence in the mountains. Autumn rains came early and the conditions on a mountain redoubt called Battaglia were appalling, although not as bad as they had been on Monte Cerasola, near Cassino, whither the Battalion had been sent after landing from North Africa, where it had fought in several bloody battles. In Italy, after the snow had fallen, we were moved to such places as Aqua Salata and Verro, known only to soldiers and shepherds.

Also in those mountains, Owen Lloyd George and I found ourselves in the middle of a minefield – S mines which sprang up and exploded around the level of the stomach. Instinct suggested I look down. We stood very still and tiptoed out of danger. Inevitably there were other narrow escapes, as with all who have fought and fight in any war.

There had been, too, a previous, fairly near miss in Palestine; but perhaps it is better to explain why 100,000 British troops were required in a place no bigger than Wales or Maryland after the Second World War, and the background both to their presence and to the whole seemingly unending imbroglio which has beset, and continues to beset, the region for more than 3500 years.

LEBANON

Lake Huleh

SYRIA

Acre

Haifa

Sea of Galilee

Nazareth

Mediterranean Sea

River Jordan

TRANSJORDAN

Nablus

Tel Aviv
Jaffa

Amman

Lydda
Ramleh

International
Zone of Jerusalem

Bethlehem

Gaza

Hebron

Dead Sea

Rafah

Beersheba

El 'Arish

Negev

Sinai

EGYPT

Petra

Jewish State
Arab State

Miles
0   10   20   30

United Nations
Partition of
Palestine, 1947

Aqaba

xviii

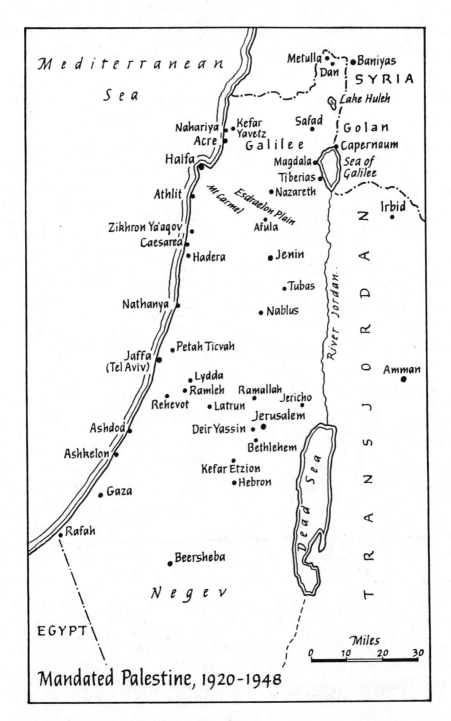

Mandated Palestine, 1920-1948

CHAPTER ONE

David's City

Long before David slew Goliath, a Philistine whose country lay by the sea between Gaza and Jaffa and gave its name to Palestine, the land of Canaan was divided into small city states and tribal entities, maintaining an uneasy relationship with Egyptian imperialism, appeased by the payment of tribute and the occasional attentions of the changing major states further north and to the north-east.

The Book of Genesis states that God inspired the patriarch Abraham to leave Ur of the Chaldees for the Promised Land (c.1750 BC). In a covenant God promised to make Abraham the ancestor of a great nation and to give him and his descendants the land of Israel, subject to certain clearly defined obligations. Some 450 years later, and a further 300 before David's arrival, the covenant made to Abraham was reaffirmed and extended to Moses on Mount Sinai; with more specific obligations required of the Jews.

Led by Moses, the Israelites, who had earlier been settled by Pharaoh in the north-east region of the Nile Delta, left Egypt (the Exodus) probably, it is now thought, during the reign of Ramses II (c.1292–1237 BC) and wandered for many years in the wilderness.

The Book of Deuteronomy is the record of Moses' farewell to his people as they were about to cross the Jordan under Joshua. The Book also recalls the renewal of the covenant with the whole population, despite their failure to fulfil their side of the agreement. Later, in Chronicles, David is reminded by God that it was He who transformed him from a simple, sling-wielding shepherd into a great king.

God's conditions, however, made it clear that His blessings were not automatically guaranteed. Nevertheless, the promise stated God's commitment to establish David's descendants upon the throne for ever. The interpretation of this promise expresses

I

the basic difference between the Jewish and Christian beliefs.

Returning, however, to the Exodus, archaeology now largely substantiates the biblical record. The Jews first settled on the east side of the Jordan, in the area of modern Amman, crossed the river around 1225 BC and Jericho fell to Joshua. Archaeologists incline to the view it was deserted at the time: if so, his trumpet was muted before walls already tumbled, as did fortified towns as far apart as Hazor on Lake Huleh and Hebron in the south.

The Jews, however, were conquered by the Philistines around 1050 BC and Samuel, the last of the Judges, was finally forced to inaugurate kingship to unite the tribes. Saul was annointed king c. 1020 BC and he, in turn, was succeeded by David. At the time there was a practical difference between the land allotted to the twelve tribes and that which they were able to occupy.

At the height of Jewish expansion under David and Solomon, a period of seventy-eight years, approximately between 1000 BC and 922 BC, the heartland of the southern part of the kingdom, later Judah, stretched forty miles west of the Dead Sea and included the Jebusite city of Jerusalem which David captured and made his capital. His territory reached the Mediterranean but excluded the Gaza strip, Philistia, and Jaffa.

The northern part of the kingdom, later Israel, went as far north as the western slopes of Mount Hermon, bordering Phoenicia, covering a forty-mile finger of land which spread northwards from Lake Galilee – Yam Kinneret in Hebrew. Further south the Jewish kingdom broadened into a wider area which went from the sea in the west, via Samaria, to well inside modern southern Syria and northern Jordan.

Under David and his son, Solomon, an empire was established which included the Negev, inhabited by Amalekites, the kingdom of Edom, and achieved military or economic control from the Gulf of Aqaba to the banks of the Euphrates. In line with God's promise to Abraham, his dependants would have all the land between that river and Egypt. Solomon built the first temple in seven years, employing 170,000 workers and 3000 supervisors. It was a typical Canaanite construction, the Ark of the Covenant excepted, with wood and an architect, Howram Abi, supplied from Lebanon. He stabled at Megiddo, it is said, 12,000 chariot horses, having both wisdom and many wives.

Solomon's glory was not bequeathed to his successors: he had centralized control of the state by breaking up the tribal boundaries into twelve administrative districts. His standing army had been considerably expanded and, as evidenced by Megiddo, equipped with chariots. In conjunction with Hiram of Tyre, he organized a

2

fleet of ships for trade in the Mediterranean, the Red Sea and the Indian Ocean. He constructed a copper refinery at Ezion-geber (Aqaba) and developed a cartel in horses and chariots in alliance with Egypt and Cilicia in the north. The Arabian kings to the south were happy to cooperate in controlling the caravan routes, trading in spices and aromatics.

All this came to an end when he died: taxes, 700 wives and 300 concubines, it is said, brought strange religions and a degree of displeasure from the Deity. Thus, not only were the tribes disillusioned, but so also was God. This was unwise in terms of the succession: Solomon's son. Rehoboam – whose name means the nation is enlarged (inappropriate under the circumstances) which is now applied to a wine bottle six times normal size – was rejected by the ten tribes of the north. He retained only Judah and Benjamin.

Israel elected Jeroboam who had formerly been Solomon's superintendent of labour and taxes, "a mighty man of valour who gave Israel to sin" and who also gave his name to a mere four-bottle (Methuselah (man of the javelin) ranks eight bottles: he did not live 969 years but 78 and 4 months. The first are lunar years, employed by Babylon and Ancient Greece: divided by 12.37, the number of moons per year in a Metonic Cycle of eight years, we have his age in calendar years).

Jeroboam was also responsible for the Israelite end of the civil war with Judah, until this was rudely interrupted by the arrival of Shoshenq of Egypt, founder of the XXII dynasty, who devastated Edom and much of the north, as well as robbing the Temple. In I Kings and II Chronicles he appears as Shishak who temporarily re-established Egyptian hegemony over the Promised Land.

Israel, in the north, lasted until 706 BC, 216 years after Solomon's death, when Sargon II, the Assyrian, claimed to have taken 27,290 Israelites as prisoners. He certainly removed the country from the map. Judah lasted until 586 BC, 336 years after Solomon and 120 longer than Israel, when a similar fate befell it after Nebuchadnezzar of Babylon (a 20-bottle man) seized Jerusalem and dispatched thousands of Jews as captives to his capital, 800 miles away.

Forty-seven years later, in 539 BC, Babylon fell to Cyrus the Great of Persia, who permitted those Jews who wished to return to do so. Shortly afterwards the Temple was rebuilt; but Palestine was firmly under Persian rule until 332 BC, when it fell, together with most of the world known to the ancients, to Alexander the Great. On his death in 323 BC, Seleucus I founded the dynasty of the Seleucids which ruled Palestine until the Jewish revolt in 168 BC under Judas Maccabaeus.

The Maccabaean expansion of Judah from a small state centred on Jerusalem was considerable, stretching from Dan in the north to the northern reaches of the Negev in the south, and crossing over to El'Arish in Sinai; both sides of the Jordan were incorporated but not Phoenicia, which was held by the Seleucid Empire. At that time the Ptolemaic rule in Egypt was weak, but, with the arrival of the Romans in Egypt, Asia Minor and Syria, the days of an independent Palestine were numbered.

In 64 BC Pompey took Jerusalem in order to pacify Judaea. He installed the Maccabaean high priest, Hyrcanus II, as Roman representative, together with Antipater, from the non-Jewish district of Idumaea as civil adviser. He was the father of Herod the Great. Pompey followed the Roman custom of making cities the administrative centres for local government and extended the system of tax farming.

Under Roman tutelage, Herod gained control of Jerusalem in 37 BC, when he defeated Antigonus, the nephew of Hyrcanus II whose granddaughter Mariamne, sister of the last of the Maccabees, Aristobulus III, he married. She was one of the ten, the first being Doris, named after the Greek sea goddess. Herod was king of Judaea under various Roman sponsors: Pompey, Caesar, Brutus, Antony (with Cleopatra) and finally Augustus. He rebuilt the Temple, had a palace in Jerusalem and managed to murder Mariamne's two sons, her brother, her mother and her grandfather, as well as sundry others including the Holy Innocents of Bethlehem. In 29 BC he murdered Mariamne. He died in 4 BC.

Three years before, Jesus of Nazareth was born in Bethlehem on 15 September, 7 BC, according to computerized research undertaken by British astronomers. His crucifixion is now considered to have taken place under the jurisdiction of the Roman procurator of Judaea and Samaria, Pontius Pilate, on 3 April, 33 AD. He was thirty-eight and a half. "On the third day He rose from the dead, as the scriptures had foretold."

In fact His coming was foretold 140 times in the Old Testament, but the Jewish leaders, as distinct from thousands of Jews, vaguely anticipating a very different kind of Messiah, were at the same time more specifically aware of the wholly temporal dangers of revolt: "the Romans will come and destroy the Holy Place and our nation. It is better for one man to die for the people, than for the whole nation to be destroyed" were their thoughts after the raising of Lazarus from the dead.

In due course Christ's sorrowful prediction of Jerusalem's destruction took place thirty-seven years later in 70 AD, following what the Jewish hierarchy feared most – revolt by zealots – when it

4

was captured by singularly ill-disciplined legionaries under Titus.

Earlier, Christ had told the scribes and chief priests, quoting psalm 118, "It was the stone rejected by the builders that became the keystone," adding, "Anyone who falls on that stone will be dashed to pieces; anyone who falls on it will be crushed. I tell you then the kingdom of God will be taken from you and given to a people who will produce its fruit." The tragic dichotomy between Jew and Christian began on that date.

In 132 AD the Jews of Judaea revolted against pagan practice when the Romans founded a colony, Aelia Capitolina, in Jerusalem, and dedicated a temple to Jupiter Capitolanus on the site of the Temple. The revolt, led by Rabbi Akiba ben Joseph and Simon Bar Cochba, ended in 135 AD. It was suppressed ruthlessly by Hadrian, who later built the Wall in Britain which may still be seen. Simon Bar Cochbar was killed in the battle of Bethar. Judaea was virtually depopulated. Afterwards Jews could enter Jerusalem only once a year.

This action completed the denationalization of the Jews which had begun under Vespasian after the fall of Jerusalem. The Diaspora (the Dispersion) from thereon was a fact and the great edition of the Talmud was completed in Babylon, 350 years afterwards, in the late fifth century.

More than a century and a half earlier, and 180 after the construction of the pagan temple, in AD 313 Constantine the Great had issued the Edict of Milan which extended toleration to Christianity. His mother, Saint Helena, Empress Dowager, was baptized in the same year and in 326 visited Jerusalem, founding the basilicas on the Mount of Olives and at Bethlehem. Her name is particularly associated with the discovery of the True Cross in a rock-cistern near Calvary. Her porphyry sarcophagus is in the Vatican.

In 638 Jerusalem and nearly all Palestine fell to the Moslem invasion under Omar, Prince of the Faithful. The Byzantines (East Roman Empire) were decisively defeated at Yarmuk, south of the Sea of Galilee in 636. Caesarea was captured in 640 and the sea coast occupied. Omar behaved with moderation, restraining his troops from pillage and leaving Christian churches intact. Some fifty years later the Mosque of al Aksa and the Dome of the Rock were built by the Emir Abd el Malek on the site of the Temple. They remain there.

Moslems regard Jerusalem as the third most sacred city after Mecca and Medina. The Dome of the Rock is considered to be the spot whence the Prophet ascended to heaven on his horse, "el-barûk". The western or Wailing Wall, the remnant of the Temple which the troops of Titus left standing in huge, Herodian blocks of stone, alone remains for the Jews to revere.

In 1099 Godfrey de Bouillon and his fellow Crusaders captured the city which became the capital of the Latin Kingdom of Jerusalem. Eighty years later it fell to Saladin. It was regained by treaty with Saladin's nephew, Malik al-Kamil, in 1229, during the Sixth Crusade, and held for fifteen years until 1244 when it was captured by Moslem mercenaries. Until Allenby's conquest in 1917, it remained in Moslem hands, the Turks having taken the region from the Egyptian sultans in 1517.

The reader will have understood that the Jews obtained their Promised Land by piecemeal conquest around 1225 BC and, through various vicissitudes with expanding and contracting areas of control, held on to it until AD 135, at the very limit, a period of around 1400 years, which matches the approximate period Palestine has been occupied by the Arabs.

The point at issue, however, is not a competition involving dates, or a numbers game, but the fact that in 1917 a Christian army under General Allenby conquered Palestine, the population of which was 90% Arab, the majority being Moslem, with undisputed legal rights to their land and possessions, and a Christian British cabinet then promised a national home for the Jewish people without prejudice to the rights of the existing population, *who, a year earlier, had unequivocally been promised independence by the British government.*

In ancient Rome the temple doors of the two-faced Janus, god of doors, were closed in time of peace. In fact, they were closed only four times before the Christian era. In Palestine, thanks to the Janiform jerks of Lloyd George and his cabinet acolytes, they were always open. Indeed they opened the doors themselves, inviting the elemental forces of human passion to enter. It was not the best way to run a temple, let alone a Mandate.

That is why, thirty years later, there were 100,000 British troops involved in the polemical gyre of Palestine, which was spiralling, after the end of the Second World War, inexorably into its mandatory mire: it was, in other words – *said entirely without prejudice to either Arab or Jewish claims* – a misguided, misconceived and misinterpreted *British* political mess from the beginning, bequeathed upon their successors by British politicians who were nothing if not irresponsible.

CHAPTER TWO

Allenby's City

The epitaph to the British Mandate in Palestine can be brief: "Founded 1920. Foundered 1948;" more than a quarter of a century of division and tragedy, arising directly from contradictory engagements undertaken by the British government between 1915 and 1917. Even if it be conceded that politics are an inexact science, Machiavelli would not have been impressed. Winston Churchill, a former Zionist, wrote in 1945: "I am not aware of the slightest advantage which has ever accrued to Great Britain from this painful and thankless task."

Pain was plentiful, and thanks were few. The fateful pronouncement which begirded British governments for thirty years, not inappropriately made on All Souls' Day, 2 November, 1917, was called the Balfour Declaration: it took the form of a letter from Arthur Balfour, serving as foreign secretary in Lloyd George's War Cabinet to Lionel, second baron Rothschild. Its consequences are far from being played out nearly eighty years later.

Chronologically, the facts are as follows: in 1914, as already mentioned, the Ottoman empire ruled the Middle East, including the accessible parts of Arabia. Egypt had been lost since 1882, in practice to the British, who also ran the Suez Canal, the short cut to India. In October, 1914, the Turks joined the war on the German side. Lord Kitchener, after leaving India in 1911, where he had been commander-in-chief, then becoming British Resident and Consul General in Cairo, had been appointed Secretary of State for War in August, 1914. As such, on 31 October, 1914, he wrote to Sherif Hussein of Mecca, the great-grandfather of the present King of Jordan. His offer, on behalf of the British cabinet, was simple: rebel against the Turks; when we win the War, *all* (Ottoman governed) *Arab lands* – 800,000 square miles in total, including

Palestine at 10,000 or 1¼% – *will be independent*. The risk to Hussein, which he took, was that we could lose the war. There were certain conditions which he studied and nine-and-a-half months later, on 14 July, 1915, he submitted his terms for entering the war against the Turks: Great Britain was to recognize the independence of Arab countries south of 37° north latitude, the present boundary between Turkey and Syria.

On 24 October, 1915, Sir Henry McMahon, Kitchener's successor and now styled as the British High Commissioner in Egypt, replied: the British government took exception to Arab claims to the Mersina-Alexandretta region. There were quibbles over Baghdad and Basra, but Great Britain promised Arab independence for all Arab populated land of the Turkish empire where "Great Britain is free to act without detriment to her ally France" who wished to "protect" portions of what is now Syria and the Lebanon, lying to "the west of the districts of Damascus" – which she later bombarded – "Homs, Hama and Aleppo".

Palestine, further south, was *not involved* in the proviso. On 5 November, 1915, Hussein accepted the British proposals for Mersina and Alexandretta, reserved his position over Baghdad, Basra, Beirut and Aleppo, and passed the political ball to the Allies. On 21 December the French government accepted the proposal of Arab administration of western Syria, including the Lebanon, their only concern, provided it was under French influence.

On 30 January, 1916, the British accepted Hussein's terms, leaving the exact status of Baghdad and Basra in the air, likewise the sphere of French influence in Syria. The agreement was signed one year and a quarter after the initial approach by Lord Kitchener, and the Arabs rebelled. In December, 1916, a week after David Lloyd George formed his War Cabinet, Hussein was recognized as King of the Hejaz and head of the Arab people.

Only three months, however, after the long-negotiated agreement with Hussein, the British Foreign Office performed a brisk fandango – a dance of courtship, only in this case with infidelity in mind – when they agreed on 26 April, 1916, with France and Czarist Russia, to establish an independent Arab state after the war, but with a British sphere of interest covering Mesopotamia (Iraq) and the ports of Haifa and Acre in Palestine, a country which would be governed internationally. This was not independence. France was to "protect" the coastal strips of Lebanon and Syria.

Courtship is only the first step: the fandango and Russia were abandoned and replaced by a lively Provençal ferandole, a duet performed by M. Georges Picot and Sir Mark Sykes. It became the established double act for thirty years: France and Great Britain

8

divided the take and signed their agreement fifteen days after its precedent involving Russia – foreign affairs could move fast when both parties wished it – and thirteen weeks after the agreement with Hussein. Lebanon and Syria went to France and the rest, except Arabia, to Great Britain.

The date of this diplomatic dichotomy and duplicity was 9 May, 1916. As a sideline, we had signed an agreement with Ibn Saud, Sultan of Nejd, four months earlier, which contradicted, in part, the one signed with Hussein. The pace was leisurely, the pressure hardly exigent: "under the exigencies of war" was a phrase later used to gloss over much that was murky and discreditable. Why was it done? Either there was no hand on the tiller, or no one particularly cared: it was a secondary game in a tertiary part of the world, compared to the desperate dramas taking place in France and at sea – the U-boat menace, which nearly ended in an Allied defeat, averted by the leadership qualities of Lloyd George and Clemenceau, exerted in this case with efficacy, and the bravery of all ranks in all services.

Meanwhile General Sir Edmund Allenby began his advance into Palestine in October, 1917. Among his formations was a Jewish contingent – no advance without security – and within whose ranks there served the young and gallant David Ben-Gurion, one of some 60,000 Jews then living in Palestine. Gaza and Jaffa were evacuated by the Turks in November.

On 9 December Allenby took Jerusalem and marched modestly into the city on foot, unlike the Kaiser in 1898. Operations were then delayed when large contingents were sent to reinforce the battlefronts in France: advances in the spring of 1918 were confined to Transjordan, where Lawrence of Arabia's irregulars harassed the enemy on the right flank, having taken Aqaba and destroyed much of the Hejaz railway link. Lawrence accompanied Allenby when he marched into the city. On 18 September, 1918, the battles of Megiddo – no chariots but masses of cavalry – broke the Turkish lines near the Mediterranean. The German *Asienkorps* under General Erich von Falkenhayn, managed to escape the encircling cavalry and made for Damascus and Aleppo, but they in turn fell on 1 and 26 October respectively. French naval forces had, meanwhile, taken Beirut on 1 October and on 30 October an armistice was signed at Mudros. On 12 November the Allied fleet, emulating the Argonauts and the disgraceful Fourth Crusade in 1204, passed through the Dardanelles and arrived at Constantinople.

Returning, however, from the Dardanelles to Downing Street – the reverse order had resulted in the disasters of 1915, when Allied troops failed to dislodge the defending Turks and Winston

Churchill resigned as First Lord of the Admiralty – the Balfour Declaration was made, as mentioned, on 2 November, 1917; it has never been denied that it was a total contradiction of our agreement with Hussein.

Given that events in the former American colonies, in India and in Ireland were firmly impressed upon the imperial psyche, we may well ask why any British government wished to risk civil unrest, rebellion and rampant terrorism in a region already prone to mercurial changes of mood, particularly involving religion. The answer becomes evident further on.

There were three Christian Zionists – a de facto oxymoron, but this escaped them – in the cabinet: Lloyd George, Winston Churchill and Arthur Balfour, *"cette vieille fille"* as Clemenceau, French prime minister, called him, the Old Testament, opportunely, having prior claim over the New, and over them. The Koran, of course, under the circumstances, was irrelevant. In the preceding cabinet Herbert Samuel, Home Secretary, was a Jew and a Zionist. The two were, and are, not synonomous. Lloyd George later publicly enthused about Hitler, which somewhat shocked his former Zionist friends, and the Righteous Gentile Award was considered inappropriate, even posthumously.

The declaration, written to Lord Rothschild, stated that the British government was in favour of the "establishment in Palestine of a national home for the Jewish people, and will use their best endeavours to facilitate the achievement of that object, it being clearly understood that nothing shall be done which may prejudice the civil and religious rights of the existing non-Jewish communities in Palestine."

The Arabs were not mentioned by name, nor was the solemn agreement with Hussein. Some Jewish Zionists hoped Palestine would be declared *the* national home, including all of Transjordan. In 1920 Balfour said publicly that he hoped the Arabs would not "grudge that small niche, for it is no more geographically, being given to the people who have been separated from it." No thought was given, incredibly, to the Arabs who were going to be separated from their own land, livelihood and way of life.

In the high noon of imperialism, when a quarter of the globe formed part of the British Empire, offering conquered land to those other than the indigenous people was already becoming outmoded, quite apart from the lack of wisdom and good faith involved in this case. Governing by fiat was finished. Diplomatic sleight of hand was both supercilious and sordid, if not in this case downright suspicious.

Lord Curzon, later to succeed Balfour at the Foreign Office, who was barred in practice from the premiership because of his peerage, immediately recognized a poisoned cup: how could a "national home for the Jewish people", however worthy an idea for an oft-persecuted race or religion, promote *British* interests? We had pre-empted Arab independence, renegued on our agreement and ensured revolt. He was strongly supported by Edwin Montagu, a Jew and then Secretary of State for India. His homeland, he said, was Great Britain.

Simultaneously, some Zionists would resent not being given what they regarded as *all* the coveted cake, of which not one crumb was within Great Britain's moral or legal compass to bestow. How could any ship of state sail in such a maelstrom? What would be the cost in lives, cash and goodwill? Lord Curzon's observations fell on the stony ground of Versailles, where his colleagues were diligently, if unwittingly, preparing the ground for the Second World War by their excessive demands in the peace treaty.

In 1920 the League of Nations, dominated by France and Great Britain, *temporarily* entrusted the two allies with the administration of all lands formerly governed by Turkey, except Arabia, "until such times as they are able to stand alone". So much for words: the self-appointed Mandatory power, Great Britain, had rendered Palestine paraplegic at birth. As an independent Arab state, she never stood at all, and the Arabs refused, in their wrath, to join the legislative council.

In 1937, some seventeen years later, the Peel Commission tried to sort out the mess. Official excuses were tenuous: it was thought Palestine lay west of Damascus, not south-south-west, and was part of the Beirut *vilayet*: respectively, geographically inexact and censurably irrelevant. *All* Arab lands were to receive independence. The areas of French "protection" were clear and agreed and bore no relation to Palestine. Thus, no marks for trying and none at all for lying.

Then there was the exigency bit: "It was in the highest degree unfortunate that, in the exigencies of war," said the Peel Commission, "the British government were unable to make their intention clear to the Sherif." The government's intention and that of Hussein were perfectly clear at the time when both sides signed the agreement. Otherwise Hussein would never have signed. The same government which recognized him as king of the Hejaz and head of the Arab people one year later revoked. Only strife could lie ahead, and it did.

In 1946 it was clear, as I stepped from the train in Haifa, glad not to have been blown up en route, that Lord Curzon's predictions had been realized: neither side could be placated: what were

Great Britain's interests in her being there? The Arabs had rebelled. Then, after much bloodshed, there was a truce at the outbreak of the Second World War when Jewish terrorism began, while the future of Jewish existence was being decided at El Alamein. A valiant Jewish Brigade was formed within the British Army, offering experience to Haganah, vital in the 1948 war. In 1945 a Russian-born Palestinian Jew in the British Intelligence Corps, Brigadier Susia Reich, was interrogating Heinrich Himmler, who called him "*mein Lieber*", near Bremen, before he crunched his concealed cyanide capsule, dying "unfortunately, quickly and painlessly," the Brigadier wrote, "in my arms!" In this manner the co-instigator of the holocaust killed himself when confronted by the Jewish Reich.

In the same year, 1945, post-war Zionist leaders realized that the 1939 White Paper would not be amended at the expense of the Arabs: allowing 100,000 Jews to enter, thus quintupling the 18,000 annual limit, at any rate once. When this was refused, as recorded in *Palestine: Statement of Information Relating to Acts of Violence. HMSO* (see Appendix 1 p. 173), Jewish strategy was planned on two fronts.

Dr Chaim Weizmann, later Israel's first president, led the political drive by recruiting support in the United States; while David Ben-Gurion, chairman of the Jewish Agency Executive, and Israel's first prime minister, mustered clandestine armed support overseas and on the ground: Haganah and Palmach, the original Jewish defence organizations against the Arabs, ad hoc allies of the British, now combined with the terrorist gangs, Irgun Zvai Leumi (IZL/Irgun) and Lehi (Stern) under a special committee, named X-Command, which directed the Jewish Resistance Movement. This arrangement eventually collapsed, terrorist paranoia being the handmaiden of hate.

In America the industrialist, Rudolf Sonnenborn, a friend of Ben-Gurion, formed the Sonnenborn Institute which provided funds and arms. In Europe Jewish agents persuaded as many Jews as possible to move west and state that Palestine was their goal: in July, 1945, there were 50,000 Jews in British and American camps. In December, 1946, there were 250,000, according to the Jewish historian Tom Segev.

On 31 October, 1945, X Command launched its rebellion in Palestine. Railway lines were cut in 154 places, three locomotives and a train were destroyed, the Haifa oil refinery slightly damaged and three patrol boats, used for intercepting illegal immigrant ships, were sunk. The Jewish Agency, the representative body of the Yishuv, or Palestine Jews, denied foreknowledge, but its telegraphic code had been broken via Sigint – signal intelligence – the speciality of the Government Communications Headquarters cryptographers at Bletchley Park and later at Cheltenham. Attlee, British prime minister since 1945, told Parliament: "We have evidence of a very close link between the Jewish Agency and Haganah, and Haganah and Irgun." (See Appx 1. page 175).

The two terrorist organizations, the Irgun and Stern gangs, were led by understandably emotionally crippled individuals, hardened by Nazi and Soviet persecution, whose families had largely been brutally murdered, and whose viewpoints in consequence were wholly exclusive to anyone else's. Their hatred for their opponents, by no means restricted to Gentiles, was visceral. Many of their acts placed them well beyond a manifestation of paranoia into the sombre world of the psychopath.

None of the leading terrorists who survived ever admitted guilt. On the contrary, it was always the fault of others. There were many cases of merciless individual assassinations in pursuit of vengeance, of indiscriminate bombings and ruthless dynamiting, a horrifying catalogue of criminality, in total contrast to the tenets of Judaism, in the name of which they claimed to be acting.

These acts were rationalized as seeking territorially and imperially an equation with the moment of transient glory during the reigns of David and Solomon three thousand years earlier. Inevitably X Command, and Dr Chaim Weizmann, lost all control; futhermore, no matter what consolation prizes the terrorist tombola might produce, perhaps the state of Israel itself, Solomon's passing glory could never be recovered: neither his temporal power both sides of the Jordan, nor the site of the Temple Mount in Jerusalem. Thus, the very heart of Zion was unobtainable.

CHAPTER THREE

An Unheralded Arrival

Whereas the matter of the Mandate undoubtedly engaged the best British minds in trying to avoid the worst, another problem concerned the Anglo-Egyptian Treaty, soon to be renegotiated: after the Canal Zone, Palestine was regarded as the next best base for our strategic reserve in the Middle East, a conception far removed from Mandatory administration.

It was in tune, however, with imperial policy, as then perceived, a policy totally confounded by the Declaration, without which current problems would not have existed, neither for the government nor for its military forces. It was now clearly realized that barbed benevolence and loose thinking did not contribute either to British interests or to peace, nor certainly to Arab interests, and to a certain extent not even to Jewish interests, as distinct from Zionist.

The twenty-year Anglo-Egyptian Treaty of alliance had been signed in 1936, but in 1945 the Egyptian government demanded revision, including the evacuation of British troops and the handing over of the Sudan condominium to Egyptian control. Great Britain stated, and carried out, her intention of granting independence to the Sudan, and agreed in 1954 to evacuate the Canal Zone within twenty months, retaining bases in Cyprus and the Gulf.

Meanwhile, in Palestine in 1945 the local security factor was becoming increasingly onerous and dangerous: 1st Division was in the north and 6th Airborne in the south. The independent 7th Infantry Brigade was near Jerusalem under GHQ command, and these forces were joined by 3rd Division. The Royal Navy and the Royal Air Force were a crucial support, as well as the Palestine Police, comprising Britons, Jews and Arabs. There were also the Transjordan Frontier Force and the Arab Legion, both based in Transjordan, but operating on both sides of the river.

17.10.45 Two weeks before X Command began its attacks, 1st Guards Brigade – 3rd Grenadiers, 3rd Coldstream and 1st Welsh Guards – landed in Haifa. Fighting terrorism, which was the matter in hand within the borders of the Holy Land for the next two and a half years, was not necessarily in the forefront of the normally resilient British soldier's mind as he formed up on the quayside at Haifa port.

Then, on 4 March, 1946, British forces were being built up, in terms of military might, when my friends and I arrived with the draft we brought with us. We had crossed France and the Mediterranean by what was then known as the MEDLOC route, sometimes called the MEDOC route. We certainly sampled the produce of France, agriculturally and viniculturally recovering from the War, as the troop train puffed its leisurely way from coast to coast.

The initial part of the journey involved a boat to Boulogne and then as unhurried trip on the train to Toulon. Hugo Herbert-Jones, Welsh Guards, and I, after learning the date of departure, then went to Cannes. We returned in time to witness the impressive embarkation of the Baron de Menasse, who was seen off by his valet, and whom we followed on board.

27.2.46 My diary entry: *"Twenty-first birthday. On board ship at Alexandria harbour."* The Baron was welcomed as Menasse Pasha by a fezzed and fervent vis-à-vis, making the traditional triple gesture of greeting with his right hand: *assaläam alaikum.* This reminded me of the tale of the Victorian gentleman, descending the gang plank, who was importuned by an ingratiating pimp, whispering deviant propositions. *"Imshi!* Go away! All I want is the British consul!" cried the exasperated Englishman. Deviance being his business, the pimp replied, "Very difficult, *Bimbashi,* but I try and fix."

Having nothing to fix, and having watched the civilians disembark, the soldiery stayed on board. We did not negotiate the gang plank until the following day. After inhaling the dust and odours of Alexandria and Cairo, my diary recorded:

28.2.46. "Disembark. Visit Barclays Bank (District Colonial and Overseas). Also Hugo and I inspect the Transit Camp and retire to Cairo. The Baron de Menasse and his wife invite us to dine at the Royal Automobile Club. Book into the Grand Hotel."

We left the P.T.-fit Hugh Stanley – he had recently attended such a course at the Guards Depot; a rather malevolent move by his adjutant at Windsor – who was in the Grenadiers, and the lean and lanky Mark Norman, Coldstream, with other enthusiastic members of the draft, to look lively and uphold tradition in the

Transit Camp, a place which Moses would have been glad to quit.

Meanwhile, with charitable recollection for those left under canvas, we ventured into the plush and pasha-packed, but most hospitable, Mohamed Ali Club, where alcohol was not forbidden, and where the Cotton Exchange members met, after fixing their prices. Their chairman, I was later to learn, was a much respected and highly intelligent Sephardic Jew, Joseph Messiqua, who among many, lost home and livelihood as the price of Israeli independence.

Then, however, Cairo was a particularly cosmopolitan, polyglot city, as was Alexandria; a ceaseless bustle of motorcars, camels and carts, laden donkeys and horse-drawn and motorized cabs driven by fezzed and usually unshaven chauffeurs, pooping their brass and rubber horns as they threaded their way through the mass. Added to the noise of klaxons was a continual cacophony of camel snorts and the cries of street vendors, mingled with the unmistakeable twangy, drumming music of the Middle East, nearly drowning the cry of the muezzin. The smells were exclusive, Turkish coffee permeating those of horse and human flesh.

Cairo was also rampant with civil unrest and a permanent plague of cockroaches. These had been the cause, with other allied culinary pests, of the kitchens being closed for two weeks at the Swiss-run Shephard's Hotel two years earlier, after an over-zealous Catering Corps colonel had carried out a pioneering inspection below stairs. Like the Nile flood, the cockroaches returned. The exercise had been pointless. The colonel's popularity diminished at the bar where, during the War, the barmen had made a passable living from information they gave to the Abwehr, largely planted by British Military Intelligence.

The next day, after our dinner with the Menasses – he was a director of the Suez Canal Company – Hugo and I went to that delightful island spot on the west bank of the Nile, reserved for the privileged, the Gezira Club, founded in 1882, to watch the races. It was later burnt down, and reconstructed, after civil unrest. All was calm, however, when we placed our bets in pursuance of Hugo's system: any horse that looked remotely normal in the Gezira ring, usually limited to no more than five or six runners, was worth a flutter. That is to say, normality was gauged when the horse was not sweating, throwing its jockey, kicking its neighbour, whinnying plaintively, or defecating excessively – the list of negative factors was long – or the jockey obviously overweight, stoned or falling off.

At the end of the day we showed a profit. The next day, at Heliopolis, we lost; the overdoped and overweight came up and we went down. We were not surprised. In fact, this form was nothing compared to what we were to witness later in Beirut. There, even a pantomime horse stood a chance.

After Heliopolis and a reasonable dinner, we boarded the night train for Haifa, crossed the Sinai to Gaza and arrived at our destination after a comfortable and uneventful journey, which is to say we were not attacked. Others were not so lucky. We were met at the station, lunched unadventurously at the officers' club, and were driven via Nazareth to Tiberias, where the 1st Battalion Welsh Guards were stationed in the "first class 'Elisabeth Hotel'" as the postcard put it.

The hotel had a remarkable view of the lake – or Sea of Galilee – and, beyond, the Golan Heights, whence the Gadarene swine had hurled themselves from the lower slopes into the water, and against which the Israelis were later to hurl themselves with great valour to defeat the Syrians. Whereas I knew about the first, the second was much in the future.

Indeed, although the present was a mixture of terrorism and tranquillity, particularly in the pastoral scenes predominant in Galilee, it was the past which permeated this land. The 35-mile journey from Haifa to Tiberias (the Mandate's broadest stretch from the Mediterranean to the Jordan River was 50 miles) passed through the northern tip of the Esdraelon Plain – or that of Megiddo or Jezreel, the alternative names – then climbed the southern slopes of the Lower Galilee hills, before descending immediately into Nazareth, nestling in a hollow. The surrounding high ground was scrubby, rock-strewn and verdant after winter rains, with masses of wild flowers.

Further on we could see the Horns of Hattin on our left, the site of the significant Christian defeat on 4 July, 1187. We were now 800 feet up, in open country, and faced with a drop, first to sea level – the Mediterranean – and then to that of Galilee, minus 700, a descent of 50 feet a minute on a carefully constructed S-bend road refined and remodelled by the Royal Engineers.

The hotel being requisitioned, we did not check in at the desk, but reported to the commanding officer, Reggie Hodgkinson and the adjutant, Jerry Spencer-Smith.

4.3.46. *"Arrive Battalion. In Prince of Wales Company commanded by Henry Coombe-Tennant. A kind and enthusiastic welcome given me by Eddie Bedingfeld in the evening. Nevertheless, I am able to find my way back to my tent."*

The hotel rooms were limited to the more senior in rank. Before too long, however, I was asked to take on the additional task, besides company duties, of looking after the mess and the allotment of rooms. So, in between tactical training and road blocks with the

17

Prince of Wales Company, the monotony of which enabled one to contemplate the mysteries of life and the administration of the Mandate, I claimed a vacant room on the grounds that both the mess and its accounts needed close surveillance.

The settling of the mess accounts, where in terms of book-keeping there had been some grave misdemeanours, led to my becoming attached and then posted to 1st Guards Brigade Head-quarters. Although, in all certainty, there were other officers in the Battalion who could add up, the Commanding Officer appeared to be impressed by my ability to discover the cause of the discrepancy and also to provide a satisfactory fare.

In fact there was nothing particularly miraculous in any of this: the number of officers, multiplied by their mess subscriptions, equalled an attributable figure, unencumbered by any deductions. This figure, translated into Palestine pounds, during the Mandate the equivalent of one pound sterling, could buy the plentiful food available in the Tiberias market. Wine and spirits were bought, and accounted for, from the NAAFI or other military sources. Once a proportion of the mess subscription was no longer siphoned off, the 7s.6d. (37½p) – the highest in 1st Guards Brigade – per day, could be spent to the evident satisfaction of all. I did the buying.

My solving this problem, as mentioned, prompted Colonel Reggie to think my career as a regular officer could be advanced by my going to Brigade. Meanwhile, other than mess and company duties, a not inconsiderable amount of officers' time was taken up in the daily exercise of the Battalion horses. These had been selected by Reggie and James Gresham, the second-in-command, whom I had accompanied when he chose the future Army steeplechase champion from a field of Cossack horses in Austria. It was later switched en route to 8th Army HQ, after being commandeered by the C in C, General Sir Richard McCreery.

We crossed our stirrups in the cavalry manner, walked and cantered clock-wise or anti-clockwise, sat facing or with our backs to the horse's head. We gripped fervently with our lower limbs, none of us wishing to fall on the rock-hard ground through inattention or the effects of a hangover. This was borne in mind the night before. Besides Prince of Wales Company, there were also two other companies at Tiberias plus headquarters. One company was at Rosh Pinna and another at Metullah on the Lebanese border. There were frequent changeovers.

We also hunted jackal, the occasional Egyptian mongoose and the fox. We had seven couple of English foxhounds, given to us by the neighbouring Ramleh Vale Hunt. The ground was largely scrub, with the odd orange grove, occasional plantations of young trees and, inevitably, cactus hedges. I put an admirable Arab mount across one of these while out with the hunt, despite my knowing it had a notable disinclination to jump anything.

We cleared this two-foot obstacle at a price: my feet brushed the hedge and became dislodged from the "pedals", as Reggie called them. The horse, pricked by the cactus spines, bolted diagonally across the field, while I clung to the saddle and reins, with most of my body underneath its belly. No Cossack could have done better. None of this was appreciated by one liverish lieutenant-colonel:

"Must you," he bellowed, obviously unnerved, "cross the field like that?"

"Does it," I shouted back, "look as if I can do anything about it?"

After this exchange, I regained the saddle. He then became quite affable; he was talking to the quick, not the dead. Off we galloped, the cry went up, the view halloo sounded: ahead Master of Hounds, the whippers in, Geoffrey Gibbon and Nigel Kearsley, and the kennel huntsman, Guardsman Phillips, who later went to the Monmouthshire Hunt, and behind came the field.

The Master wore a black velvet cap, otherwise we were all bareheaded. An enterprising local Arab tailor offered to run up two khaki hunt frock coats, inspired by *Baily's Hunting Directory*, of which he had obtained a copy, but the Joint Masters declined.

Nigel Kearsley's 1862 hunting horn was sent to him by Arthur Heywood-Lonsdale. Nigel reminded me that the ploy was to put the animal up, then chase it by view with Reggie's large Saluki, Mick, for about a mile. At that point Mick usually packed up and the hounds took over. This was the normal procedure. There is, however, a shameful entry in the Welsh Guards War Diary, dated 2 February, 1946: "Commanding Officer's Saluki was chased by a jackal". Sentence: confined to kennel on biscuits and water, but no bone.

When the Welsh Guards left Galilee the hounds were returned to the Ramleh Vale and the horses dispersed. They had been obtained from a pool of ex-remounts of 1st Cavalry Division which was so equipped until early in the War. Some, bought from Arabs, were good polo ponies. Nigel and others played on them, mostly against the Transjordan Frontier Force.

On the shores of Lake Tiberias Reggie had rented the Villa Melchett for £5 a week from Lady Reading. I went there first with Mary Rosner, a delectable girl I had met in Tiberias. The staff comprised a sergeant and four guardsmen. Orange and grapefruit groves surrounded the place and two sailing whalers, transported from Egypt, were moored alongshore.

Further north, on the lakeside, was Magdala, where Christ ate with Simon the Pharisee. His feet were anointed by a woman considered unvirtuous and whose sins He forgave. She is thought by many liturgists to be Mary Magdalen. A little further on is the Plain of Genesareth, then Ain Tineh, where Christ told the parable of the mustard seed, and five others; then Tabigha, where the stones of an ancient wharf can still be seen. Here Matthew, called by Jesus to be an apostle, probably collected duty for Herod Antipas, as goods were landed there, including fish caught in the lake.

The tax man cometh at all times, and wouldst fain be known to Simon Peter, who lived at Capernaum, and other fishermen. There were at least six genera of fish in the lake considered clean. Those without scales would not have been eaten by Jews. Capernaum lay at the north end of the lake. The ruins of a Byzantine church and a synagogue, where Arab shepherds grazed their flocks, were there. The synagogue was funded by the Roman centurion – *Domine non sum dignus:* Lord I am not worthy to receive thee – whose servant Jesus healed through the appeals of Jewish friends and his own faith.

I often bathed from the shore nearby, more rock than gravel at that point. A soldier drowned in the vicinity. As the Welsh Guards report no loss of life, he must have been from another unit. Northwards is the road to Metullah and the Lebanese border. On the left is the Mount of Beatitudes. Not too far away, across the Jordan as it enters the lake, is the Plain of Bataiha where Christ performed His miracle of the loaves and fishes.

I remember shooting duck there – Mark Norman behind me bringing down the wind-driven high flyers I missed – and running out of cartridges. Even though "not a sparrow falls" without divine cognizance, and certainly not a duck, who was I to ask for a miraculous replenishment? Then I remembered a dinner conversation with the theologically alert Father Murphy, the Irish priest at Brigade Headquarters. He told me, in some confidence, with the air of a man who was knowin' a fact 'n all, after deep thought and a deeper draught of the port,

"The rain falls gently, like God's grace, on all parts and on all men!" Presumably also on all women. A poetic phrase he had learnt before leaving Ireland, somewhat inapplicable to the Sahara. Then he added, "Remember, my son, yer can't put a gun at God's head!"

It had never entered my mind to menace our Maker in such a manner, even when I ran out of cartridges, and the gun, *ipso facto*, was unloaded. In fact, I asked Julian Paget, the Coldstream adjutant, who was leaving the shoot, if I could borrow his gun – 12 bore, for which there was no cartridge shortage; mine was 16 bore – and he replied, quite correctly, that he never lent his gun. There was no miracle there either.

Other off-duty activities included religious expeditions, arranged for all ranks: churches and sites being plentiful in Palestine, despite the turmoil of centuries. These trips were curtailed towards the end. Besides bathing in the Sea of Galilee there were outings to the Mediterranean, and for the curious to the Dead Sea, where no fish could survive, swimming was arduous, and only floating possible, as one gazed towards the mountains of Jordan, 4000 feet up, or those of Judaea at 3000 feet. The Dead Sea was 1300 feet below sea level at its surface, and another 1300 feet to the bottom, which we did not explore.

Nor did we see Sodom or Gomorrah. They had gone to ground. Nor any pillar of salt, nor a Bedouin emerging from a Qumran cave, offering to sell scrolls from which the latest arcane mystery of the Essene sect could be unravelled and its significance disputed by the experts, who would not be experts if they could not dispute.

Leave parties also went to the Lebanon until the frontier was closed, theoretically, in mid-April, 1946. There were, however, Cyprus and to a certain extent Egypt, whither we could go. Nearer base, games of all kinds were organized: rugby, soccer, cricket and boxing. One round with Colonel Reggie. Any takers? Also Reggie and James Gresham organized and financed the hiring and showing of suitable films in the cinema attached to the Elizabeth Hotel, nothing exotic, erotic or erosive to morale, all good clean stuff previewed by the Censors: the reverend padré and the very reverend RSM, Arthur Rees.

As far as the officers' mess was concerned, the immediate challenge which faced me was the arrival of the Regimental Lieutenant Colonel, Sammy Stanier. I wrote to my mother, coping with post-War rationing and food coupons: *"We dined well, beginning with consommé, followed by Galilean fish, then roast beef with roast potatoes, liver savoury, ice cream, Turkish or French coffee. As for wine and liqueurs: anything ordered!"* The Medical Officer was on hand.

Three days later, on 23 March, we lunched with Sheik Mohammed el-Masri, the muktah of el-Muftkra, in the Huleh valley. The veiled ladies ululated, while the men galloped full tilt at one another, firing their old Turkish rifles into the air. At lunch, sitting on the ground under a large tent, we set to as portable hillocks of rice and mutton were borne before us and put down – four men to each gargantuan plate – while the women peeped from behind a dark canvas screen. Their cooking was appreciated.

Our host was impressed by the carrier which, for some reason unclear to me at the time, bore Colonel Sammy to the feast. The Muktar wished to acquire it. "It's the King's carrier," said Sammy, obviously an old hand at this sort of thing. "When I return to England, I will ask him." Honour, if not gratification, was wholly satisfied. The Muktar then offered Sammy the sheep's eye which it was his dubious privilege to eat. I was unsure whether he did so, or conjured some simulated motion with his hand, and let it slip down his battledress front.

Then, on 27 March, our Colonel having recovered his digestion, the officers' mess offered him and the Major General Commanding Brigade of Guards, Sir Charles (Budget) Loyd, whom I had last seen in Italy, a sensible five-course affair, which did not vary much from the first, on 20 March. Duck, however, replaced beef. With others, I had accounted for 25 brace in the Huleh and, nearby, some black partridge.

The Huleh, now irrigated after Jewish settlement and minus the Muktar and his clan, was then largely marshland, and an obvious attraction for migratory and resident duck, as well as snipe and quail. I had bought my 16 bore double barrelled shotgun for £5, sight unseen from a Coldstream officer of my height, reach and modest needs. He had liberated it in Berlin. It was made by Forster and served me impeccably.

The only problem was the supply of cartridges: NAAFI dealt in 12 bore. This matter was overcome in one way or another, of which I recall one. I bought 2000 of various numbers in Italy, some of which I shared with Bill Gore-Langton, the Brigade Major, who shot with his left arm. The right was lost at Salerno. Armed with my 16 bore Forster, I used to go with a friend or two, rather than with a group if I could, and walk snipe, by far the most enjoyable sport for me. We would then wait for the evening flight of duck. Arab boys were always there and were duly rewarded.

More adventurously, the shoot at Azraq, 50 miles east of Amman, an outpost of Lawrence of Arabia during the Arab revolt against the Turks, involved a longer expedition from Palestine. Dick Chaplin, Coldstream, and I went once, though I had been twice before while in Transjordan. On this trip, avoiding Jerusalem, we went through the hills via Nablus, then dropped below sea level to Jericho, a lush oasis of palm and banana trees, and crossed the Allenby Bridge over the muddy, meandering, slow-moving Jordan.

We then climbed 4000 feet until we reached the Jordan plateau and stayed the night with the Transjordan Frontier Force, the British cavalry regiment mentioned earlier, with a large and extremely courteous Circassian contingent, who had left the western Caucasus in the nineteenth and early twentieth centuries. They wore red-striped, grey breeches, grey shirts and Karakul-lamb kalpaks. Duties were to guard the frontiers and the pipeline which ran from Iraq to Haifa. It also had an internal security role, as did the Arab Legion, then commanded by Glubb Pasha – Major General Sir John Glubb.

The Legion was technically a Transjordanian formation under the Emir Abdullah, son of Sherif Hussein, king of the Hejaz and head of the Arab people. After 1946 Abdullah became king. The duties of the Legion, in addition to posting the royal guard, were similar to those of the TJFF. The rank and file, then as now, were largely recruited from Bedouin tribes. The officers, then, were either British or Arab. Brigadier Teal Ashton, formerly Welsh Guards, was second-in-command of the Legion.

Dick and I were the guests of the TJFF commander, Colonel Shan Hackett, then aged thirty-seven, and his Austrian wife, Margaret. After dinner we played liar dice, in the course of which my hostess cast doubt upon a fundamental factor about my call. I shook the five dice again. They fell exactly as before. The odds on this happening are long. The dice, in passing, belonged to the Hacketts. Our shoot went well.

In the years which followed, Shan Hackett, better known as General Sir John, became Deputy Chief of the Imperial General Staff and made the transition, in the 1960s, to Deputy Chief of Staff, Ministry of Defence: the Empire was gone, but the Army carried on. Indeed, the Army carried on in Palestine until its final withdrawal in June, 1948, when 1st Guards Brigade Group sailed out of Haifa harbour on board ships of the Royal Navy.

The Army suffered casualties, both in the conquest from the Turks and during the Mandate. The Arab rebellion between the Wars was led by Haj Amin el-Husseini, Grand Mufti of Jerusalem, whom Herbert Samuel, first High Commissioner, had appointed. In the Second World War he allied himself with Hitler and narrowly escaped death at the hands of the British SOE while travelling on the Orient Express. He was also photographed inspecting a Bosnian SS Mountain Division. The Palestine Police – British, Jew and Arab – also lost many dead and wounded both before and after the War. The civilian population, too, suffered many casualties: Palestine was not a paradise of peace.

During the Second World War and its sequel, when I was there, it was the extremist Jewish elements who, by their savagery, shamed their co-religionists. As X Command learnt early, it required greater central control than it could exercise to stir up violence. Thus, the Jews were faced with the moral question of the means used to obtain the end. Many wished not to face the question. Some felt it did not even arise; but many, both Sabras (Palestine-born) and immigrants recognized the obvious British dilemma: the Arabs had rights to their own land and employment in their own country. Why should they be dispossessed? Was it wise to dispense with the Mandate? Was violent degradation the right and righteous way to achieve a certain ambition?

Furthermore, Zionism was not and never has been a 100% equation with Judaism. First, although few Gentiles were Zionists, they existed: some British for personal reasons and certain American politicians, largely concerned with votes. Secondly, among Jews, some religious sects were opposed in principle; others were wary of the idea of an independent state. Thirdly, many Jews were used to getting on with their neighbours in Arab countries, such as the Sephardim in North Africa, descendants of those who arrived at the time of the Diaspora in the 1st century AD.

After deliberate Irgun provocation, nearly all lost their homes and livelihoods. The Sephardim were aghast at the Nazi slaughter in Europe, but saw no reason why Palestine should be the exclusive sanctuary for the survivors: a Zionist tactic to put pressure upon the Mandatory power, hasten the establishment of a Jewish state and arouse the eternal enmity of the Arabs.

Many Jews living in Syria, Lebanon and Iraq were descended from those taken into captivity by Nebuchadnezzar. They did not return when Cyrus of Persia conquered Babylon and released all who wished to leave. These Jews lost the fruits of twenty-six centuries of shared citizenship and mutual respect, through many vicissitudes in twenty-six days, perhaps twenty-four hours, when Jewish terrorists, almost exclusively Ashkenazi or European Jews, provoked Arab reaction in order to force their return to Israel. In fact, many Sephardim passed through on their way elsewhere.

In 1945, three years before these dramas, and Harry Truman's re-election (president since Roosevelt's death in April), the British government informed Truman via the usual channels that his humanitarian viewpoints were appreciated, also the importance of the Jewish vote. But the gates of America were not being opened to Jewish refugees. Rather, they were encouraged, with the concurrence of the Jewish Agency, to go to Palestine. This made the British administration more difficult and totally ignored Arab rights. It was proposed that he cooperate.

Thus, the "buck stopped", to use his own phrase, on Truman's desk: of the choice between playing Cyrus – go whither thou wilt – or Nebuchadnezzar – I take thee unto mine own in Babylon's Big Apple, New York City. Truman chose the Anglo-American Committee.

CHAPTER FOUR

Palestine 1946 – Background and Foreground

6.3.1946. The Anglo-American Committee of twelve not particularly apostolic nor evangelic gentlemen – six from each country – arrived, unarmed, in Haifa on a Wednesday, two days after our draft. Perhaps they felt safer. It was the fifth or sixth effort, depending on how many official reports, White Papers, Commissions, capers and Committees are included, set up to investigate and recommend a solution to the insoluble: a political situation fundamentally flawed from the beginning.

The reader need not feel robbed of any suspense if I reveal that the Committee observed and listened, cobbled a report and failed. Nevertheless, they delved deep enough to obtain facts relating to dissidents and terrorists. The committee was followed by two more, before the British government handed over the matter of the Palestine Mandate to the successor organization of the League of Nations, whence it had received the Mandate in the first place, namely the United Nations.

Rejection of all proposals and Papers was the only point upon which Arab and Jew ever agreed. Their cooperation began nine years earlier, when both effectively rejected the 1937 Peel Commission proposals: partition and restricted Jewish immigration. (Although accepted by the World Zionist Congress, stultifying provisions were added. Non-Zionist Jewish opinion denounced it.) A year later the Woodhead Commission reversed the proposition, declaring partition to be impractical. Jewish immigration was restricted – in 1939, after acceptance by the British Parliament of which thirty Jews were members – to 75,000 over five years, giving the Jews one third of the population, an advance on 10% in 1917. Known as the *White Paper*, it was blackened and vilified by both Jews and Arabs, the latter, in 1930, having received the unconsoling British admission of the injustice done to them, arising from the dual, contradictory commitment.

In 1937, the obvious and digressive geographical fact that Palestine lay south-south-west and not west of Damascus, was, as mentioned, admitted. There was also the aforementioned abstruse reference to Palestine's position under the Turks: Jerusalem was a *sanjak* and the remainder part of the Beirut *vilayet*. These facts bore no relevance to the independence agreement signed with Hussein in 1916. In an ongoing tragedy, they were as much farce as fallacy.

The Nazi persecution of the Jews and their being deprived of German nationality in 1935 was neither. The War followed. Estimates of casualties and exterminations run into tens of millions in Asia, Europe and Africa. Certainly the largest number of civilians was in Russia and China. In Europe, on 20 January, 1942, the extermination of the Jews was planned in the annexe to the villa at 16, Kleiner Wannsee, on the lake near Berlin – Interpol's temporary Gestapo-dominated headquarters – the sequestered property of a Jew. It was convened by Reinhard Heydrich, self-appointed head of Interpol, Himmler's deputy and soon to be assassinated. Nazi death camps accounted for around twelve million souls, of which half were Jews.

As for Palestine, it soon became clear to all parties that the agreement made in 1916 with Sherif Hussein on behalf of all the Arabs was nullified by the 1917 Declaration. Since this decision cost the lives of hundreds of British soldiers and civilians, as well as thousands of Jews and Arabs before the Mandate ended in May 1948, and brought no benefit to Great Britain, why was it made?

In most political matters, however obscure, established policy in foreign affairs is founded on a clear grasp of the country's best interests: the Cossacks, for example, were expelled from Austria in 1945 to appease Stalin. Many were non-Soviet citizens and therefore wholly extraneous to the Yalta Agreement. It was considered objectively and dispassionately by the perpetrator, Harold Macmillan – admitted in detail by him and by his biographer – a patriot and later prime minister, to be in pursuit of policy: the Palmerstonian principle which maintained that the least risk for any country was always run by working closely with the country most feared.

Subjective, special pleading to the contrary, with selected omissions and irrelevancies, is unhistorical. Humanity, as admitted by Harold Macmillan, was not an issue, any more than it was in bombing Dresden or Warsaw. Humanity, on the other hand, was the primary reason posited for the conception and announcement of the Balfour Declaration. This was certainly not in British interests, nor was it policy. There were four reasons :

1. Assumed obligation by David Lloyd George: cordite = commitment (see below).
2. Zionist lobbying, plus generous, generative funding.
3. Sympathy for Zionist ambitions in London political social circles.
4. Gross underestimation of Arab feelings, abilities and reactions.

First: David Lloyd George states in his *War Memoirs* that supplies of cordite were dwindling. In the First World War cordite was derived from wood alcohol: shipping losses had cut timber imports. Lloyd George, minister of munitions, met Dr Chaim Weizmann, who isolated an organic substance – acetone butyl alcohol – from which cordite could be made. He declined an honour, says Lloyd George, but requested that the British government facilitate Jewish immigration into Palestine.

Lloyd George became Prime Minister in December, 1916. The Declaration followed eleven months later. It was a cabinet decision. In 1937 Lloyd George appeared before the Peel Commission. A year earlier he had appeared before Hitler, whom he publicly admired. As for the Commission, he told its members that Weizmann undertook to rally Zionist support for the War and added, tangentially, that the Zionists kept their word. In an off moment, Horace might have called this an *harengus ruber*, red herrings being known both to the Roman palate and debate. Politics, nevertheless, being the art of the artful, this rhetoric endeavoured to make the meaningless meaningful.

In fact, patriotic Jewish support was manifest long before Zionism offered its help. Zionists could not sink U-boats, reinforce three million men in France, save the Russian government, which included several Jews in 1917, nor encourage Jews in Germany and Austria-Hungary to betray their countries. Weizmann would have agreed.

The power of Zionism was two-fold: its ideals were largely, but not wholly, supported by the Jewish vote in New York. This gave it political power. Secondly, it could raise funds. Politicians took account of both: they were positive factors, but negative if the Peel Commission, for example, were to consider they influenced the initiators of the Declaration. Thus the cordite commitment, which most historians now regard as tenuous, needed wadding. Lloyd George therefore emphasized the War effort and Zionist support. In saying Zionists kept their word, he diverted attention from his own government's failure to keep theirs to the Arabs – whose direct and effective contribution to the War was in accordance with *their* word and Allied interests, as well as their own.

Secondly, Jewish support for the War was prompt and patriotic. More directly, in terms of Palestine, Zionists undertook legitimate lobbying in and out of Parliament, where Jews sat in both the House of Lords and the Commons. Contributions were made, quite legally, to both Coalition parties.

Thirdly, Zionist ideas were received sympathetically at influential, white tie, political dinners. Sadly, for future peace and stability, no Arab could, at that time, be invited to these gatherings, beset by the fog of cigar-fumed philanthropy in post-prandial pursuit of Allenby's conquests, to state plainly that the idea, in practice, meant the medusoid acquisition of Arab homes and Arab land – *their* homeland – by a third party, who fervently postulated a biblical claim. This was uniquely considered to be superior to anything temporally legal. It was equally unacceptable, indeed both absurd and even blasphemous to a Moslem. Melpomene, the muse of tragedy, was coming on stage.

Thus, the *political* foundations of this racial and religious imbroglio were built not on sand, which is manageable, but on quicksand, which is not. The cabinet knew the civil and religious rights of the "existing non-Jewish communities" – 90% Arab – must be prejudiced *ab initio*, by the Declaration. The proverbial die, however, was cast: in a mood of nonchalant, *déjà vu* imperialism, with disregard and deliberate disrespect for the prior agreement, the cabinet implemented what they declared to be a policy, which in fact was an idea, presuming all difficulties could be resolved by decree.

Fourthly, a distorted idea of Arab civilization, and a gross miscalculation of Arab ability was prevalent in ministerial deliberations. As late as 1935 Churchill told Malcolm MacDonald, as reported in a conversation with Nicholas Bethell: "You are crazy to help the Arabs. They are a backward people who eat nothing but camel dung." Even allowing for Churchill's frequent inebriation with his own command of language, this was immoderate. The Jews, he expected correctly, would make the desert bloom, although details of its legal acquisition and the consequences, were not seriously considered. They could also replant, after purchase, Naboth's vineyard, while Jezebel could be revamped, and her talents disinterred, within the confines and constraints of the kibbutzim.

Nine years later, in 1944 after the assassination of his friend Lord Moyne, Churchill warned: "If our dreams of Zionism are to end in the smoke of assassins' pistols and produce a new set of gangsters, many will have to reconsider the position we have maintained. These wicked activities must cease, and those responsible rooted out." Among the triumvirs who ordered Moyne's death, who were not rooted out, were Yitzhak Yiszernitsky (Shamir) later prime minister, Nathan Friedman-Yellin (Yellin-Mor) and Israel Sheib (Eldad) the executive of the Lehi/Stern gang. The three met again, four years later, to order the murder of Count Folke Bernadotte, the UN Representative in Palestine.

A year after Moyne's murder, in 1945, President Truman, needing, as he admitted, the Jewish vote, quixotically proposed the immediate entry of 100,000 Jews (the Zionist conference demanded a million) when the limit was 1500 a month. This last figure, established by the Woodhead Commission – the White Paper's precursor – remained throughout a minimal Mandatory obligation, preventing further injustice to the Arabs, who demanded none. Neither Clement Attlee, nor Ernest Bevin at the Foreign Office, were best pleased. The British political position, however, was weak, and from the beginning impossible to maintain: a *ménage à trois* was not a British speciality, even though Lloyd George may have been induced to attempt it.

The War had momentarily ruined Great Britain – pre-War oversea assets accounted for £5.5 billion; post-War debts were £2 billion – while the American economy was flourishing, having produced in the War nearly 300,000 aircraft, 71,000 ships and 86,000 tanks. Thus, Britain was indebted to an America antipathetic to British overseas possessions, of which it once formed an integral part, and after independence expanded with considerable exuberance to continental proportions. In this case, what was good for the goose was definitely not good for the gander: whereas transriparian imperialism was acceptable – one more river to cross and a few more Indians to kill – transmarian colonialism was not, Hawaii excepted. The fact that Palestine was a Mandate and not a Colony was irrelevant.

Anti-British *colonial* feeling was, therefore, not difficult to arouse. This was doubly irrational: first, had the British run Palestine as a true democracy, the Arab majority would have voted the Jews out. The latter were lucky it was run as a Colony. Secondly, American imperialism, both permanent and vast, like its Russian, Latin American and Chinese counterparts, was considered heroic and freed Americans from other imperialists. Yet, in 1946, Americans were still alive who were born slaves. Segregation was legal in many states. Half Mexico was taken barely a century earlier. In 1898 America attacked Spain and seized the Philipines, Cuba, and Puerto Rico. Hawaii was annexed and its monarch deposed. The construction of the canal in Panama province followed a classic act of subversion against Colombia.

This frontier spirit of amoral achievement was successfully

exploited by Zionist interests. In the minds of many, perhaps more unconsciously than consciously, a chord was struck and recalled by American gentiles whereby the Arabs were likened to the Amero-Indians. Arab rights were never discussed. The Arab case was not even judged by default. Certainly the standard of living, the agronomic and economic skills of the two communities – Arab and Jew – were incomparable. In consequence, Jewish political pressure was applied not only through the horse trading of votes in New York, but also psychologically: how could the remnants of Nazi bestiality be refused admittance to the Promised Land when much of it was waiting for their skills and workmanship?

There was, nevertheless, a dichotomy in American thinking: the war of independence, termed a revolution, was basically about an exchange of excisemen, the nearer in the end being dearer. The rapturous reception given to George VI and Queen Elizabeth in 1939 – ticker-taped in New York as only the Big Apple could – was in contrast to the mythologized feelings expressed towards the great-great-great grandfather of their honoured guest, George III, the engineered, collective archetypal ogre, whose known sympathies for his American subjects were drowned in the discord expressed and exemplified by his incompetent government, and the hostility and introversion of Parliament, passing detrimental, fiscal colonial legislation, precluding recourse or representation.

In 1939 Americans were perhaps, unwittingly eager to make amends for the affront given to the father figure they had wronged. An emotional people, they became easy prey to propaganda. Playwrights and copywriters put pen to parchment. Not all their creativity was judged exemplary :
"Every time a British soldier is killed in Palestine, I make a little holiday in my heart" was the inept and inelegant comment of an aspiring Jewish American playwright, Ben Hecht, who vilified the British and martyrized their language. He was, however, appreciated on Broadway. Hecht was a member of an Irgun gang front organization, the American League for a Free Palestine. It was disavowed by the main Zionist groups, who also raised money.

This was the acid fruit of a double engagement, thirty years earlier, which unlike the caprine escapades of its progenitor, Lloyd George, became impaled upon the horns of its brazen indiscretion. Into this remarkably unnecessary and unrewarding mess, the uncomplaining, phlegmatic British soldier was precipitated. Indeed, as a form of welcome to the Anglo-American Committee's duodecimal 1946 act, X Command launched attacks against three airfields between 20 – 26 February, when the author and his draft were on the high seas. Seven aircraft were destroyed and eight damaged. Then Irgun attacked the 3rd Hussars' camp at Sarafand. This failed. Two attackers were held and later hanged.

The Anglo-American Committee, meanwhile, heard the Arab viewpoint lucidly presented by Albert Hourani, of the Arab Office in Jerusalem: neither the Jews nor the great powers had the right to impose the burden of Jewish refugees on Palestine, nor to create a Jewish state in a predominantly Arab territory. Injustice had already been done. As for the introduction of a further conflicting factor – the maintaining by Great Britain of a strategic reserve in Palestine, if the Egyptian bases were abandoned – this was, luckily, not on the agenda nor within the Committee's brief.

7.3.46. At the grassroots level of military activity, I took a Prince of Wales Company patrol around a Jewish village, with nothing much in mind, it seemed, but to show the flag. Cordoning and searching, of which all battalions in Palestine had their share, was a more complicated operation. Sometimes arms were found, sometimes not. Either way the searched expressed resentment. Not least they asked among themselves, who, among the Yishuv, had informed the authorities? And the searchers, while not being unsympathetic, were aware the arms might be used against them if the security situation deteriorated, the defined difference between an armed terrorist Jew in Tel Aviv and his kibbutz co-religionist being blurred.

While the Anglo-American Committee attended to their appointed task, I was asked to collect five armoured vehicles – White scout cars – from Egypt. Two broke down in the desolate Sinai desert, a crossing of two hundred miles undertaken more slowly at the time of the Pharaohs. We reached, however, a deep well of hospitality at Beersheba where we spent the night, after a reasonable evening meal, with the local military. In the morning, before leaving for Nazareth, I noted the wells which Abraham knew, some small shacks, the military encampment, a Government House, a few scattered trees and a bust of Lord Allenby, which the Bedouin regarded with superstition as an unnecessary graven image to a great warrior.

We left the brown hills surrounding Beersheba as we drove north into the coastal plain, where Arab shepherds and their flocks were replaced by citrus groves and Jewish agricultural development, keeping on the direct road north until we reached Hadera when we struck off north-east, across the southern stretches of the Carmel range, then descended into the Esdraelon Plain, passed through Afula and climbed the southern side of the Lower Galilee Hills, before descending into Nazareth.

I had known Micky Boyd, Irish Guards, to whom I delivered the vehicles, in Italy when he was listing the sick and wounded in his regiment, after severe casualties at Anzio. In a few months I was to become his successor at Brigade Headquarters. Meanwhile, as mentioned, I was ordered to divide my time between Prince of Wales Company and running the mess.

29.3.46. The Major General and the Regimental Lieutenant-Colonel Commanding the Regiment having departed, and my reputation remaining momentarily intact, Hugo Herbert-Jones and I received permission to explore the Lebanon, at that time – until 15 April, 1946 – still retaining the rearguard of French and British troops. We went via Metullah, on the frontier, where Support Company, Welsh Guards, commanded by David Lawman, was stationed. We then descended towards the coast, arrived in Beirut and checked into the Normandy Hotel, run by an androgynous young man called Roger the Corkscrew.

The following day we made for the mountains, where I ski-ed for the first and last time, although, on reflection, this is an exaggeration. Even on the gentle slopes and sliding on my behind, I seemed to hit the trunks of the few remaining cedars. Sitting on a bar stool was both safer and warmer. In the mountains the temperature was around freezing. At sea level it was hot. We decided to descend. In Beirut there was bathing, some shopping, and the racecourse which welcomed us enticingly in English: "Today's events: exciting flat horse steaks!"

The owners' enclosure provided a scene of men in varied dress: wide striped suits, worn with a fez or panama hat, a sheik or two in robes and headdress reminiscent of the Hejaz and even a chap who looked as if he had fled Newmarket before the Stewards' decision. At any rate, we judged the man by his surroundings. The jockeys entered and left, after a brief dialogue with the owners. Trainers were not in evidence, which raised the question of their being required.

The first race was a walkover. The second differed considerably. An owner standing next to us appeared horrified to see his horse in the lead. He rent his racecard, for what the gesture and the card were worth. His jockey was in the race but well outside his instructions. A convincing performance was one thing; too convincing was another. The horses were only required to run from start to finish. Not all of them managed even that.

The jockey suddenly remembered the form, pulled back his mount, and looked over his shoulder while the stewards trained their glasses on the blonde in the President's box. The designated winner sweated its way to the front, its jockey with the whip out. It was a close run finish. Our neighbour relaxed. We had had enough excitement – without betting – and left. The blonde in the President's box presented the cup.

We returned to the Battalion by the coast road, before turning inland for Tiberias. Hugo heard he was being posted to Greece. My dual duties were unchanged.

On 23 April, Saint George's Day, the Irgun gang attacked Ramat Gan police station, near Tel Aviv. One of the terrorists was killed and another arrested. Two days later, the Stern gang, in an assault comprising thirty men and women, murdered seven members of the 6th Airborne Division, commanded by Major General James Cassells. Lieutenant General Sir John d'Arcy was then GOC Palestine. He shortly handed over to Lieutenant General Sir Evelyn Barker, who soon introduced some tough measures.

29.4.46. The Anglo-American Committee's recommendation of an independent state with autonomous areas was rejected by both Jews and Arabs. It had posited the admittance of 100,000 Jews who would have been given 1500 square miles to absorb and sustain them, when, at that moment, 82% of Palestine Jews were living in a 90 square mile area. The 1500 square miles, a 1666% increase, would have included the best land, 85% of the citrus-growing area, the only deep water port, Haifa, most of the coast line, and a considerable amount of the main water supply.

Weizmann, who together with all Zionists had begun with very little before the Mandate, called it worse than the Peel Commission proposals of 1937. The United States senate heard such statements as "it was a betrayal of the Jewish homeland", a "conscienceless act of treachery" and "confinement inside an economically non-viable ghetto". The Arabs, hardly, if ever, considered by Zionists, also rejected it.

Meanwhile, unable to make any progress in Palestine, Great Britain recognized the independence of Transjordan and on 25 May the kingdom of that country was proclaimed with Abdullah as king. I attended the celebrations on 1 June, with Johnny Lascelles, a Grenadier and 1st Guards Brigade Headquarters' Intelligence Officer.

The Arab Legion laid on a pageant of armoured cars, passing in columns, preceded by the Legion's cavalry and camels. We noted the presence of Ibn Saud's sons. It was their father who had ousted Hussein, Abdullah's father, from Mecca, and with him the Hashemite dynasty, now installed in Jordan: a consolation prize for a younger son from the British. Another received Iraq. Their independence, agreed in 1916, took some time to arrive *de jure*. The Palestinians waited in vain.

33

Another pageant was held in Tiberias on 13 June, when the Welsh Guards celebrated the King's Birthday Parade. Other units did likewise throughout Palestine. Colonel Reggie invited Crown Prince Talal of Jordan to take the salute, suitably mounted on a grey charger. They had been at Harrow together and later at Sandhurst. The Arabs were delighted. The Jews refused all invitations.

The parade, under the new adjutant after Jeremy Spencer-Smith's departure, Peter Leuchars, was impeccable; both adjutants, appropriately, later became Major Generals. The Regimental Sergeant Major, Arthur Rees, became Major and Quartermaster. Talal became king for a year. He was considered unstable. I liked him when he dined at Brigade, whither Reggie had sent me on attachment in June.

This began at a leisurely pace. I watched a parade of Polish school girls and boys in Nazareth, the progeny of Poles who had fought under General Anders in Italy, among whose forces were many women drivers and nurses. I then shot some dove with Brigadier Eddie Goulburn in the Jordan Valley. We swam the river to the opposite bank where some of the birds had fallen. In Nazareth, I played tennis with Willy Whitelaw, Scots Guards, the DAA & QMG, Edward Imbert-Terry, in the Coldstream, who was GIII, and Johnny Lascelles, on the District Commissioner's court, above the town. A predecessor, Yelland Andrews, had been assassinated by Arab terrorists in 1937. The residence was now guarded by an alert soldier in the Arab Legion, his rifle resting on sandbags piled on a circular pillbox before the entrance gate.

Off the tennis court, in the real world, all battalions and units were warned on 15 June of imminent terrorist attacks. Our intelligence was usually accurate, which meant the so-called Jewish Resistance Movement had been penetrated. Since terrorism was more or less part of the daily routine, we carried on our normal activities and mine, on this day, included a trip to Sarafand to hear Field Marshal Montgomery's address to senior officers. I accompanied the Brigade commander.

The great Field Marshal's words escape me, but I recall his water glass was empty. Flurried generals sought the nearest tap and, no doubt later, the chap in charge of slaking the thirst of the Chief of the Imperial General Staff. As for terrorist attacks, none came, nor did they for most of the following day. Certainly those officers who dined out considered it to be a false alarm.

16.6.46. Edward Imbert-Terry was on leave. I was acting, attached GIII. I was also the duty officer. After dinner, which was considerate, X Command, specifically Haganah, in conjunction with Lehi/Stern in Haifa, launched a concerted attack. Our intelligence had been correct: nine bridges, five road and four rail, linking Palestine with Jordan, Syria and the Lebanon were destroyed. 1st Division Headquarters telephoned and I immediately went to the operations room, where I was joined by Peter Smalley, 60th Rifles, as my assistant.

Peter was a keen, likeable fellow who "blew up" a tenth bridge with considerable enthusiasm. This displeased, or disappointed, the CRE, who investigated and found it intact. He rang me and blew me up in its place. I consoled him, however, with the fact that the other eight were genuine losses. He seemed happy with the news: engineers like building bridges. One Royal Engineer officer, however, was killed while defusing a delayed action mine placed on a bridge across the Jordan.

In due course, the others returned: Brigadier Eddie Goulburn, Bill Gore-Langton, the Brigade Major, Willy Whitelaw, Johnny Lascelles and Micky Boyd. Other officers were not concerned with operations. They had dined with one or other of the three battalions. They now sat down, watched and listened. I offered to hand over. This was declined. The duty officer then dispatched troops, via battalion headquarters, to various points, as reports came in, encouraged Peter Smalley to stick the right flags in the right places and said a private prayer of thanks for the signals officers and the Royal Corps as a whole that the telephone lines were open and clear, lines which Haganah had neglected to cut or were unable to find.

On 18 June five British officers were kidnapped while lunching in Tel Aviv, and a sixth in Jerusalem. They were liberated.

On 23 June General Barker, GOC Palestine, informed divisional commanders of countermeasures. The next day I was driven by jeep to the Coldstream headquarters at Acre, with a sealed envelope in my hand and a cocked tommy gun on my lap. I gave the envelope to Bob Coates, commanding, who was in the orderly room with David Chetwode, his second-in-command, and Julian Paget, the adjutant. Other officers were sent to the Grenadiers at Hadera and the Welsh Guards at Tiberias.

On 29 June Operation "Agatha" was launched: 100,000 troops and the Palestine Police were involved. The Jewish Agency was occupied; twenty-five Jewish settlements were cordoned and searched; 2659 men and 59 women were detained. Even so, Operation Agatha achieved very little: it solidified the opposition of the Jewish community, the Yishuv, to the Mandate which many of them, but by no means all, were beginning to feel had served its purpose and had ceased to be of any further use. The Germans had been defeated, the Americans were backing them, and the Arabs were comparatively impotent, at any rate politically.

35

On the day the operation was launched Chaim Weizmann, playing his role of injured innocence to perfection, and with chutzpah, told Sir Alan Cunningham that the British reaction to Jewish violence was a battle against world Jewry. Not all Jews would have agreed. In any case, the following day Ben-Gurion called a meeting of X Command, the existence of which was well known to Weizmann.

Palmach, the offensive wing of Haganah, had prepared a plan to destroy, as a political gesture, as these acts are described, part of the building in which government offices were housed in the southwest wing of the King David Hotel, Jerusalem. At the meeting were representatives of Palmach, Haganah, Irgun and Stern. It was decided the operation should be undertaken by Irgun. X Command issued written instructions. On 1 June, Menachem Begin, the Irgun terrorist leader, began planning the King David Hotel outrage.

6.7.46. Weizmann summoned about thirty undetained Jewish leaders to his house at Rehovot, some twelve miles south of Tel Aviv. They included Israel Rokach, Mayor of Tel Aviv, Gershon Agronsky, editor of the *Palestine Post* and Goldie Meyerson (Golda Meir) later prime minister. She advised Weizmann that a counter-demonstration was needed, to avert, as she put it, Irgun and Stern doing something "far more serious".

In fact, something far more serious had been launched a week earlier. At this 6 July meeting, as recorded in *History of the Haganah*, Weizmann was privy to the plot. He demanded a postponement until after the Jewish Agency August meeting in Paris. Begin paid no attention: "too dangerous" he said. The IZL went ahead.

On 7 July, the day after the Rehovot meeting with Jewish leaders and his request for postponing the King David Hotel operation, Weizmann assured Sir John Shaw, Chief Secretary, that there was no liaison between the terrorists and Haganah, except for an occasional effort to restrain them, a situation which John Shaw knew not to be true. Weizmann also assured Shaw that he was a friend of Britain (FO 371.52542).

At 12.37 on 22 July – all electric clocks were stopped – the bombs went off. Ninety-one people were killed, including seventeen Jews. I had an appointment in the bar arranged for 12.30.

CHAPTER FIVE

Seven Milk Cans and a Pilgrimage

Not being on X Command's distribution list, and thus unaware of this counter-demonstration, I left Nazareth for Jerusalem on Saturday 20 July, two days before the bombing. Alan Barton, BEME, Guardsman Heaver, Irish Guards and the Brigade interpreter, Issa S. Sa'ad, a Christian Arab and father of fourteen, who lived ecumenically and no doubt economically in the German Colony, Jerusalem, and myself formed the party of four.

We began early in our jeep and the journey took us through the hills and the beautiful Vale of Shechem, before we reached Nablus, a town of some 20,000 inhabitants, which lay in a gorge between the mountains. Its alleys were narrow, packed with donkeys, camels and the usual street impedimenta of the orient. It was also the centre of the remaining Samaritans, ruled by a High Priest who supervised the annual sacrifice of lambs on the summit, at 2400 feet, of the neighbouring holy Mount Gerizim.

The antipathy between the Jews and Samaritans dates from the return of the exiles from Babylon who found those Jews who remained had intermarried with the Assyrian colonists. Whereas the Samaritans disliked the Jews – Samaria, the ancient capital of the Northern Kingdom of Israel, was close by – they regarded the Arabs who had arrived in 638 AD as interlopers.

Sa'ad, who was a source of some erudite, even arcane information which I later checked, told me Alexander the Great had ordered the Samaritans to build statues to himself throughout their land. This offended the Mosaic law which forbade graven images. He returned later to find none. Furious, he arrived at Shechem and sent for the High Priest, demanding an explanation. The High Priest called out "Alexander!" Immediately numerous small boys appeared in front of him, all of the same age. They had been named after the great Macedonian. "We made you," said the High Priest "living statues! Not dead ones in stone!" He kept his head.

A mile-and-a-half outside Nablus, on the side of the road among a few trees, we found Jacob's Well at Sychar, where Christ met the woman of Samaria, a lady who had coupled five gentlemen and was living with a sixth. Many centuries later, a Greek church, surrounded by a wall, was built over it and the well, in turn, was surrounded by pillars of earlier churches, including one built by the Crusaders in which the high altar was directly over the well.

Fig trees grew in the garden, overlooked by the stony slopes of Mount Gerizim, itself crowned by a ruined tower, the remains of the Samaritan Temple erected in rivalry to that of Jerusalem. The well is about seventy feet deep, below the crypt, where soft rain water collects at the bottom. The nearby village of Aksar, formerly Sychar, is supplied by the hard limestone water of 'Ain Aksar. The sexpartite Samaritan lady preferred a longer walk to obtain better water and was rewarded for her pains, encountering "the spiritual rock, whence life's water springs".

The road from Jacob's Well to Jerusalem winds for fifty miles through the hills. We approached Ramallah, its main street lined with eucalyptus trees, if I remember correctly, then passed the airstrip of Kalandia, before first catching sight of the Holy City. We overtook, with care, the usual flocks of sheep and goats, their shepherds walking ahead on this journey, and not droving behind, often mounted on donkeys, uttering strange sounds which were both understood and obeyed by the flock.

Jerusalem approached from the north, or south, is not so impressive as from the east or west. The Kedron Valley to the east is virtually a sheer drop of several hundred feet, emphasizing why David took the Jebusite fortress and made it his capital. Approached from the west, after a climb from the coastal plain, Jerusalem appears on the spur of the central hills upon which it is built. North and south, these hills maintain a fairly constant altitude, becoming higher near Hebron, to the south, at nearly 3000 feet.

The eye falls first on the gilded Dome of the Rock. Built on the old Temple Mount, it is the most obvious feature. One or two minarets stand out, glimmering like polished silver sugar casters. The twenty-foot, castellated walls around the Old City were built by the Turks in the sixteenth century, after its capture from the Egyptian sultans in 1517. We skirted them as we came in via Mount Scopus. Our first call was entirely practical. We found that there was no room at the inn, the effectively unguarded King David Hotel, under Swiss management, epitomized by Mr Hamburger, the manager, and we booked in at Jasmin House, soon leaving for Bethlehem.

Some two miles on the road south we stopped at the Magi's Well, sometimes termed Mary's Well or the Well of the Star, so called because the Magi, or Wise Men, were said to have lost the star they were following, but rediscovered it when they saw its reflection in the water. There were a few trees surrounding it, and under them was a stone basin, which enabled shepherds or camel drivers to provide water for their animals.

The star, or, more specifically, the mysterious bright light, is now considered by astronomers, helped by computer work at Sheffield University, to be the alignment of Jupiter with Saturn in the constellation of Pisces, which occurred on 15 September, 7 BC. To the Magi, Jupiter was the planet of Kings, Saturn the protector of the Jews, and Pisces the Zodiac sign associated with Palestine. Christmas has, thus, been celebrated three-and-a-half months – and six years – late by the Christian Church, more in the spirit of supplanting the heathen celebration of the winter solstice than in terms of theological accuracy.

At this point on the road, we could see, to the east, the sudden and remarkable drop from our own altitude of around 2200 feet to the Dead Sea, at 1300 feet below sea level, a dramatic descent of 3500 feet, over a wilderness of bare hills, shimmering in the heat, to the elongated, spherical patch of salt water, way beneath us, on the further side of which towered the waterless Mountains of Moab, on the Transjordan side of the valley.

In our open jeep we soon became covered in the limestone dust which lay on the road and all about us. The airless heat surrounding Rachel's Tomb – white-domed and revered by Christians, Jews and Moslems – made us think of the shade we hoped to find in Bethlehem, only a mile further on. Sa'ad, however, drew our attention to a ruined aqueduct which at one time ran from Solomon's Pools, south of Bethlehem, to the Temple, and to the Roman barracks when troops were quartered in Jerusalem.

It was built by Pontius Pilate who had financed its construction by sequestering funds from the Corban, or Temple funds. There was a riot when this became public knowledge, and several Jews, notably Galileans, were killed in Jerusalem in the process. Pilate's career in Palestine ended when he over-reacted to a Samaritan religious assembly, which he broke up with the usual Roman brutality under such circumstances – rubber bullets were not a Roman form of dissuasion, even had they been known – and consequent large loss of life. The Samaritans complained to his superior, Vitellius, Legate of Syria, who sent him to Rome. On his way the

39

emperor Tiberius died, in 37 AD. His successor, Caligula, was presumably not interested in such a minor massacre.

A mile further on we reached the slope which leads slightly uphill to Bethlehem, a small town of flat-roofed, white houses, bell towers, convents, monasteries and orphanages. There was one minaret. On either side of the narrow main street were shops and workshops, the artisans tapping and sewing their wares, working under wide open arches. Bougainvillaea cascaded from the white roofs, the red and purple bracts overhanging, like the fabled gardens of Babylon. In the main square we saw a massive wall, at the bottom of which was a small door. It was too small for a horse to enter when open, the basic reason for its construction in troubled times, and we crouched as we crossed the threshold.

Inside was the Church of the Nativity, architecturally a stern, disciplined Roman basilica, with little ornament and even less reconstruction. This was the Church which Constantine the Great built in the fourth century. Subdued, red stone Corinthian pillars supported the roof, forming the nave and aisles. Faded gold mosaics could be seen on the walls. In the fifteenth century the roof was in danger of collapse, so the Yorkist king, Edward IV, dispatched oak beams and lead to repair it, through the intermediary of the Venetian Republic and the Franciscans.

Two centuries later the Turks, it is said, melted down the lead and used the resultant bullets against the Venetians. In the Candian War, Venice lost Crete. In the Morean War they captured Athens and retained the Morea, which they lost thirty-four years later. Nevertheless, Venice retained the Ionian Islands and the Dalmation coast. The Church of the Nativity, meanwhile, retained its purity: the high altar was built directly over the cave where Christ was born. In fact, this cave or grotto was sacred to Christians before the time of Hadrian, who built a temple above it to Adonis. Constantine destroyed it.

We descended one of the two staircases on both sides of the altar to the cave below, which was about twelve feet wide and forty feet long, nearly five hundred square feet. Behind the tapestries, permeated with incense, was rock. Embedded in the floor was a star surrounded by a Latin inscription which in English translates: "Here Jesus Christ was born of the Virgin Mary". There was a series of adjoining, interconnected underground passages. In one of them, with the help of a few candles, Saint Jerome translated his Vulgate from the Greek in the fourth century.

Sa'ad, our erudite interpreter and guide, pointed out other caves in Bethlehem, level with the road but underneath single-roomed old houses, carved or naturally present in the limestone rock. They were the same, and no doubt as old, as the Nativity grotto, which was certainly, 2000 years ago, at ground level, possibly in some form of bowl-shaped depression of the land surface, now built over. The houses were reached by stone steps, while the caves were used as stables or byres. In most were stone troughs – mangers – hewed out of the rock; iron rings dangled from the walls, to which the animals were secured at night.

The dress of the Bethlehem women we saw was unique. It dated from the Crusades, and the blue-eyed, fair-haired inhabitants strongly resembled Europeans. The headdress was high, supported by a small fez, and covered with a veil, pinned under the chin, and flowing over the shoulders, down the back. Around the fez, and unseen, were small coins, I was told, sewn into the material; but more particularly, after marriage, ten coins were suspended from a pendant. These represented the bride's dowry and formed the basis for Christ's parable: "What woman having ten pieces of silver, if she lose one piece, doth not light a candle, and sweep the house, and seek diligently till she find it?"

We returned to Jerusalem, climbed the old walls near the Zion Gate and had dinner at the King David Hotel. After dinner we met Alan's successor at Brigade, Arthur Butler, and a friend of his Rosemary Walsh. She was secretary to her father, the Economic Adviser and Food Controller. We arranged to meet again at the King David Hotel bar at 12.30, Monday 22 July. Seven minutes after this appointed time, the X Command, Irgun-detonated, terrorist bombs exploded.

On Sunday we walked through the Old City by the Via Dolorosa, the traditional route along which Christ carried His Cross to Golgotha, a bare limestone hillock twenty yards from the west wall of the city, from which it was in all probability separated by a ditch. The site of the Crucifixion and the tomb of the Resurrection are not really in dispute, but the route of Christ carrying the Cross depends upon whether Pontius Pilate held court at the Antonia Fortress next to the Temple, in which case it was by the Via Dolorosa and a journey of around 600 yards, or in Herod's Upper Palace. In the latter case, a shorter more direct route would have been taken. Either way, the Romans made a thorough job of destroying Jerusalem in 70 AD. The Via Dolorosa, its rubble cleared and re-used, is so narrow that we had to press against the walls to allow a donkey laden with a sack of flour to pass. Overhead are arches, and on each side are the usual artisan shops and little doorways.

We passed through Saint Stephen's Gate, with its graceful Saracenic arch, as H. V. Morton described it in *In The Steps of the*

Master. It overlooks the rocky gorge that leads into the arid Kedron Valley. We descended on a narrow road, turned right at the bottom and entered the Garden of Gethsemene, which is surrounded by a wall. Behind us, in the morning sun, were the Turkish ramparts of Jerusalem, the blocked Golden Gate and the Dome of the Rock, several hundred feet above, standing in stark contrast to the rural simplicity of our surroundings.

The Garden of Gethsemene is tended by the Franciscans who also administer the colourful Church of All Nations, the light – of the Gentiles – shining brightly through its windows, and if the olive trees in the garden be not two thousand years old, they certainly must be half that age. The cypress trees, too, are ancient, but not nearly as old as the olives. In the garden was a monk, tending the flowers and raking around the roots of the eight ancient olives from which new, green shoots were sprouting.

We left and began our climb up the Mount of Olives. It is slightly higher than Jerusalem, and appeared at first to be rather bare and inhospitable, with white limestone tracks twisting among the rocks and the occasional patch of cultivated land, terraced by limestone walls, with scattered olive trees. Yet, when we climbed it and reached the Ascension Stone, whence Christ ascended into Heaven forty days after His Resurrection, the place exuded peace.

To the north of the Mount of Olives lies the British War Cemetery for the dead of the Palestine campaign. It is east of Mount Scopus, and unlike most War cemeteries, it faces west – it is east of Jerusalem – and contains the graves of 2,180 soldiers of the United Kingdom of Great Britain and Ireland, 143 from Australia and 34 from New Zealand. One Welsh Guardsman is buried there and a Scots Guardsman. Among the dead is one woman, an Australian, Nurse Charlotte Berrie, of Neutral Bay, Sydney.

Rosemary hedges were growing between the graves and we saw one of the few places in Palestine where an earnest effort was being made by the gardeners to grow flowers with some success in a climate which did its best most of the year to wither them if they were not watered regularly. We were also in need of water, or perhaps something a little stronger, by the time we returned to Jerusalem where, on the way back to our hotel, I bought a rug in the souk. It was difficult not to buy something.

We had an excellent lunch with Sa'ad and his family and posed for our photographs afterwards, taken by Alan, to whom I remain grateful for all the photographs he took on this trip. As the reader will learn shortly, taking a batch of them the following day deflected by a fraction the arrow of fate which was winging its way in our direction

Lunch over, we left for Jericho and took the old road. In the tradition of Christ's parable, it was not difficult to see why the route was a haunt of bandits and the Good Samaritan was moved to perform his act of great charity. It turned and twisted, while boulders protruded onto the road, which was bounded by a tractless wilderness on both sides, of which one soon merged into a towering-rock-faced mountain, studded with caves. We could see a Greek Orthodox monastery built into the cliff face, clinging to the surface like a termites' nest. How it was built heaven alone knew, and no doubt heaven helped in its construction.

At a certain point the road rose slightly and on the crest was the Inn of the Good Samaritan. It was a Turkish khan, or small caravanserai, built to offer shelter to travellers, with a rock cistern at the back, which stored water. It must have been the site mentioned by Christ, because there was no other place to match it, and there was no other inn. The route was well known to Jews going up to Jerusalem, coming from across the Jordan and from Galilee, whence pilgrims would pass by way of the Jordan valley and Jericho, to avoid the dangers and defilement of Samaria and the Samaritans.

We were now entering a region of fierce, dry heat. This was not the climate we had just left, of the Mediterranean, and it was 1300 feet below the level of that sea. The Jordan plain is about fourteen miles across in the Jericho area. The river, or rather the tamarisks, willows and green bushes and reeds on its banks, resembles a grass snake, albeit a harmless one, for such it must be in so holy and baptismal an area. The Sea of Galilee lies sixty-five miles north, but the river course covers two hundred miles, or three times longer than if it flowed directly.

The Dead Sea, from our vantage point, looked blue and sparkled under the sun, its waters nestling between the distant Mountains of Moab, their dry, steep valleys streaked in shadow. The dun coloured Hills of Hebron were behind us, descending steeply over rock-strewn ground from heights of 3000 feet.

Jericho was not exactly as it was in the time of Cleopatra to whom it had been given by Antony, and who, in turn, rented it and its balsam groves to Herod the Great. There was not much balsam about when we were there, but there were palm trees, banana groves and herds of black goats. The heat was stifling and the ground shimmered as we drove to Allenby Bridge, the original steel structure, wooden planked but damaged during the recent disturbances, and then on to the Dead Sea, where we bathed, or rather floated.

There are no birds, because there are no fish, nor is there any vegetation, no plants or weeds, and the shore carries no shells. Anyone bathing can only float – Titus had some chained slaves thrown overboard to prove it – as a result of the concentration of salt, five times that in the open sea, because the Dead Sea is a huge basin of chemicals for which there is no outlet. Nearly every day the Jordan and its tributaries pour seven million tons of water into this catchment area, which contains nitrous and sulphurous matter that cannot escape. It evaporates in the great heat, depositing salt and other chemicals.

After an essential shower, provided by a Jewish entrepreneur who had rigged up fresh water in a wooden shack, we went in search of the traditional place of Christ's baptism, which can never be known for certain. We found, nevertheless, a spot on the banks between the tamarisks and reeds which, for what it was worth, another Greek entrepreneur, felt was the place. Dusk was approaching in a part of the world where twilight was not prolonged, so we began our return. On the way back we stopped to observe the Mountains of Moab at sunset, rose-coloured and purple, the valleys now navy blue. Ahead the Palestine hills were darkly silhouetted and difficult to define. In Jerusalem the street lights were turned on and we dined quietly, later joining most of the inhabitants of the Eternal City in our slumbers.

In Tel Aviv Begin's Irgun gang began their operation early on Monday 22 July, while Jerusalem and the author slept. At 05.30 they stole a Jewish taxi and a Jewish truck. They then drove to Jerusalem where at 11. 00 they stole a pick-up lorry and loaded it with seven milk cans, a significant number in Jewish tradition. Then, dressed as Arabs, armed with Sten and Tommy guns, they drove to the King David Hotel at 11.45. They descended the slope to the unguarded entrance, rounded up the staff and unloaded the explosives packed in the milk cans.

Meanwhile, wholly unaware of this unfolding drama, Alan Barton, Sa'ad, one of his daughters, our driver, Guardsman Heaver and myself walked once again through the Old City, this time to see the Wailing or Western Wall, the Dome of the Rock and the Mosque of Al-Aksar.

The Crusaders allotted the Wailing Wall in the twelfth century to the Jews as a place of prayer, which the Moslems later respected, it being then, as now, Moslem property. Above, on the site of the old Temple, are the Dome of the Rock and the Mosque of Al-Aksar, which are approached by an immense, flag-stoned courtyard, empty at the time of our visit, which was in conspicuous contrast to the bustle and push of the Old City.

At the entrance to the Dome of the Rock our shoes were covered with large slippers, provided for the occasion. Sadly, Sa'ad's

44

1. The author in 1946.

2. 'We found Jacob's Well at
   Sychar, where Christ met
   the woman of Samaria'
   (p.38).

3. 'We had an excellent lunch with Sa'ad and his family' (p.42). The author is at the rear, Sa'ad on the left.

4. The Dome of the Rock, Jerusalem. *Left to right*: the author, Sa'ad's daughter, Guardsman Heaver, Captain Alan Barton (see pp.37-42).

5. 'Allenby Bridge, the original steel structure wooden-planked but damaged during the recent disturbances' (p.43).

6. Bill Gore-Langton, Eddie Goulburn and Willy Whitelaw at 1st Brigade Headquarters, Summer, 1946.

7. The King David Hotel,
   Jerusalem, 'At 12.37 the seven
   milk cans blew up. The whole
   south-west corner of the Hotel
   collapsed' (p.47).

8. 'Everyone loved Ivor' (p.56).
   Captain Ivor Roberts, the Welsh
   Guards Quartermaster.

daughter was not allowed in. Rather absurdly, the old man in a brown frock who welcomed us said she was a Jew. Obviously he knew she was not, but it saved him from saying she was a woman.

Inside, in contrast to the light of the Church of All Nations, this exquisite, octagonal example of Moslem art was dimly lit by streaks of blue and red light coming from the stained glass windows beneath the dome, which was supported by columns of breccia, porphyry, marble and other coloured stones.

These materials were recovered by the Moslems from Roman, particularly Byzantine, Jerusalem, many of the columns retaining the original capitals, some still bearing the sign of the cross. In the centre, behind an intricate lattice work metal screen, was the rock itself. Black and polished, it once formed part of the threshing floor of Araunah the Jebusite, from whom king David had acquired it.

Two hairs of Mohammed's beard were preserved in a gold casket which we were shown with great reverence. The rock itself, as mentioned earlier, was the place whence the Prophet galloped to heaven, Moslems maintain, on his horse Lightning or el-Baruk. On one side some steps descend into a cavern whence a channel cut in the rock drained the blood of Jewish sacrifices and carried it into the Kedron Valley. We were shown a flagstone which, when struck, gave a hollow sound. What lay beneath it remained a mystery; no archaeologist had ever received permission to delve and dig. What treasures might it reveal? Perhaps those hidden in 70 AD and not carried off to Rome for the triumphal procession of Titus, even maybe the Ark of the Covenant.

We blinked in the sunlight as we left the Dome and crossed the vast pavement to the Mosque of El-Aksar. This resembled a Christian church, not least because the materials of Saint-Mary-the-New, built by the Crusaders, were used by the Moslems. As we entered we could see this mosque was an exceptionally large building, built on the Roman pattern, its roof supported by imposing Byzantine columns. The floor was entirely covered with rugs. I was particularly interested by a stone in the central aisle where a guide pointed out a defaced inscription. Beneath it were believed to lie two of Saint Thomas à Becket's four assassins, one of whom, Sir Richard le Breton, was said to be an ancestor. After papal censure by Alexander III, the quartet left for the Holy Land; but which one of his two companions, Reginald Fitz Urse and William de Tracy (Hugh de Murville returned), might have lain with him, were he there, required further research, not so far accomplished. Crusading, as an act of atonement, bestowed automatic redemption.

What was accomplished was our photograph being taken with the aid of Alan's camera, as we posed on the large open space, known as the Temple Mount to the Jews, or Haram al-Sharif, the Noble Sanctuary, to the Arabs, where King Abdullah was assassinated five years later. Some sanctuary! The time was 12.15 and we should have been going to our appointment to meet Rosemary Walsh at the bar of the King David Hotel.

Alan, however, was an electrical and mechanical engineer and disliked being flustered; the girl might be late and so on; all the excuses of a man concentrating on the job in hand, and not particularly punctual. His concentration was interrupted around 12.20 when the first – diversionary, as it turned out – bomb exploded. The city siren sounded, then the all-clear at 12.31. We remained, watching Alan. Then at 12.37 there was a very loud explosion indeed.

Guardsman Heaver cocked his Tommy gun. I advised him to uncock it. We were not going to shoot our way out of the Old City unless someone attacked us. Alan stopped taking photographs. The Old City shop shutters were clanging shut, and the place became as silent and still as death, except for one woman at the Western Wall – forbidden in this anti-feminine environment to pray aloud – who wailed for all she was worth. She had reason. More than ninety people had just been killed, including seventeen Jews, in the Hotel and one terrorist found by the police.

The terrorists had, as noted, arrived at the basement of the King David Hotel at 11.45, placing the seven milk cans containing the explosives along the corridor underneath the government Secretariat offices where, with many others, Rosemary Walsh and her father worked.

Two orders had been ignored by Irgun, the first being that the operation was to take place out of office hours to avoid, hopefully, any loss of life; also a warning must be telephoned in good time. It was, even so, a dangerous, uncertain, unprincipled and ungrateful act against the one country which had gone out of its way, however unfairly to the Arabs and disastrously for its administrators, to help the Zionist cause. It was, too, organized at the highest level of the Yishuv. The planting of the bombs, and consequent planned destruction of government offices, was an extension of the rebellion, undeclared and never admitted, against the Mandatory power. British intelligence, however, was well aware of the existence of X Command and the identity of its chairman, Ben-Gurion. The King David Hotel operation did not have the destruction of documents as a prime objective: they were not filed exclusively there and those removed from the Jewish Agency had been copied. It was a pointless counter-reaction of provocation which backfired. It was also cold-blooded premeditated murder by the Irgun gang.

46

Ernest Bevan and the British government were conversant with the Zionist strategy to obtain their State, both from public pronouncements and from decryptanalysis:

1. Calculated use of violence and, when the occasion demanded, denunciation of the violence initiated by X Command or its affiliates.
2. Condemnation of government response, provoked by violence, as being – to use Weizmann's words – a declaration of war against world Jewry.
3. The Arab position to be ignored.
4. American support to be rallied in both political and financial dimensions.

The government's knowledge of facts, nevertheless, could not provide a solution. If a solution was acceptable to the Jews, it would not be to the Arabs, therefore not to the Mandatory power. Thus, the strategy and tactics of obtaining the end by the means outlined above continued: terrorism – condemnation of terrorism – government reaction – condemnation of this reaction – more terrorism. Neither the ambition to obtain the goal, nor the blood lust which went with it could be either controlled or assuaged.

No one knew this better than Israel Levi who was in charge of the party which placed the bombs. He connected the timing devices, and also a booby trap, duly announced, to discourage defusing. He and his gang were disturbed by Captain A.D. Mackintosh, Royal Signals, whom they failed to overcome. They then shot him in the stomach. He stumbled towards the staircase and was found by a porter to whom he gave the facts. The porter informed the manager, Hamburger, who told security.

Thus the Hotel security, alerted through the heroic efforts of the Royal Signals officer, knew at 12.10 that "an officer had been attacked. Armed Arabs were in the basement". A security officer then peered through a grill. He was fired at. Irgun withdrew at 12.15. The Hotel alarm bell alerted Jerusalem Police Headquarters. Hotel security fired on the Irgun lorry. It was abandoned. The occupants fled on foot. Two were hit.

Minutes later, between 12.20 and 12.25, the smaller bomb we heard in the Old City, intended to divert attention and block access to the Hotel, was exploded. At 12.37 the seven milk cans blew up. The whole south-west corner of the Hotel collapsed; six floors and twenty-eight rooms were reduced to rubble. Robert Newton was in his office when the ceiling fell and the wall behind him disappeared. Below was open space; beyond had been the lift shaft, the typists' room and an adjacent office in which a colleague had worked. Everything and everybody had disappeared. The girls in the typing room and his colleague were buried under the rubble, dead.

Superintendent K.P. Haddingham had just arrived from Police Headquarters. He was injured and placed on a stretcher. He then saw, with horror, on the wall of the Young Men's Christian Association opposite, the bodies of two middle-aged men, flung by the blast, like plaster, against the stone, their blood streaming in rivulets, their crucified remains splayed and contorted sixteen feet above ground, resembling some sick mural, stuccoed and silhouetted in high relief. They were his friends, Postmaster General G.D. Kennedy and Assistant Secretary E.W. Keys, who had been standing at the Secretariat entrance.

About fifteen minutes earlier the first so-called diversionary bomb had been detonated outside a car showroom, owned by a Christian Arab, a few yards from the Hotel. It failed to set off the ancilliary incendiary devices which would have fired the whole street. The second diversionary bomb failed to explode and was dismantled by the police, always a dangerous job. It was some diversion. It had been placed north of the Hotel in a nearby street, outside a shop named Deen's Indian Taylor. It contained TNT and inflammable wadding. Four petrol cans were on top.

Meanwhile we made our way back to the New City through the deserted, winding ways of the Old and soon passed through a police cordon where the car containing the second so-called diversionary bomb was being searched and the bomb dismantled. We collected the jeep and went to the Hotel. The bar was a shambles of broken glass and blood. The barman told us no one had been killed there, so Rosemary Walsh was safe. Arthur Butler was cut about the knees. Had we been there we would not have been killed, but flying glass can damage more than knees.

Rosemary's father was buried under the masonry and presumed dead. He was not among those missing who miraculously survived, one of whom was dug out twenty-four hours later. He shook hands with the High Commissioner and was taken to hospital where he died of shock.

After lunch we returned to examine the damage, having no idea of the numbers buried, dead and alive underneath. There was no noise as soldiers and police began the prolonged job of digging into the rubble. The police, in the meantime, had found the two terrorists hit by the Hotel security: one was dead, the other wounded. He was arrested, later tried and hanged. They were the *soldati*. The *capi* escaped.

The warning ordered by X Command, with whom the ultimate

48

responsibility for the outrage rested, was, in practice, ignored. The first warning was given two minutes before the main explosion, and repeated twice afterwards, by which time it was an epilogue. The Irgun gang had instructed Adina Hay-Nissan, a young adherent, to warn the Hotel, the French Consulate and the *Palestine Post*, after she heard the first bomb, between 12.20 and 12.25. The impartial, wholly corroborated evidence of six witnesses, recorded in the report, signed by Assistant Inspector-General J.P.I. Fforde, stated she began at 12.35, when the Hotel operator took her call.

The manager was informed at 12.37, when the explosion took place. At the French Consulate the operator received a warning at 12.42, five minutes after the main explosion. The Consulate Secretary confirmed it. The *Palestine Post*, whose editor, Gershon Agronsky, attended the meeting with Weizmann on 6 July, received a call after the main explosion. The information was passed to the duty officer at Police Headquarters immediately, at 12.50.

In sum: the terrorists fled from the Hotel at 12.15, after being there for half-an-hour, during which time they placed and primed the bombs. The diversionary explosion occurred between 12.20 and 12.25. The first of three warning calls was received at 12.35. The main explosion occurred at 12.37: 91 dead, including 41 Arabs, 28 British, 17 Jews and 5 others. Our rendezvous with Rosemary Walsh saved her life. She would otherwise have been in her father's office. Weizmann's cordite had come full circle.

The *Palestine Post* wrote: "The outrage committed yesterday in Jerusalem has neither sense nor apology. It was unqualified evil and will be judged as such by honest men in every part of the world. It is a challenge to the Jewish cause itself, a challenge that must be taken up in the interest of the cause."

The Jewish Agency, of which Ben-Gurion was a senior member, and Vaad Leumi, the Jewish elected body, issued a joint statement expressing "their horror at the dastardly crime perpetrated by the gang of desperadoes. The Yishuv in Palestine is called upon to rise up against these abominable outrages."

Israel Rokach, who attended the 6 July meeting at Weizmann's house, and the Tel Aviv Municipality issued a similar statement, as did the Histradut, the Yishuv trade union organization. Menachem Begin and IZL admitted their responsibility. In their pamphlets, appearing in Tel Aviv, they stated they had given half-an-hour's warning. It was, thus, entirely the fault of the British authorities.

In the afternoon of this black Monday Alan and our party returned to Nazareth, a journey of 75 miles, without any further sightseeing. We had seen enough sights and witnessed the Calvary of 91 people as well as those injured and severely shocked. In one week's time Tel Aviv was surrounded and searched. It was some days before all the dead were dug out, among them Rosemary's father. The Sappers were working with masks and spraying the ruins with DDT. The smell of the dead was overwhelming.

One factor does, however, raise a question in the author's mind: seven milk cans, packed with explosives and a duly announced booby trap were left in the basement of the Hotel. The staff, and Captain Mackintosh, could not have imagined the "Arabs" were there for any purpose other than terrorism. They were certainly not delivering milk. A security officer had been fired at shortly after 12.10 and the Hotel security, in turn, had shot and hit two terrorists when they left in haste at 12.15. What communications failure occurred between the basement staff and security between 12.15 and 12.37, a long twenty-two minutes, and why, in any case, did security not investigate the basement situation *immediately*?

30.7.46 General Barker launched "Operation Shark". The police information was clear: the terrorists had fled to their lairs in Tel Aviv, whence they had come in the first place. Before dawn on 30 July four brigades, with additional troops and police, in all some 20,000 men threw a cordon around the city and searched the homes of 170,000 people. The IZL leader, Begin, was not found, although soldiers were encamped outside his house. They were trained to street fight, but not to house search. The Palestine police would have found Begin.

Yitzhak Yisernitzky (Shamir), however, was caught, disguised as a rabbi: some holy man! He was the Stern gang/Lehi's number two, and, like Begin, a future prime minister. Five weeks later, true to their mafia-like practice of personal vengeance, Sergeant T.G. Martin, who had recognized Yisernitzky, was shot while playing tennis in Haifa. Yisernitzky was sent to Eritrea but not to the gallows. He told Nicholas Bethell, "I was not consulted, but I would have approved."

In Nazareth, earlier in the month, on 1 July, Eddie Goulburn, the Brigade commander, was promoted to Major General, and left to head the British Military Mission in Rome. Rodney Moore succeeded him. He had commanded the 2nd (Armoured) Grenadiers in Guards Armoured Division during the War, while Eddie commanded the 1st Battalion.

Their views differed about the future of the Mandate. Eddie was pro-Arab, while Rodney was the reverse. I got along with both and maintained that I was pro-British. Willy remained as DAA & QMG. I was acting GIII, and in August, when Bill Gore-Langton and Edward Imbert-Terry were away simultaneously, acting Brigade Major.

In September my contemporary at Mons, Lawrence Verney, Grenadiers, left. I succeeded him as Camp Commandant, for nearly three months, before taking over from Micky Boyd as BTO/Staff Captain "Q" on 1 December. Micky's legal "A" duties were given to my old friend, Andrew Gibson-Watt, who joined us on 31 October as Staff Captain "A". He was exceedingly competent and actually enjoyed the work – courts martial and such like legal matters. I was later termed the Staff Captain and acted as DAA & QMG during the absence of Lewis Dawnay, a Coldstreamer, who succeeded Willy Whitelaw on 12 October.

A month earlier, in September, I had been promoted Captain. I was beginning to feel that picking up the political pieces in Palestine, and sometimes the bodies, following the War in Italy was ageing: I was twenty-one-and-a-half.

CHAPTER SIX

Diverse Functions

9.8.46. My diary refers to many disturbed nights, following Jewish terrorism, largely condoned or controlled at this stage by X Command, in pursuit of Zionist policy: the establishment of an independent state covering as much of Palestine as could be obtained. On this date Bill Gore-Langton left for a month's leave at the quite early hour of 06.30, driving to Port Said. In consequence, as Edward Imbert-Terry had not yet returned, I assumed the duties of Brigade Major for just under a month. Willy Whitelaw was there if advice was required.

13.8.46. " *Ride with brigadier in early morning. Government announcement stating in future all illegal immigrants will be shipped to Cyprus. Riots, as a result, in Haifa. Seven Jews died, after police baton charges.* "

Meanwhile the idea of a Middle East base in Palestine, to replace the Canal Zone, now seemed unlikely to be realized, although there was a post-Partition hypothesis of retaining the Negev, through the intermediary of Jordan's taking possession of the place, an idea abandoned when it was occupied, forcefully, by the Jews.

Thus, events were moving to their finale: the London Conference was being prepared for its convening in September. At the same time, the spiralling vortices of distress and destruction continued on the ground, while the soldiery, exceptionally well disciplined, with only rare lapses under the most extreme provocation of murder and bestiality, exercised remarkable restraint.

18.8.46. So far, death had not arrived on the doorstep of 1st Guards Brigade Headquarters, nor were corpses usually kept in the storeroom. There was, however, an exception on this day, inconsiderately on the Feast of Saint Helena, mother of the Emperor

Constantine, and Christian pilgrim, aforementioned, to the Holy Land in 326.

As for the guardsman in charge of our storeroom at Nazareth, he was unable to attend Camp Commandant's memorandum because he had fainted after tripping over the bodies: he was found in his temporary morgue, irregularily and in an unsoldierly manner, flat out on the floor, and was placed in close arrest. The dead were carried out.

It transpired that the duty officer, Tony Lake, soon to depart for Rome, had ordered the two dead soldiers to be placed in the storeroom in the early hours. It was better than having them laid out on our dining room table. He retired to bed. Neither he nor the guard warned the storeman, who upon entering was confronted with blood and bodies. "Gor-blimey!" he muttered before he passed out, and was, as the not unsympathetic Company Sergeant Major explained on his behalf, "Shook rigid!"

Brigade Headquarters was billeted in a two-storied Austrian Hospice, near the road leading out of the town as it climbed northeast towards the hills, before its 15-mile descent to Tiberias. If you climbed westwards, you were on the right road for Haifa, some 20 miles away; if south-west, in the normal course of events, you were heading for the plain of Esdraelon, sometimes called Jezreel or Megiddo, whence you could make your way south. The name of the plain was unimportant. The name of the game was to stick to the road. Short cuts were inadvisable.

This, sadly, was where the driver of a Parachute Regiment White scout car failed. He and his four companions had refuelled themselves, if not their heavy armoured car, in an alehouse, somewhere in the town. Subsequently the driver, while descending four hundred feet on this winding Esdraelon road, was unable to negotiate a bend with any evident success at a moment when his vehicle was reaching breakneck speed. Indeed, the resulting accident broke two necks and severely injured three others. They were taken to hospital in Haifa. We were left with the fully broken.

Next to the storeroom was the chapel of the six or so remaining monks. They kept the key. Otherwise Tony Lake might have had the bodies dumped in the aisle. The chapel adjoined the officers' mess anteroom, dining room and kitchen, the whole ground floor on the south side being linked by an open, colonnaded stone passage. This was most pleasant as a form of annex in the summer heat. It looked on to an olive grove, beyond which were wooden huts, used for military purposes, and a pleasing, not too uncomfortable, four-seater latrine for officers.

There was a twelve-seater affair nearby for other ranks. Natural functions in the Army, at any rate in camp, were always accommodated according to rank, the ratio differential decreasing from the bottom up. The Brigade Commander, for example, had one to himself, which he shared with a nocturnal, semi-feral tomcat. Latrine supervision was one of the more tedious jobs of the Camp Commandant, or camp comedian, a burden I carried for eleven unwilling weeks after Lawrence Verney's departure on "B" release, and before taking over from Micky Boyd.

Brigadier Rodney's latrine was otherwise impeccably maintained by a guardsman, especially picked for this duty, whose unofficial title is best omitted. The Commander's complaints about the cat were usually levelled at me over luncheon. Thus, as much in my own interests as Rodney's, I had the place wire-netted. The animal, however, was not discouraged: it simply marked its presence – the liquidity factor, as bankers call it – by climbing on the roof, backing onto the door, or anywhere else it could target. In its queer way, it just loved Rodney. Our departure for Transjordan at the end of September terminated the affair.

In Nazareth the natural liquidity flow came from a spring whence the Mother of Christ drew water for the Holy Family. The Greeks built a church over the source, and I could hear the water gurgling as it emerged from the rock. The stream then ran in a conduit to the Virgin's Fountain, on the right, next to the road, as we entered the town from our hospice Headquarters. The dignity of the Christian women, straight-backed, one arm akimbo, the other supporting a full pitcher on their heads and wearing long, multi-coloured dresses, was impressive. It was their sole source of water and they made the journey more than once a day.

Our hospice was one of several large buildings associated with religious institutions in a largely Christian Arab town of some 12,000 inhabitants. It had been taken by Saladin, after his victory at the nearby Horns of Hattin, in 1187, captured by the Turks in 1517 and visited by Napoleon Bonaparte in April, 1799, who supped therein after the little known Battle of Tabor in which General Kleber, with 1500 men, held 25,000 Turks from dawn until noon. Then, as the battle raged in the plain on the site of the Crusader castle of Faba, the commanding general, Bonaparte, led 600 cavalry over the ridge to the rescue.

Whereas Bonaparte left Alexandria for France within four months in a fast clipper, nearly intercepted by the Royal Navy, his army had to wait until 1802, and shot off the nose of the Sphinx while passing the time. Meanwhile Nazareth slumbered for a further 119 years under Turkish rule, until it fell to the British in 1918. It was a town of whitewashed houses, lance-like cypresses with dark green leaves and rounded cones. Its terraces produced olives and figs, and the two dominant churches were the Carpenter's and the Church of the Annunciation with attendant caves, in one of which the Annunciation may well have taken place.

There were many narrow streets in the town, one entirely devoted to carpenters, where the artisans worked in open archways. The more up-to-date made furniture and shaped wood for the building trade. They also carved rocking cradles. The more traditional used tools known to Joseph, and they met the carpentry needs of the nearby Arab villages, undertaking to maintain what they made for a year. Their reimbursement was in kind: a down payment of grain and an annual one of olives, wheat, barley, figs or sesame. It was hardly taxable.

As for our hospice, there was not much left unoccupied by the Army. Our vehicle park was at the rear, but the monks did retain a small walled garden and a piggery. The layman in charge never washed. We concluded he must be doing penance, in which to a certain extent, we became involved. Lawrence Verney played chess with him. The pungent odour of pigs and unwashed flesh wafted across the board and permeated Lawrence's uniform. In terms of loyalty, he stuck to his game: in terms of stench it stuck to him. In terms, however, of hygiene, after our complaints, he either played in his underpants, or changed his clothes. I trust his soldier servant was adequately recompensed.

Other than chess, sport and relaxation were available to all ranks. My diary also refers to many games of tennis on the court of the District Commissioner, Charles Evans. He was married and had three daughters. There were also visits to, and dinner with, Christian Arab families, drinks in the officers' club, a first floor room overlooking the main road, as well as trips to Haifa for lunch or dinner, or to visit 1st Division Headquarters.

Hugh Stanley had joined us at Brigade as a Liaison Officer, also Andrew Wemyss, Scots Guards, who was my second-in-command while I performed the duties of Camp Commandant. Andrew liked motor-cycles. He dismantled one or two and certainly one he was unable to re-assemble.

In 1949 I received a note from Archie Fletcher, a Scots Guardsman who joined us later and succeeded Andrew Gibson-Watt in Tripoli after we had left Palestine, mentioning there was a sum outstanding of £14, following a court of inquiry. A proportion of the blame, as O.C. motor-cycles, was laid at my door. I coughed up and, some forty-five years later, I remembered this when I saw Andrew – in fact we had often seen one another, but I had forgotten – and proposed a private arrangement, which was honoured, which let him off the capital sum, plus compound interest.

In terms of occupying off-duty hours, neither bridge nor cricket were compounded by any interest of mine. Nevertheless, *esprit de brigade* necessitated my agreeing to umpire or score, while others played on the hard ground of Esdraelon, whenever they were able to peer through the dust. These efforts came to a natural conclusion when we went to Jordan for military exercises; also, after our last game against the KDG, Edward Imbert-Terry said we would have won had I not been umpiring. It was time to pull up stumps.

In a more unusual field, I spent the night in a monastery. Father Philip Dyer was the Roman Catholic padré, succeeded by the afore-mentioned Father Murphy, who was inspired to influence what the Church calls the most hardened hearts. In pursuit of this unlikely goal, he most kindly invited me and three other officers to the Fran-ciscan basilica on Mount Tabor, built in 1923 on a much older structure. It was not too far from Nazareth. There, on 6 August, Mass was celebrated on the Feast of the Transfiguration. Reli-giously it was inspiring. In terms of food and locally produced wine, we wanted for nothing.

21.8.46 "Bloody awful night," I wrote in my diary. *"Woken up regu-larly: Jewish terrorism."* We did not suffer casualties and I did not record the details. There were other explosions besides those initi-ated by terrorists. In the Welsh Guard lines both the Battalion War Diary and my memory recall a series of fires which seem to have broken out, following inexplicable exothermic reaction. More sim-ply some overheated stove or burner blew up. On 23 August Prince of Wales Company changed billets with Support Company at Metullah where they had "lost a lot of kit". On 3 September Ivor Roberts, the Welsh Guards Quartermaster, reported the loss of 13 motor-cycles and £800 worth of damage, following a fire at Bat-talion headquarters. We were more than a little suspicious, but everyone loved Ivor. At least he had not added a couple of jeeps to the inferno.

Just before Christmas RSM Rees lost all his personal kit and the prizes for the Christmas draw. Before this, on 29 October, two days before he joined us at Brigade, Andrew Gibson-Watt, acting com-mander of No 3 Company at Rosh Pinna, followed Peter Beckwith-Smith's departure in September, lost his cookhouse and two messrooms – but not his cooks nor a young officer seeking immolation in the flames. This time Ivor Roberts, certainly the prince and most humorous of provisioners, was able to provide all immediate needs without their catching fire on the way.

1.9.46. "Lunch with Brigadier and Rachel Saphir at Astoria Restaurant, Haifa." It was owned by a Viennese lady, Lilli

Manheim-Winkelkotte, who came to London after the Mandate ended. Another restaurant was Pross' where I lunched occasionally, sometimes with Hugh Stanley, who, like Francis Widdrington, Welsh Guards, a very large man indeed, loved his food. Pross' was run by Mrs George, who knew a cousin, Evelyn Brutton, who ran the Portsmouth Conservative Association until a great age, with both charm and firmness.

After Edward Imbert-Terry returned I was relieved of my responsibilities as acting Brigade Major, and I also handed over the GIII side of the act to Michael Robertson-Young, Grenadiers. My duties as Camp Commandant were not over-taxing. Of 143 men, most were specialists: mechanics, electricians, signallers, Military Police, a Master Cook, a sanitary engineer of sorts, and other assorted jobs requiring expertise. The Company Sergeant Major was a castaway from the Coldstream. The Brigade Commander felt I could take a few days off, but, before touring the northern parts of Galilee with my jeep and driver, I asked Sa'ad to take me to a nearby village, four miles north-east of Nazareth, just off the road to Tiberias. It was called Kefr Kenna, the site of Christ's first recorded miracle when He turned pristine water into vintage wine: "There was a wedding at Cana in Galilee. The mother of Jesus was there, and Jesus and His disciples had also been invited. When they ran out of wine, since the wine provided for the wedding was all finished, the mother of Jesus said to Him: 'They have no wine'. Jesus said: 'Woman, why turn to me? My hour has not come yet'. His mother said to the servants: 'Do whatever he tells you'. There were six stone water jars standing there, meant for the ablutions that are customary among the Jews: each could hold twenty or thirty gallons.

"Jesus said to the servants: 'Fill the jars with water'; and they filled them to the brim. 'Draw some out now,' He told them 'and take it to the steward'. They did this; the steward tasted the water, and it had turned into wine. Having no idea where it came from – only the servants who had drawn the water knew – the steward called the bridegroom and said; 'People generally serve the best wine first, and keep the cheaper sort till the guests have had plenty to drink; but you have kept the best wine till now'."

There were two small churches in Cana, one Greek and the other Franciscan. The Greek was simple and contained two stone urns which, whatever the priest may have believed, were dubious and no more ancient than the sixteenth century. The Franciscan church was built on the site of a former edifice, extant in 726 AD, and reckoned to be the place where the wedding feast was held. The Franciscans started negotiations with the Turks in 1641. In 1891 they were permitted to build their chapel, in the crypt of which we were shown an ancient cistern and a Jewish waterpot or pitcher which could well have been contemporary with the time of Christ.

The finds of archaeological digs were displayed in a small museum: Byzantine mosaics and coins showing the head of Constantine. The Franciscans were certain they had unearthed the Byzantine church which, in turn, was considered most likely to have been built on the site of the wedding feast, after which Christ went with His mother and His disciples to Capernaum. After returning with Sa'ad to Nazareth, I went to Rosh Pinna in Upper Galilee.

The countryside in those parts was rocky but not barren. Both in biblical times and now vines have been grown on some of the higher slopes. The principal town which I visited was Safad, which was situated on a white, chalk mountain, 2700 feet up. It was always particularly sacred to the Jews. Nearby was Rosh Pinna, where No 3 Company, Welsh Guards, was stationed. I went there on 14 September and my diary records: *"Royally entertained by Peter Beckwith-Smith, Andrew Gibson-Watt, Michael Bonn and James Bowen."*

Rosh Pinna was 2500 feet above sea level. Only five miles away the Sea of Galilee was nearly 690 below, a downward plunge of 3190 feet.

On the following day we shot in the Huleh and I then went on to the attractive Russian Jewish village of Metullah, where I stayed with Henry Coombe-Tennant and the Prince of Wales Company. The camp was actually in the Lebanon, just beyond the frontier post. We rode in the surrounding hills; and as we controlled the frontier, travelling to Beirut presented no obstacles. There, Irena, the younger daughter of a White Russian who kept a modest tavern called *Nuits Rouges*, seemed always pleased to see me. We had met at a dinner given by a Druse family. Until the Palestine influx, the ethnic and religious mix in Lebanon was harmonious.

Trips to Beirut ceased when we moved south in January, 1947. But before this, I took advantage of the unimpeded access, visited the Bequa'a Valley, staying at Ba'albek, later the site of a successful festival, until the civil war, when it became the site of scenes and actions much more militant.

East of Metullah was Dan, on one of the Jordan headwaters. Beyond, over the Syrian border, was Baniyas, a rather depressing Roman ruin, where the sheik's house was built of collapsed, horizontal, Corinthian columns. Marble and stone were mixed together. Like many ruins, it had acted for centuries as the local quarry for any construction not made of mud. Nearby was the ruined Crusader castle of Subeibeh, erected on a conical hill, but only occupied from 1130-1165, when it fell to Nur al-Din of Damascus.

Baniyas was better known as Caesarea Philippi, built by Philip, son of Herod the Great, co-named after the Emperor Tiberias and himself. Here Jesus came with His disciples whom he asked: "Who do you think I am?" Peter replied; "You are the Christ, the Son of the Living God." Thereupon, Christ charged Peter with His Church: "You are Peter and upon this rock I will build my church."

Beyond, northwards, was the towering 9000-foot peak of Mount Hermon, the slopes of which being a much more likely site for the Transfiguration than Mount Tabor, despite the Franciscans' reputation for accurate research. I had no desire to climb it, unlike my friends Carol Mather, who took command of No 3 Company, and Andrew Gibson-Watt. On the contrary, staying with the Prince of Wales Company, after an early morning ride, we had breakfasted with the TJFF – "A" Squadron commanded by Roddy Shaw – then, on the border near Maleikeir, we shot the local French partridge, chukor. I then drove back to Nazareth for dinner.

On 23 September I went with Willy Whitelaw to Transjordan where we lunched with the DCLI. A military exercise was being planned to take place in Transjordan during the month of October. There was a major and a minor gaffe preceding this operation: first we had forgotten that the country had been independent since June, had ceased to be a Mandate, and the minimum courtesy due to King Abdullah was to ask his accord to our entering his country. He had, I think, also forgotten. The British Army had been comfortably close in Transjordan since his arrival as ruler.

The minor gaffe, however, was the main reason for our going: our latrines were near the road. The King was informed of this indiscretion by his consorts: there were three. Although suitably accommodated in three separate mini-palaces, they shared a large Wolsey motorcar for their afternoon ride, which changed little – Amman to Zerqa and back or a return journey to Irbid – as there were only two roads. It was during one of these rides the consorts observed the exposed posteriors of the soldiers. Yashmaks were lowered, as were the guardsmen's trousers. Excitedly, the ladies reported the affront to their sensibilities. Willy and I were dispatched to paper up the cracks.

Willy seemed to be suffering from the after-effects of a party at the Villa Melchett. He was not, however, at all vague about the latrines. Revealing his powers of practical common sense and considerable diplomacy, given the exigency which faced us and the bare-bottomed affront we had given the consorts, he ordered the immediate erection of a canvas screen. Exposure, now discreet,

59

was, nevertheless, not for long. A side effect of the wind and sun on the Jordanian plateau, 3000 feet above sea level, was that it scorched the skin.

30.9.46. "Leave for Transjordan." 1st Guards Brigade crossed the Jordan and Allenby Bridge remained intact. "Sand and bloody blue sky" was how a guest, Colonel Micky Lindsay, had described Jordan to its Crown Prince, Talal, when both were dining in good form at Brigade in June. The vague idea then was to open a race course. Now we were bent on churning up dust in the course of one or two military exercises, devised by James Gresham. Successful in their fashion, more interesting was Abdullah's lunch at Brigade headquarters.

We were, to the manner born, under canvas and under pressure to get things right, to begin with the correct standard to be flown. We got this wrong. We had been given the flag by the Arab Legion which Abdullah's father had flown at an auspicious moment during the Arab revolt – Hussein's side of the bargain, which he kept – which was, apparently, inappropriate. It was a little arcane. What was not, however, was its being flown upside down. This is sometimes the fate of the Union Jack when hoisted by the uninitiated. We rectified the second error. We were stuck with the first.

Colonel Peter Clifton, commanding 3rd Battalion Grenadiers, provided the guard of honour, as well as the battalion corps of drums, both under the watchful eye of Alan Breitmeyer, the adjutant. The main job of the musicians was to offer a convincing version of the Transjordan national anthem. It was only ten bars – anthems, I suspected, being a western imposition upon Arab culture – and sounded like an orchestra tuning up. There were also other behind-the-scenes functions to be organized.

My diary entry for 11 October reads: *"Willy Whitelaw preparing two EPIP tents for H.M. to prepare himself. He prays at 12.45 and may also perform a natural function without paper, but using a smooth stone with his left hand."* We had, of course, been carefully briefed by the Arab Legion, supposedly in the know. The two EPIP tents adjoined. I was placed in charge of this operation for the following day. I slipped several sheets of brown paper underneath the third stone down. The Guardsman Sanitary Engineer in Residence was not entrusted with this delicate operation, other than digging the hole next to the single, wooden seater, also holed, which had been borrowed from the Brigadier.

King Abdullah was in good humour when he arrived, and even better when he left. He went immediately to his prayer tent. Willy and I had checked the kiblah and placed the prayer rug in the direction of Mecca. His entourage of prime minister, Glubb Pasha,

60

commanding the Arab Legion, Sir Alec Kirkbride, British resident minister and others in attendance, immediately started smoking.

Unluckily for the addicted, H. M.'s prayer was brief. Cigarettes were out and we were inside the mess tent. The King sat next to Brigadier Rodney. Glubb Pasha translated. Johnny Lascelles, who had organized the lunch, sought anonimity next to me, well below the salt. It seemed to be my place to sit at the end of trestle tables.

The matter of Abdullah's three consorts arose at what was basically a boys' lunch: one was black, one was white Circassian, the third, khaki, was Arab. He told Brigadier Rodney that he slept with the black lady in summer; she was cooler. As for the food, John Lascelles provided roast lamb, ritually slaughtered and bought in Amman. The cheese came from an excellent source, next to the Villa Melchett, a first class Stilton, certainly equal to the original. The King, knowing its provenance, said it was delicious and smelt like a Jew's foot. He then asked for the address.

In the Noble Sanctuary, Jerusalem, as mentioned earlier, this erudite and intelligent Hashemite prince was assassinated five years later. Next to him was his grandson, Hussein, now King of Jordan.

On 12 October, the successful luncheon over, a sad event occurred, summed up in my diary: *"Willy Whitelaw leaves. Very sorry to see him go."* Willy was much missed. He was an instinctively kind man, tolerant of inexperience, intolerant of incompetence, fair in his admonishments. No one resented a rocket from Willy. Exuberant and extrovert, he was also loyal to both seniors and juniors, admittedly the norm, but when I experienced the reverse, it was Willy who spoke for me. He was politically perceptive, not only over the general situation, not too difficult to analyse, as distinct from solve, but I remember his comments on General Barker's irate message, self-admitted to have been precipitate, understandably delivered after the King David Hotel carnage.

His successor, Lewis Dawnay, was a competent and likeable Coldstreamer, but introvert. Much pained him, including, occasionally, the author. He was, as my observant friend and fellow staff captain, Andrew Gibson-Watt, wrote in *An Undistinguished Life*, "Highly strung, and usually on the verge of a nervous breakdown." The same could never have been said of Willy.

We did our best to keep Lewis this side of sanity. Like many of his disposition, however, much tension was caused by self-imposition of unnecessary trivia and needless minutiae. One example was his pertinacious avoidance of initials and acronyms.

Lewis announced himself, initially, on the telephone as the Deputy Assistant Adjutant and Quartermaster General. Once, when he asked for his superior at Division, Jack Sanderson, Scots

Guards, the AA & QMG, whose job title, like Lewis's, ended in General, he was put through to the General, "Windy" Gale. He then sadly came to the conclusion that it was a plebeian world, and with stoic resignation reverted to DAA & QMG. There were, however, limits. We had much to do with Middle East General Orders – MEGOS: "Me no go too!" MEGO was out and so was BEEMEE (BEME) the Brigade Electrical and Mechanical Engineer. Lewis, against his innate disposition, compromised: the Brigade EME was the outcome.

After Lewis' arrival, Willy's departure and the luncheon with King Abdullah over, four others and myself were permitted to fly to Petra the following day. My companions were Johnny Lascelles, Bill Pease, Gordon Kennedy, the Signals Officer, and Stafford Floyer-Acland DCLI. We chartered a plane, my first flight, and planned ahead.

On 13 October, a Sunday, we left camp at 0700 and arrived at Amman airstrip forty-five minutes later. We took off in a de Havilland Rapide and were airborne, to my considerable relief, without hiccups. We reached Ma'an about 0900 and checked in at the Station Hotel whence we left by taxi, the maintenance of which was nothing if not haphazard. After one-and-a-half hours we arrived at the police post of Wadi Musa. Thence, we made our way on horseback to Petra, dismounting at the entrance to the narrow gorge leading to the ruined city.

Some Bedouin women greeted us, but quickly fled when Stafford Floyer-Acland tried to photograph them, a not infrequent reaction, sometimes modesty and sometimes concerned with the evil eye. The first of the two-thousand-year-old monuments to be found, on the right as we entered the entrance gorge, a split between ten to twelve feet wide, in the towering, rose coloured, sandstone rock, was the Kasr el-Bint Temple.

The ladies having disappeared, we crossed the 1½ square mile open space, surrounded in varying degrees of proximity by the adjoining mountains, in the walls of which were carved tombs, a theatre, temples and caves for their former inhabitants, We climbed to a point near the 2nd century AD Roman theatre – thirty-three rows of seats, with stage and dressing rooms: touring the provinces must have been quite a performance in the Roman Empire – while below us, in the Wadi Musa, was a young Bedouin and his child bride.

They were unaware of our presence. The young shepherd left his flock to graze untended, while he took the girl by the hand and led her to the confines of their black, goatskin tent. She screamed, maybe literally and not ritually. He dragged. She screamed. He persisted. They disappeared. I hope he was kind.

The Reverend John William Burgon's description of Petra as "a rose-red city – half as old as Time!" was vaguely correct in its colour, although roses vary and sandstone, too, depending on the time of day, but he was chronologically inexact. In fact, the Nabataeans emerged from the Arabian desert around 600 BC and would almost certainly have dispossessed earlier dwellers. Their rose-red city was on the King's Highway or Royal Road, namely the caravan route from Mesopotamia to Egypt and Arabia.

The Nabataeans were the toll keepers: pay up or push off home. Coming or going, the caravans paid up. The Nabataeans had the wisdom to keep in with the Romans. Caesar, as *capo di tutti i capi*, was rendered unto. The odd extra god in the pantheon could be fitted in. Caesar was accommodated. Christianity, nevertheless, arrived in the 2nd century AD. Petra had a bishop, and one of the great tombs was used as a church. The Moslem tide swept over the place in 630 AD.

The Crusaders held it for ninety years, until 1189, when it fell to Saladin. We could see evidence of a more recent conquest: the initials of British and Empire-Commonwealth soldiery of two World Wars, with accompanying graffiti. I asked our guide about drainage. He waved vaguely at the Wadi Musa, flowing with nothing in particular at that moment, which was probably just as well.

On 14 October we returned whence we had come and boarded our plane. The pilot suggested we fly, first, over Petra, and then the Dead Sea. In fact, with an air current suddenly sucking us earthwards, we nearly joined the Bedouin, dropping like a brown hawk from the sky, as would a falling stone. Only, unlike the hawk, we would not have been up and away in a flash. The pilot controlled the plane, or the air current subsided, and it was thought better to pack it in. We then flew more sedately over the Dead Sea, its salt-permeated waters glistening under the sun, between the brown hills and mountains of Palestine and Transjordan.

On the east side of the Dead Sea the pilot pointed out a virtually indistinguishable conical hill which was the site of Machaerus, the fortified palace of Herod Antipas where John the Baptist was beheaded following Salome's request to her stepfather, Herod. It was near a small Arab village, which carried the resonant name of el-Mashnaka: the Hanging Place. We then turned in the direction of Amman. Beneath were all the signs of ancient civilization, even field boundaries, but the land was now largely desert. This was the route of Moses, and near that of Lawrence in 1917. Nearer Amman we could see the ruins of the citadel of Shaubak, built by Baldwin I, king of Jerusalem. He called it Mont-Réal. Saladin took it in 1189.

My diary records some difficulty in landing at Amman, due to donkeys on the landing strip and a strong wind. Neither factor delayed us for long. At one end of the earthen runway there was a steep drop. It was from this end we approached, at first to buzz the donkeys away from our path and then to land. We made, I suppose, one or two dummy runs, always with the dual intention of neither hitting the cliffs nor the donkeys. Air currents were not our best friends, but we made it.

We found the GOC 1st Division, "Windy" Gale, staying with us at Headquarters. Also a friend of mine in the Coldstream, Torquhil Matheson.

The military exercise followed. The Bedouin joined in. One isolated Welsh Guards company was to be supplied by camels and mules, meticulously hired with their owners and duly inspected by the Quartermaster, Ivor Roberts. They set forth into the night, expertly loaded with the company's food, water, blankets and greatcoats. Everything was expertly unloaded by the Bedouin, who also set forth into the night. They never, as a later British prime minister remarked, had it so good.

Two days before we left Transjordan I dined with Lewis Dawnay, Edward Imbert-Terry and Johnny Lascelles in Amman, none of whom were to reach particularly old age. The old name for the capital was Philadelphia, and we inspected the amphitheatre before our dinner. On 26 October we left Amman for Jerusalem, descending from the high plateau via the twisting road, almond and pomegranate trees, reddish-brown in colour and green fig trees on either side, until we reached the Jordan valley and arrived at the ironclad Allenby Bridge, its cross planks clattering as we drove over them.

We reached Jerusalem after two-and-a-half hours' driving. The King David Hotel was no longer functioning as an hotel, but had been wholly requisitioned by the government. We returned to Nazareth. The exercises had gone well. Some had roughed it more than others. I had arranged for my iron bedstead to be transported across the Jordan and back. It belonged to the monks, but it had become rather attached to me.

My diary entry for 29 October reads: *"The Brigadier is seen very little these days, and spends most of his time in Haifa. He is a charming man and very capable."* Rodney was then 41. His capability was to take him to Malaya as Chief of the Armed Forces Staff and Director of Border Operations. Before that, he was GOC London District. His final appointment, as a full general, was Defence Services Secretary at the Ministry of Defence. In Palestine, it was apparent from the moment he arrived at Brigade on 1 July, and what we knew of his immediate past in the Mandate, he was taking a greater interest in matters outside his official command than, for example, had his predecessor.

It appears that Rodney was assigned by the Foreign Secretary and the High Commissioner, to both of whom he reported directly, the task of *sub rosa* communications with the Jews. Ernest Bevin hoped, even after referring the matter to the United Nations, to hold the ring. It is possible, therefore, that the discussions continued until Rodney left in July, 1947. Undoubtedly he was fully briefed about X Command, and probably had no illusions about the Jews wanting nothing less than their own state.

He, nevertheless, carried on, while knowing the depths of complicity in which the so-called peaceful Jewish leaders were involved in controlled and uncontrolled acts of terrorism. His primary role, therefore, under the guise of discussions, must logically have been to garner information and act as a covert channel of communication rather than negotiate, although he may well have gone through the motions to establish his *bona fides*.

Weizmann, as Rodney must have known, had initiated with Ben-Gurion the official form of terrorism under X Command. The future Foreign Minister, Aubrey (Abba) Eban, wrote: "Weizmann accepted the use of violence only as a controlled calculation to achieve a political end. He probably thought Haganah had it about right." All terrorists, of whatever hue, would subscribe to that. All perpetrated, and perpetrate, their acts with controlled calculation – otherwise it is anarchy – but X Command, in any case, lost control.

It is a moot point whether Rodney's contacts limited terrorist attacks against 1st Guards Brigade officers, men and installations. The evidence indicates it did not, although no one ever mortared our camp at Petah Ticvah. He left no records. I lunched many times with him and the presumed liaison lady, Rachel Saphir. On these occasions the conversation was not concerned with his discussions. All of us, however, witnessed "conferences which went far into the night" to quote Andrew Gibson-Watt, at our Petah Ticvah headquarters, whither we moved in January, 1947.

The background, however, was that Weizmann and his fellow Zionists had rejected the Anglo-American Committee proposals. They were now demanding the unconditional admission of 100,000 Jews and were receiving increasing support from the White House, as distinct from the State Department and the Pentagon. President Truman stated on 4 October, when we were in Transjordan: "The American government, for domestic and other reasons, would find it easier to support, in the United Nations and

65

elsewhere, the solution of the Palestine problem calling for partition and the setting up of a viable Jewish state." This speech ran contrary to the principles of article 76 of the United Nations Charter which stated that self-government should be granted to all countries according to the freely expressed wishes of the people concerned. This was a point which the State Department emphasized: the Arab majority was two to one, reduced from ten to one in 1918.

In fact, the British Mandatory power throughout ignored the majority factor, which it would not have found so easy to do had the Arabs joined the legislative council proposed in 1921. They refused, because they were informed that the council would not legislate on immigration. Later, when they wished to join, they were told the moment had passed for such matters: so much for democracy in the Mandate. The French, in their administrated territories further north, called in the artillery, in 1945, to reassert their protection. Having bombarded intransigent Parisians during the commune, who, by comparison, were the Damascenes to complain? They did, and demanded independence.

Meanwhile, in 1946, Weizmann continued to repeat the tactics and policy of Herod the Great. He appealed to whomever pulled the silken ropes of power in the imperial capital – a judicious admixture of opining, dining and wining. He had begun with Lloyd George and continued with successive British ministers, never losing sight of his objective; then switched to Washington, whither the imperial power had moved in 1945. There was, however, a significant difference: Weizmann was not, unlike Herod, alone. He was backed by Zionism, and imperial leaders sensed the power if not the glory. Secondly, unlike Herod, he could climb Mount Snowdon with his first collaborator, the Welsh Wizard, but he could never set foot on the site of Herod's Temple.

More mundanely, and in the light – or shadow – of my recent scatological experiences, I was due for some leave from the strains and stresses of serving in the Mandate. I boarded a plane for Italy after the Remembrance Sunday parade.

CHAPTER SEVEN

Remembrance Day and Christmas

Eighteen months earlier Italy had been the scene of bitter battles against two German Armies in which I played a humble role as a platoon commander in the 3rd Battalion Welsh Guards, as described in *Ensign in Italy*. Now, after eight months in Palestine, it was a place of rest. Indirectly, this was the intention of X Command.

A few days before I went on leave Andrew Gibson-Watt joined us, on 31 October, 1946. I was most pleased to see him. He was, as mentioned, due to take over the "A" side of Micky Boyd's activities. I was to take over the "Q" on my return from Italy. There was, however, an intervening incident on Remembrance Sunday, when five men fainted on the parade ground, and in so doing dropped their rifles, two very serious offences.

10.11.46. The word "faint" was mentioned in my diary. It was not used in Brigade of Guards Standing Orders. Therein and thereunder, men fell out – never down – without permission. These orders were specific and had not changed overmuch since the Crimean War. Another instruction, for example, was: "When capturing a redoubt, Guardsmen will be ordered not to shout 'Hurray!' but 'Hussar!'" In this case the dead and the wounded were graciously exempted.

The Headquarters' quintet were much alive, although momentarily unaware of it. Obviously, they were not as fit as their battalion counterparts, also on parade, namely contingents from the Grenadiers, Coldstream and Welsh Guards. The three battalions were lined up on the football field before the arrival of the Brigade Commander. Meanwhile, before the command "Fall in the officers!" I remember chatting, in an orderly and soldierly manner to Johnny Norton, Grenadiers, whom I had not seen since Italy, and to others whom I knew.

Although the *effect* is of primary interest in such matters – all men were taught to place their weight on the ball of the foot, and not on the heel, which hinders circulation – the *cause* was presumed to be dissipation, namely a hangover. Here, however, there was another reason: the words of the Army chaplain strayed from the Christian message, not too difficult to invoke in Nazareth, and approached the seditious. The five could well have been "shook rigid". The unfortunate padré criticized the British Empire. It was, he said, "already too great!" The five men fainted.

After they fell we marched past Rodney, whom I could sense, without any particular intuition, was going to put us all through a rough lunch; for Rodney's charm melted when military matters were flouted, here flagrantly. A classic example of five men biting the dust, for dust was everywhere in Palestine, even in November before the rains.

Rodney's ranging shot was fired over me: "Are those men in close arrest, Philip?" I said that I would check with the Company Sergeant Major, which we both knew was not good enough, not least because we knew this unfortunate sergeant major was over-promoted.

"Put them in close arrest," said Rodney, "or you'll be in close arrest yourself!" The right action was taken and the men were awarded – the military phrase – a week's confined to barracks and seven extra drills – *extra* being a euphemism as there were few drills at Brigade Headquarters – in order to employ the company sergeant major, much to his chagrin.

The shot, however, which required no ranging preparation and was spot on target, was his call to whomever commanded the griping clergyman. He was dog-collared out of Palestine immediately. There was no Armistice for him. Perhaps he in turn telephoned Attlee and advised him to give away India, effected in 1947. He was not on the same plane which flew me from Lydda to Cairo on my way to Rome, via Tobruk and Malta, in a Dakota.

I have described the details of the War trials then taking place in Rome in an appendix. In Cairo I met the bride of an Irish Guards officer I knew, Giles Vandaleur. Jean was not his first spouse, nor he her first husband. They had just tied the brief knot with the official help of my friend and contemporary, James Denny, Grenadiers. James had not taken holy orders, nor did he wear a surplice and an air of long experience and incomprehension of the mysteries he was supposed to explain.

James was twenty-one, as I was. His job, as Staff Captain "A" at MELF, was to marry people, not of course in the middle of the desert, but in the Semiramis Hotel, Cairo. The bridal suite contained a desk and three chairs – one for James. Most couples preferred to spend their honeymoon elsewhere. Marriage for girls not possessing British passports – their would-be husbands, *ipso facto*, were serving in the British Army – involved an often pregnant pause of six months. In the case of Giles and Jean, six minutes took care of the ceremony and six hours later Giles was off on urgent military matters, as we understood it. In consequence, I lunched with the bride at a place called the Saville and we dined at the Champagne Club.

The reader will be relieved to know I left the Club at 0200 on 12 November, after winning a few piastres at poker dice off Mrs Vandaleur, to catch my plane for Italy. There I spent two weeks staying with my friends the Sorbellos and seeing General Eddie Goulburn and his ADC, Tony Lake. I then returned to Palestine on 28 November at 0830 at the same moment as the CIGS, Field Marshal Montgomery, wearing his Airborne beret. I soon arrived back at Brigade in Nazareth and learnt that, in my absence, Lewis Dawnay had been offered first choice of Staff Captains by Bill Gore-Langton, as to whether I was to be GIII under Bill, or Lewis' Staff Captain "Q" and BTO. Andrew Gibson-Watt was already designated Staff Captain "A" and Welfare Officer, a combination of courts martial and comfort.

Either Lewis confused me with the other chap, or he made one of his few blunders. I became Staff Captain "Q" and later, as mentioned, following some obscure War Office ruling, *the* Staff Captain. These were dizzy heights. I had a jeep and a staff car, itself a cause of dizziness, in which I was careful to sit in the back, far to the left or right, as it was, I considered, only a matter of time before the big end of the connecting rod came up through the floor.

Rodney and I once travelled in this vehicle together, the other staff cars being either off the road or otherwise taken, in which it was frightening enough going at a reasonable speed, let alone the Brigade Commander's idea of acceleration. "Faster driver! Faster!" he ordered, as the guardsman pressed the pedal down to the floorboards. The car began to sway, as I knew it would, and became as lopsided as Rodney's cap, which he always wore at a rakish and unregimental angle. The choice, it seemed to me, now lay between the big end coming up or the vehicle snapping in two. I forget where we were going. We not only made it, but returned even faster, scattering a flock of Arab goats and its herdsman, in safety. I felt the driver deserved a DCM.

On the day after my return from Italy, 29 November, the Irgun terrorist gang blew up the income tax office in Jerusalem after attacking it. This caused a degree of satisfaction among the Yishuv, but the taxes they faced in two years time were a great deal heavier than those currently imposed. Also, the currency dropped in value by 50% and transfers abroad became difficult.

1.12.46. "Standing in for Bill Gore-Langton as Brigade Major."

2.12.46. "Begin taking over from Micky Boyd on the 'Q' and transport side." This was a leisurely affair. We drove around the rock-strewn but green hills of Galilee, in many ways unchanged since the time of Christ, a pastoral countryside, some 2000 feet above sea level, dropping suddenly to the depths of the Sea of Galilee, with the heights of Syria and Transjordan beyond its eastern shores. The Arab villages were in stark contrast to Jewish settlements. The first were virtually devoid of sanitation; water was drawn largely from wells; scant ploughing scraped a living from the topsoil and life was pursued at a pace commensurate with the philosophy of Islam: *umshala!*

In contrast, the Jewish settlements, whether in the Jordan Valley or high in the hills of Galilee, were run on co-operative lines. Each kibbutz had its committee and leader. Water and drainage systems were installed; produce was marketed in Haifa, Jerusalem or Tel Aviv. Except in winter, the settlers wore little other than khaki shorts and shirts, shoes and socks. The women shared the work of the men. The children were placed in crèches and saw their parents in early morning and in the evening after work. Meals were almost invariably taken in the communal hall.

A tricky point which, on the whole, the British authorities mismanaged, was the question of arms for their defence. During the Arab rebellion before the Second World War, which was the direct consequence of the Balfour Declaration, Jewish settlements came under attack and both Haganah and Palmach were acknowledged to have a *raison d'être*. On the other hand, the possession of unlicensed arms was a capital offence, if the Mandatory authorities wished to pursue the charge. Thus, the British Army was responsible for the defence of the kibbutz.

At the same time, and this was the viewpoint which predominated, the arms could be used for terrorist purposes. Hence any information which was received which led the authorities to believe there were hidden arms within the confines of any settlement was followed by a search. As the terrorists were not short of arms, supplied by means of surreptitious sympathetic funding from America, it might have been better to leave well alone.

The tour with Micky Boyd –Irish, fairly tall, blue eyed with a sandy moustache and keen sense of humour combined with considerable shrewdness – incorporated much of northern Palestine. In terms of the whole country, it is often described as being divided

70

into six strips, running from north to south: the coastal plain begins at the northern tip of the Bay of Haifa. Initially it is only three-and-a-half miles wide, but broadens to nearly eight miles as it nears Haifa. There the Carmel range, Mount Carmel dominating the port and oil terminal near the town, cuts it in two. South of Haifa, for a distance of eighteen miles it is only two-and-a-half miles wide, sometimes less. South of the Tanninim stream it starts to broaden to about twelve-and-a-half miles at the Hadera valley which leads into the central hill country. The coastal plain continues south to Gaza and then merges with Sinai and the Negev. Running along-side it, to the east is the Shephelah, the second strip, a countryside comprising a succession of broad valleys and round hills, with routes running north and south as well as east and west. Adjoining, further east, are the central hills, all of which in pre-biblical times were covered with evergreen oak forest, while the coastal plain and parts of the Carmel range grew deciduous (Tabor) oak. A modest start at re-afforestation had begun under the Mandate.

The central hills begin in the north in Upper Galilee, where the range reaches heights of 3300 feet. Military roads had been built by the Royal Engineers, but communications in the hills were lim-ited. In Lower Galilee – Nazareth and its environs were on the periphery – the central hills are divided by a number of broad val-leys which run from east to west, across country, thus providing routes from the river Jordan and the Sea of Galilee to the coastal plain. South of Lower Galilee is the Valley of Jezreel – the Plain of Esdraelon – which is heavily cultivated with cereals and citrus farm-ing as well as being the site of the Beisan fishponds. It is about fifteen miles wide at its broadest point.

Further south, the hills begin to increase in height, reaching 3000 feet in the central Samarian countryside, where sheep and olive groves predominate economically. In their midst lies Nablus, and to the south are the Bethel hills, the town of Ramallah, and then Jerusalem, both lying at 2500 feet above sea level. South of Jerusalem, after Bethlehem, the hills increase in height to over 3300 feet, until they begin to slope rapidly towards the Negev, arid and eroded in many parts with hills rising again to 3400 feet in the high, central area, in which there is a crater nearly twenty-five miles long and five miles wide, reaching a depth of 1650 feet. It is fantastic scenery and, after winter rains, covered, like so much of Palestine, with wild flowers and small shrubs.

To the east of the central hills and the Negev lies the fourth strip, the rift valley, which forms part of a fault which runs to East Africa. At water level, the Sea of Galilee is already 690 feet below sea level, and, as mentioned, the Dead Sea reaches a depth of 2624 at rock bottom, below sea level and 1312 feet at water level. Except for the area immediately bordering the River Jordan, the land ranges from being semi-arid to arid and desert. To the east, the fifth strip, lie the hills north-east of the Sea of Galilee which reach 3600 feet before becoming the plateau which stretches to Damascus. Further south, on this east side of the Jordan, the hills build up to 3000 feet and become the Jordan plateau where we trained on two occasions.

These eastern hills are pierced by deep-cut valleys running from east to west through which rivers run, some keeping their flow during the summer months. Then, beyond this plateau, effectively beyond the borders of modern Palestine, is the sixth strip which is the Syrian desert, then as now patrolled by the Arab Legion and when we were there, aided, as described earlier, by the Transjordan Frontier Force.

In Haifa, where we lunched on more than one occasion –Pross' in the lower part of the town, or at Lilli Manheim's, half-way up the Carmel and well within the Jewish quarter – the Royal Navy had the unpleasant and unrewarding job, during this first week of December, 1946, of transferring 3900 illegal immigrants to Cyprus. Equally, it was neither pleasant nor rewarding for the would-be immigrants, although many an Englishman dreamed of passing his winters in Cyprus. This was not the viewpoint held by the Jewish refugees, and to emphasize the point Haganah organized violent demonstrations. Meanwhile, Jewish leaders, still detained at Latrun and Rafiah, following Operation "Agatha", were being released.

In contrast to the events in Haifa, I spent the day, 7 December, hunting jackal with the KDG, across easy country. After six hours in the saddle, we dined at a Jewish settlement and were most hospitably received and entertained.

On 13 December, the intransigency of a horse caused a false alarm in Nazareth. I had gone to the Nazareth police barracks, a fortress compared to our own defences, to collect a pony with the intention of riding it across country to the Cypriot Mule Company. This was a matter of a couple of miles in admittedly rather rough and rocky country which should have taken a couple of hours. The horse had other ideas. Despite careful checking and tugging before mounting, the metal point in one of the stirrup leathers came out of its socket. The horse sensed this, decided it was the moment to be difficult, bucked and bolted. I came off. It was dark by the time I caught up with it, after being a little concerned that some Arab might have taken a liking to both horse and saddle. Meanwhile, I had retrieved the stirrup leather and iron, and considered myself lucky to have found the horse.

It was now docile, probably contrite, and certainly glad of my company. I had to lead it down a trackless hillside in the general direction of the Mule Company lights inside the camp. I telephoned Brigade. Lewis stood down the alert he was about to make general. He ordered some whisky and a little water. Well, at least Lewis had missed me, or, perhaps more accurately, had noted I was missing.

While I was trailing after a recalcitrant horse, the Zionist conference was forgathering in Basle. There harsh words were said about Chaim Weizmann's conduct of affairs, which were singularly inappropriate, considering that his actions and ideas, from the Zionist viewpoint, were exemplary. In a subsequent tally he was outvoted and he resigned as president of the conference, which refused to attend the London gathering, being planned by the British Foreign Secretary, Ernest Bevin, in yet another attempt to solve the insoluble. In fact, Ben-Gurion, and others, went unofficially.

Back in Galilee, where 1st Guards Brigade had suffered no casualties and comparative peace reigned with moderate tranquillity, news reached us that we were soon to be transferred to the more stressful, urbanized coastal plain further south, covering such places as Tel Aviv, Petah Ticvah, Nathanya and points in between. that is to say 1st Division, under Major-General "Windy" Gale, and 6th Airborne, under Major-General Bols, were changing stations.

The largely pastoral north, except for the coastal strip, was mostly, but not exclusively, as recent events had proved, the domain of Palmach and Haganah: training camps in the remote Galilean hills, arms caches buried in the kibbutzim and a strong presence in Haifa, which later, in the ever-changing kaleidoscope of Palestinian politics, was to work to our advantage *vis-à-vis* the terrorists. The southern area, by contrast heavily cultivated in the coastal area, growing citrus fruit, dates and figs, as well as being the centre of the diamond trade, had an underworld shared by the Irgun and Stern gangs, from the bowels of which was emitted the stench of fanaticism, decay, mental decrepitude and terror, long recognized by Haganah as endemic.

Irgun and Stern were the two other legs of the unholy, unwise and by now rather loose quaternity, under the direction of X Command and Ben-Gurion. They all, however, had one ultimate aim in common: for better or worse, richer or poorer, the end of the Mandate and the establishment of a Jewish state, even if some members of the Jewish Agency were still pussy-footing about total independence. Logically, their actions and intentions could lead only to this one goal, and the first move was to rid themselves of the referee.

On 21 December I left early in Bill Gore-Langton's car, with my jeep as escort – there was an amber alert – to recce the new area, and subsequently advise Brigadier Rodney on the disposition of the two thousand or so men under his command. I arrived at 0900 at 1st Parachute Brigade Headquarters; and at Citrus House, Tel Aiv, saw Mike Jenkins, my contemporary in the Grenadiers, and now adjutant of 1st (Guards) Parachute Battalion, commanded by John Nelson, also a Grenadier, who had commanded his battalion on Battaglia, in the Apennines "with a field telephone in one hand and a pistol in the other" so close and fierce was the fighting.

I made a wider tour of our new area: the Divisional Training Centre at Sarona, near Tel Aviv, the 7th Parachute Battalion at Lydda, and stayed the night at Citrus House, where, over dinner, I proposed myself, and was accepted, for the Guards Parachute Battalion. A short time later, slightly to my relief, this idea was vetoed by both Lewis and Rodney Moore.

The next day I returned to Lydda where I found no great problems to solve except that the 7th Parachute Battalion shared the officers' mess with the Royal Air Force. Lydda, not unreasonably, was an RAF base, which the Para officers said was more like a transit camp. The combined messing and maintenance was 2/4 (14p) per day. The food was commensurate with the outlay, in itself three times less than the average in Brigade of Guards messes.

"*I can't*" I wrote in my diary "*really imagine this working out at all. Luncheon with Royal Engineers at Bir Salim.*" In the evening I lost £6, fifty-two days messing at Lydda, playing poker. Normally I won, but there had to be exceptions.

On 23 December the Brigadier, Lewis and Bill Pease, the LO "P", arrived at the Divisional Training Centre and were taken on a conducted tour of the various camps. We had a picnic lunch, the weather not being too bad, even in December, and I casually pointed out the bungalow – two-roomed with kitchen and bath-room – that stood isolated in the Petah Ticvah camp, also officially administered by the Air Ministry, but this only took the form of one civilian, known to one and all as "Woody". My objective, which I achieved, was to persuade the Brigadier to put 1st Guards Brigade Headquarters in the Petah Ticvah camp which was the most suitable and salubrious for our functions: adequate office accommodation, messing facilities and hutment (the military term) sufficient to install officers and other ranks in considerable comfort. It was obvious the RAF looked after its own. We returned to Nazareth, a journey of sixty miles, via Hadera and Afula, in just over an hour. Rodney did not like dilatory driving.

The next day was Christmas Eve. Rodney invited 200 guests to

Brigade Headquarters. Max, the barman at the Astoria, who made a delicious creamy cocktail called an Alexander, "*did the necessary*", I wrote home. My old Prince of Wales Company commander, Henry Coombe-Tennant, turned up from Cairo. He was then bound for Saudi Arabia on a military mission, later retiring from the Army, taking orders as a Catholic priest and becoming a monk. Henry was not the only Welsh Guards officer sent to Arabia: one, hesitant in manner if not in action, Gavin Young, failed to galvanize the vacillating Iman of Yemen to advance and defend his throne. He was soon deposed. Even Lawrence of Arabia might have failed; fat bellies without fire cannot be ignited.

On Christmas Day Andrew Gibson-Watt and I were invited to lunch with the Battalion at Tiberias. Colonel Reggie Hodgkinson had left on 12 December and James Gresham was acting as commanding officer. Physically they were very different. Although both were of average height, Reggie was blue-eyed and lantern-jawed with a distinct cavalry gait, whereas James, keen and brown-eyed, looked and remained the fair but finicky inspector of men, horses and their equipment. He had also been a superb commander in the field and possessed a considerable sense of humour.

James asked me to carve the ham, not to be found locally from either denomination, while he dealt with the turkey. I thought it wisest to say I had not carved a ham before, having been a boy of fourteen in 1939 when I last saw one. Logically, it should not be too difficult, but, with James's perfectionism in mind, I played safe. He most kindly explained. It was not too difficult.

Paper hats being part of the ritual, setting alight to mine was not a temptation James could resist. No damage was done to hair or scalp and the laughter was commensurate with the diversion. We finished at the respectable hour of five o'clock and went to see our friends Francis Widdrington and Jim Jerman some little distance away with their company. Cold ham and a bottle of champagne were loaded into our jeep and the driver, commendably sober, drove us back to Nazareth where, on the morrow, the Brigadier and four of us dined with the Khouri family, who were Christian Arabs. The next day we sat down to our own Christmas lunch.

Friday, 27 December, the feast of Saint John, the Apostle whom Jesus loved, was also the day of physical chastisement for two Irgun members, too young to be condemned to death. They had been arrested during an armed bank raid with every intent to shoot their way into and out of trouble, had they been given half a chance. They were not. Each one was given eighteen strokes of the cane and eighteen years imprisonment, which effectively meant eighteen months. In terms of the cane, it was an instrument which most boys of all nationalities in those days had experienced at some moment in their lives. The IZL gang felt, however, that, whereas their boys had their licence to kill, no one had the right to punish them. In fact they were lucky: by comparison to the cat, a rope whip with nine knotted thongs, or the birch, the cane was virtually a tickle.

Seeking revenge, the IZL seized the Brigade Major of 2nd Parachute Brigade and three sergeants whom they whipped in retaliation. This was an error. The flagellants were caught *in flagrante delicto* with arms and whips in their car when stopped at an Army checkpoint. One died and the others took a long time to recover before their trial. Major Brett and the sergeants were none the worse for their experience.

There was a reaction to this terrorist activity in Great Britain. Public opinion was becoming increasingly indifferent to the future of Palestine, where it could see, certainly more clearly than the British government at that moment, there was no British interest. What use, even as a military base, was the place when the bulk of the troops stationed there were wholly engaged fighting terrorists? Little backing was given to any possible political decision ordering the Army to use its full force.

"Rule or get out!" was Churchill's cry, in opposition. A logical conclusion was impending, following a train of events forecast by Lord Curzon in 1917, long before the additional horrors of the holocaust and the transmogrification of the Empire into the Commonwealth and its consequences, both political and strategic, had materialized. There was also the well orchestrated Zionist drumbeat resounding in the ears of President Truman to whom votes were as precious as all the accumulated gold in Fort Knox.

The year 1946 had seen 212 deaths, including 45 British soldiers, 29 British police, 14 British civilians, 63 Jews, of whom 26 were armed, 60 Arabs and one other. The King David Hotel bombing accounted for 45%. Nor did the New Year bode well.

9. 'Bill Tilleard (*left*) took over from John Lascelles (*right*) as Brigade Intelligence Officer' (p.81).

10. 'Rodney Moore took seven Grenadier officers ot the Tel Aviv Opera. All were recieved by the Mayor, Isreal Rokakh' (p.88). The Brigadier is in the centre, the Mayor on the left.

DAILY EXPRESS

No. 14,708   Lighting-up: 10.50 pm to 5.23 am   FRIDAY AUGUST 1 1947   Weather: Bright periods, thunder   One Penny

TEL-AVIV SHOTS: FIVE JEWS KILLED, MANY INJURED   *ATTLEE MAY TELL OF CUTS IN BREAD AND BUTTER*   *HOLIDAYS ABROAD BARRED FOR BRITISH CHILDREN*

HANGED BRITONS: Picture that will shock the world

6,000 holiday trips stopped

Paralysis scare

Express Staff Reporter

CONTINENTAL holidays for 6,000 British children were suspended last night.

The World Friendship Association stopped three bookings to Belgium, fearing infantile paralysis sent back 300 children on Wednesday. . . . Other arrangements—Other

4.30 a.m. LATEST

'INVADERS ARE ON THE WAY'

Food from abroad is cut

BUTTER RATION MAY BE HALVED

By GUY EDEN

MR. ATTLEE, in his speech to the Commons next Wednesday in the two-day state-of-the-nation debate, is expected to announce these cuts in the drive to save dollars:

BUTTER ration down by a half —if now represents a weekly average of 3oz.

BREAD allowance down by a quarter—to an average of 27 B.U.s a month.

PETROL ration down by a third — the Basic unit to revert to the one-gallon value instead of being worth 1½ gallons as now.

MEAT is also likely to be cut from today's 1s. 2d. worth a week (4d. worth in corned beef). The cut will not be severe as first but the ration may have to be reduced again later.

SUGAR is also believed to be on the Premier's cuts-to-come list. But the MARGARINE (introverted) average at present is 3ozs.—may be slightly increased.

Food on our land is wasted

Cabbages fed to sheep

By KENNETH PIPE

FARMERS in the West Country dealing with a better-than-expected early harvest, are finding markets glutted with vegetables . . .

Food in Argentina is rotting

Senor Miranda burns the oil

BUENOS AIRES, Thursday.—Half a million tons of wheat have rotted in the Argentine because of inefficient transport, said Senor Miguel Miranda, new head of the Economic Council today. . . . —Reuter.

£100,000,000 lost in ten minutes

Holders of gilt-edged stock lost about £100,000,000 yesterday in a ten-minute "bessel" torrent of the Stock Exchange . . .

£11,000,000 to spend

Britain, despite coming economic cuts, is to spend £11,000,000 next year on a new holiday fund last night. This is planned over and above the August Bank Holiday . . .

Dust-coat men raid store

MEN wearing dust-coats to look like furniture removers raided a bonded store in Bury St. Edmunds, Suffolk, yesterday, and got away with kegs of spirits . . .

Shots in Tel-Aviv: 5 Jews die

STAY-PUT SHIPS FOR CYPRUS?

Express Political Correspondent

THE Cabinet is considering several other landing places for the 4,500 Jewish illegal immigrants off the French coast if it proves impossible to land them in France. . . .

ANOTHER TRY

F. J. Tarkfield telephones from Port de Bouc—

One more attempt is to be made today by the French to persuade the Jews to leave the ships . . .

Horse lost— stable locked

Collar a horse which can be stabled in the 3.30 at Goodwood yesterday, provided two unclothed mysteries before the race . . .

Waiting

Earlier through the Palestine High Commissioner Sir Alan Cunningham had called to Government House Mrs. Golda Meyerson . . .

Cripps asks: Free Empire trade

PARIS, Thursday.—Sir Stafford Cripps, President of the Board of Trade, flew to Paris today to drive with America's Under-Secretary of State Mr. William Clayton, and told him that Britain could win through if she is allowed to co-operate in the Empire trade at the expense of the rest of the world . . .
Express News Service.

Two ways out of the crisis

By Max Edwards, Parliamentary Secretary, Ministry of Labour, said in the Commons last night.
It may well be that the whole of the crisis in our economy the country will have to decide whether or not we have direction of labour or an absolutely open door for the employment of Poles and European voluntary workers. . . .

Cancel Viceroy

Because there will be no V-ceroy when Lord Mountbatten's office lapses as a Governor-General next month, the Viceroy will be abolished . . .

IN A GROVE OF EUCALYPTUS . .

RADIOED from Jerusalem last night, this Daily Express picture was taken in a eucalyptus grove south of Nathanya, Palestine.

The bodies of murdered Clifford Martin and Mervyn Paice—British security sergeants—hang from eucalyptus trees.

The hands of both victims are bound behind their backs. Pieces of shirt have been wrapped round their heads.
To one body is pinned a notice: "This is the sentence of Irgun's High Tribunal."

A booby-trap explosion threw the photographer to the ground after this picture was taken. The film was salvaged from his smashed camera.

Wanted for murder

MENACHEM BEGIN

THIS is the Irgun thug commander who issued the warrant orders for the hangings.
When Mr. Creech Jones, Colonial Secretary, announced from the window of the car, and caught the gang's thugs . . .

Mr. Silverman (Soc., Nelson) asked Mr. Silverman, and Colonel said that he had tried to awaken sympathy for it.
Later he expressed his deep shame and humiliation that the hangings should have been stained with innocent blood.

Late last night Government and opposition leaders made provisional arrangements for a full debate on Palestine next Friday.

I spy a witch

JOHANNESBURG, Thursday.—In the language of African from killing three suspected of witchcraft Northern Rhodesia is changing. . . .

Fifty Colorados

Fifty Colorado beetles were kept caught yesterday on another on being a witch doctor . . .

'Tell Dutch to go back'

NEW YORK, Thursday.—The way is now clear for the U.N. Security Council to order back to their original positions India's spokesman Mr. H. B. Sen told the Security Council today. Otherwise the Dutch would have set up a "de facto" administration when the time came for talks. . . .

999 AT MIDNIGHT

Woman held

Express Staff Reporter

THE burglar alarm started to ring at 12.15 this morning in a gown shop in Old Brompton-road, S.W.

It often does. Every time it goes off one of the neighbours dials 999.

This morning it was a doctor who ran to the phone.
Police found panes of glass smashed in the shop which is owned by Lettice D. B. Braddock. People in the flats above waved from their bedroom windows and saw them chase a man down a side-street. He got away.
Later a woman was taken away in a police car. She was detained at Chelsea police station.

Baby, 1½lb.

A baby weighing one and a half pounds has lived six days in cotton wool at St. Thomas's Hospital, S.E.

ABBEY WEDDING FOR THE PRINCESS

On November 20

Express Staff Reporter

PRINCESS ELIZABETH and Lieutenant Philip Mountbatten will be married at Westminster Abbey at 11.30 a.m. on Thursday, November 20, it was announced from Buckingham Palace last night.
The King last revealed this at a Privy Council meeting earlier in the day when he gave formal consent to the marriage. . . .

DRIVE IN STATE

'Snap' colonel cashiered

HAMBURG, Thursday.—Lieut.-Colonel R. N. J. Warren, Commanding Officer of 17 Vehicle Company, Hamburg, alleged to have photographed a Danish girl in the nude in the gardens of his mess, has been cashiered. . . .

'Scared' man stops runaway pony

A pony, breaking away from its overturned trap, bolted for four miles through the traffic along the Great Cambridge-road yesterday . . .

'I'll teach you, said the boy of 7

Seven-year-old William McCrary of Newton Stewart, Wigtownshire, fell over a 30-ft. shelf of mud to reach two children on whom he drew . . .

Seagull in plane injures pilot

A seagull which flew into the cockpit and struck him in the eye. The second pilot landed the plane . . .

Dutch 'warship sunk'

BATAVIA, Thursday.—The Dutch admitted today that Indonesian planes had dive-bombed and set fire to the Malang base, which had been captured from the Indonesians. . . .

'Undeclared war'

NEW YORK, Thursday.—Greece tonight charged Albania, Bulgaria, and Yugoslavia with waging undeclared war against her and demanded action by the Security Council.—Reuter.

CENtral 8000

... countries may die the same and we cannot risk more parties being turned back.
The children who were going to France include Holland, Denmark ... other mothers back or photos, when ... strange holidays start again.
An equal number of Continental children were now due to holiday in Britain have been stopped too.
NOTE—The World Friendship Association announced on Wednesday they turned back 300 children and were sending infantile paralysis. But although a doctor had passed them all fit, he could not risk it with 300 in a party. . . .

YESTERDAY . . .

MR. BEVAN, Minister of Health, said yesterday that at least 300 cases of infantile paralysis having for the first time ever. One child died in Epping Forest; another in Hoyland Yorks.

THE FUTURE . . .

LLOYD'S underwriters are today issue an insurance policy against infantile paralysis. For payment of 30s. a year any person can get cover up to £1,000.
An insured person who gets the disease will be paid £10 a week and recovers. If he is certified a half-disabled the balance of the £1,000 will be paid to him.

PRECAUTIONS . .

THE British Medical Journal says that Britain looks like having for the first time an American experience of infantile paralysis.
The Lancet says that summer assemblies, particularly of children, should be avoided.
A sensible precaution is the avoidance of excessive exertion of children at sports and games. A contributory cause is also dangerous because over-exertion and chills will develop any tendency to the disease.

BACK THEY COME

ONE BY ONE

The children are playing again on the golden shores, and building their sand castles to their hearts' content. The old peace-time joys are returning. Things are getting better for everybody.
In particular the '57 Varieties' are returning with all their freshness, goodness and appetising flavour.

HEINZ 57 VARIETIES

ALREADY ABOUT: Baked Beans, Spaghetti, Salad Cream, Mayonnaise, Soups, Sandwich Spread, Pickles, Vinegar, and Strained Foods for Babies.

---

11. Front page of the *Daily Express*, 1 August, 1947 (see p.102).

12. 1st Guards Brigade Headquarters, June, 1947. Brigadier Moore front row centre: front row right, the author and Andrew Gibson-Watt.

13. 'In Transjordan, at this moment, were two journalists, a married couple, Alexander Clifford, the *Daily Mail* chief foreign correspondent, and his wife Jenny Nicholson' (p.111). Seen here with the author on the steps of the Philadelphia Hotel, Amman, December, 1947.

14. The author, second from right, with Fawzi-el-Kaoujki on his right, at Tabas (see pp.118-134).

15. Saint David's Day, 1948. On the left is General Sir Alan Cunningham, the High Commissioner: to his left Colonel Billy Malcolm: behind him Lieutenant-General Sir Gordon Macmillan, GOC Palestine: rear right the author.

CHAPTER EIGHT

The Move South

The beginning of 1947 was not a particularly good moment, either, for Chaim Weizmann. He had resigned the presidency of the Zionist conference and had expressed his fear to Aubrey (Abba) Eban that " terrorism would destroy the liberal and humane elements in Zionism, thus leading to a chauvinistic lack of realism".

Yet, as Eban confirmed, Weizmann condoned and encouraged Haganah acts of violence, and attempted to introduce a liberal and humane element into terrorism in 1945 with Ben-Gurion, when X Command was created. Human elements and terrorism, however, were and are mutually exclusive.

In contrast, the United Kingdom had not only opened the floodgates to Jewish immigration into the British Isles and the Empire, but had also, by the Balfour Declaration, begun a similar process in Palestine. All this took place at a time when anti-semitism, the precedent of Zionism, was rampant in Russia and festering in other parts of Europe.

Great Britain, whose passport Weizmann carried, was the country for which Weizmann's son, Michael, gave his life, serving in the Royal Air Force. Nevertheless, throughout the saga of the Mandate, Weizmann's and the Zionist objective remained, first, to maximize Jewish immigration, having already achieved a national home for the Jewish people, and then, secondly, a Jewish state, after it became evident that the Mandatory power was trying to honour its obligations to the Arabs, already hard done by, and in no way the beneficiaries of democracy.

Thus, by its own definition, Zionism was logically chauvinistic and irredentist. It had no reason to be created or exist otherwise. In terms of realism, the psychopathic fringe was hardly the personification of liberal and humane action or ideas. The outcome,

77

however, of *all* brands of terrorism, by definition both illiberal and inhuman, was the establishment of the State of Israel. Terrorism was the bellwether; and the bell tolled for the liberal and humane elements in Judaism, not least when Irgun strangled two young British sergeants, in July, 1947, after kidnapping them and incarcerating them in a sealed, underground cell for seventeen days. Herod, by comparison, was compassionate.

In the same manner as Lloyd George was induced to conjure his own Mephistopheles in the form of the Mandate, preceded by the Declaration, so too Chaim Weizmann chose the dark side, although he tried to convince himself it was grey, and hoped his *deus ex machina*, controlled terrorism, would only be benignly malevolent. If the phrase be an oxymoron, so too was the thinking of Weizmann, as revealed by Eban, unless the view be taken that he knew exactly what he was doing and why. Machiavelli would have smiled, Talleyrand would not have despised the duplicity, and Palmerston would have noted he was working closely with the opposition under the guise of amiability, at first with Great Britain and then with the United States.

Chaim Weizmann endeavoured, also with limited success, to link any action which was contrary to Zionist aims as being anti-semitic. Thus, after the launch of Operation "Agatha", a direct and legitimate response to X Command-directed murder, Weizmann informed the High Commissioner, "British reaction to Jewish violence is a battle against world Jewry." That is to say, Jews could be violent and law-breaking, but their legal government must abdicate its responsibilities. Other than extremists, few Jews or Gentiles would have agreed. Once again, on the evidence, was Weizmann playing a Machiavellian ploy, or was he schizoid as well as being, it would seem, paranoid? Either way, no one doubted his particular brand of intelligence, and in 1948 he obtained his objective.

In his definitive book *The British Empire in the Middle East 1945-1951* William Roger Louis writes: It is difficult to sustain the argument that anti-semitism explains British policy towards the immigration question. Bevin was fully aware, in his own words, that 'the plight of the victims of Nazi persecution, among whom were a large number of Jews, is unprecedented in the history of the world'. But neither he nor his advisers drew the conclusion that the future of the Jews lay in Palestine. Bevin, and other British leaders, including Churchill, consistently advocated the revival of Jewish society on a basis of equality with other Europeans within Europe itself. The Foreign Office was indeed anti-Zionist, but not antisemitic."

In other words, refugees were categorized by nationality and not religion. Obligations to Arabs were cardinal factors in the Mandate's administration. This obligation was never recognized by Zionists, who, at the same time, were well aware that American immigration policy was hostile. Meanwhile, the attentions of the State Department and the Foreign Office were drawn, respectively, by the Joint Chiefs of Staff and the Imperial General Staff to increasing Soviet hostility, and the question of Arab oil in an area of exceptional strategic importance. Closely linked to this factor was the matter of British military bases in Egypt and the prudence of finding an alternative.

Fundamentally, however, throughout this continuing drama, British administration, exemplified by the competence and probity of the last Chief Justice, Sir William Fitzgerald, was an exercise of *pax Britannica* without any chance of success. *La vieille fille* – Britannica Balfour – had from the beginning made peace impossible. Thus, an executive which had governed India with only 2000 civil servants was unable to cope with the shackling pre-conditions formulated in 1917 and codified under the Mandate.

Chaim Weizmann, once he observed the dependence of the post-War British economy on an American bridging loan, and in turn the dependence of the American President on the New York Jewish vote and the abundance of funds being provided for Zionist aims by American Jewry, must have been aware then that it was only a matter of time. The undoubted horrors of Nazi persecution certainly accelerated the process and, in January, 1947, there were only sixteen-and-a-half months to go.

In his authorized but secret dealings with the Jewish Agency, Rodney Moore had not been provided with a crystal ball by the Royal Army Ordnance Corps, but he must have realized the writing was on the wall for the Mandate – in Hebrew. Meanwhile, life, and death, continued in its normal abnormal manner in the Holy Land when, as referred to earlier, five Jews were caught in a car on New Year's Day, armed with whips and pistols. One died subsequently and according to the official statement the others were "not in a fit condition for trial at present."

The next day, 2 January, an IZL adherent, Dov Gruner, who had been wounded and arrested on 25 April, 1946, during an attack on a police station, was condemned to death. On this same Thursday Lewis Dawnay and I went south to continue detailed arrangements for the move from Galilee. Two jeeps were blown up – not ours – and John Nelson's 1st (Guards) Parachute Battalion headquarters at Citrus House was attacked by Irgun. The Airborne reaction to this followed five days later, when some 65 men from a Tel Aviv quarter were taken to Sarona camp and made to run the gauntlet

79

while being beaten with sticks. None of this was good news for anyone.

In Galilee, at this juncture, there was comparative peace: riding, some shooting, tennis, John Lascelles' twenty-fifth birthday party on 11 January in the Astoria restaurant, and a dinner with the KDG. One of their officers, Robin Sheepshanks, later a neighbour of mine when I lived in Suffolk, was Johnny's cousin. We went to the cinema in Haifa, and all ranks were prone to reminisce with a degree of nostalgia about the more temperate times in the north.

On 14 January this came to an end when we moved south to the camp at Petah Ticvah I had reconnoitred three weeks earlier. I left with Andrew Gibson-Watt. We visited the large cantonment at Sarafand and had tea with John Nelson. Meanwhile the Brigade moved into camps allotted by Brigadier Rodney Moore: the 3rd Grenadiers left Hadera for Lydda; the 3rd Coldstream, now under command of Lieutenant-Colonel Billy Steele, my commandant at Mons, and who had commanded the battalion in Italy during the winter of 1944/45, moved from Acre to three areas.

Citrus House contained two Coldstream companies; another was at Sarona, a mile away; the two remaining companies were first at Petah Ticvah, then at Sarona. The 1st Battalion Welsh Guards, soon to be commanded by Billy Malcolm, went to Sarafand.

On 26 January the imminent execution of Dov Gruner provoked Irgun into kidnapping two British civilians: a retired officer, Major H.A. Collins, whom they chloroformed, hit on the head and pushed into a sack. Then, on the following day, they kidnapped Judge Ralph Windham from his courtroom in Tel Aviv. At the same time, pending an appeal to the Privy Council, unbeknownst to the condemned, the execution was postponed.

28.1.47. "*Judge Windham returned*" my diary entry states. He later became Chief Justice in Tanzania. Meanwhile the military and police operation against the terrorists continued. The authorities let it be known that they would impose complete civil stagnation and martial law in the Petah Ticvah and Tel Aviv areas if disorder continued. At this moment the detailed planning of Operation "Elephant" began – the sealing off of ten miles by five of the area concerned.

29.1.47. "*Kidnapped civilian, Collins, still not returned. Martial law will be declared in certain areas at midnight tomorrow if the man is not released. The Ramleh Vale Hunt meet cancelled.*" In fact, late at night Collins was set free. He was suffering from excess inhalation of chloroform and died later of emphysema.

On the same day the Commander-in-Chief, Middle East, General Sir Miles Dempsey, came to lunch at Brigade with General

Gale and I received a letter from my older friend, Molly Berkeley, who lived in Assisi that she had decided she would not come to Palestine for the moment. How wise! Had she decided otherwise, she would, in fact, have been crossing the frontier in the opposite direction to 3000 women being evacuated in the exodus know as Exercise "Polly". This was in preparation for "Elephant" which the authorities felt was an inevitable sequel to anticipated terrorist violence. The exercise began on 2 February, preceded, in some cases, by a dance at the officers' club in Sarafand where I, according to my diary, supported the wife of CREME on the dance floor.

On 3 February, not necessarily in the form of compensation for the loss of the ladies, Lieutenant-Colonel Billy Malcolm arrived to command the Welsh Guards and the following day Peter Clifton gave up command of the Grenadier battalion and was succeeded by John Davies. On a lower level, Bill Tilleard took over from John Lascelles as Brigade Intelligence Officer. Even more important during such times of stress and deprivation, the Ramleh Vale Hunt resumed its activities. In passing, the Jewish elected body, Vaad Leumi, said it would fight terrorism.

On 6 February, while the world waited without much hope for the Arab and Jewish reaction to the final British proposals for the future of Palestine, 1st Guards Brigade held a court martial. Its members – John Lascelles, Richard Carr-Gomm and Julian Paget – were given lunch and hopefully the accused was fed as well.

The next day, to no one's surprise, the proposal of a British trusteeship administering divided Arab and Jewish zones in Palestine was rejected by both sides. The British government then decided to refer the matter of the Mandate to the United Nations which it did nearly two months later. On 8 February we received the draft "Elephant" instructions. Military planning was thorough and precise.

Meanwhile, the three IZL members caught carrying arms on the night Major Brett and the three sergeants were flogged were condemned to death on 10 February. The sentences were confirmed by General Barker. He left Palestine two days later on 12 February. On the same day Bernard Fergusson, the Assistant Inspector-General of the Palestine Police, submitted his counter-gang plan to seek and hunt the terrorists. Two war heroes were recruited: Alastair MacGregor and Roy Farran, who had operated behind the lines in France.

It occurred to me at the time that it was not going to work. Despite the Vaad Leumi's statement that it would fight terrorism, there were too few gaps in the Jewish population through which a countergang operation could pass and infiltrate any terrorist cell without leaving a trace of their means of entry. Although many Jews were wholly against terrorism, even an independent state, none, or hardly any, would take the mortal risk of cooperating with *goyim* to that extent, if it were likely to be traceable.

On the other hand, police and military intelligence often had wind of terrorist intentions, which indicated that their organizations were not impenetrable. Yet, when asked to cooperate openly and with loyalty to their own government by Henry Gurney, Chief Secretary, Goldie Meyerson (Meir) replied that the Yishuv was not going to encourage anyone to "spy on its own people". In fact, she was paraphrasing the daily prayer known as the Eighteen Blessings which includes the sentence: "There shall be no hope for the informer."

Nevertheless, in an ambivalent situation, Farran made some contact, and a Stern gang member was abducted and disappeared. In a careless moment Farran left his hat near the scene – undercover agents in 1947 wore hats in February – and he left for Syria, but returned voluntarily. He was tried for murder but was acquitted: you cannot cross-examine a hat. Stern as usual, sought vengeance, deliberately misinterpreting the thrice mentioned biblical phrase "an eye for an eye, a tooth for a tooth" concerning which rabbinical teaching was clear: justice must be administered by the law and not outside it by individuals.

Stern, regardless, sent Farran a parcel bomb. His brother opened it and was killed. Stern conceded that they were satisfied. Roy Farran went to Canada where he became solicitor-general of Alberta. There was no hint of subversion there.

Plans, in the meantime, for "Elephant" were being formulated, and Brigade staff were heavily involved. It would be 1st Guards Brigade Group which would carry out the operation. It was being described as a punitive plan, evolved by General "Bubbles" Barker, before his departure, and likely to be put into operation by two Zionists, namely General "Windy" Gale and Brigadier Rodney Moore. In fact, an understanding of Zionist aspirations by both officers did not equate with condonation.

Interspersed with planning for "Elephant", I had time for a day's hunting with the Ramleh Vale. James Gresham and "Mac" Reynolds, Welsh Guards, were both out, so too an apparent exception to the female exodus under Exercise "Polly" in the lithe form of Miss Felicity Archdale. I described her as a plucky rider, but who became divorced from her horse at a later stage. Hounds found two jackals, but the scent was bad. My horse "Prince" went well, but tossed his head. Miss Archdale was swept off her feet and onto her horse by a gallant in the KDG.

General Barker's successor as GOC Palestine was Lieutenant-General Sir Gordon Macmillan of MacMillan who lunched at Brigade, after touring the area on 19 February. Our mess at Petah Ticvah was shared at this moment with the aforementioned Royal Artillery 651 Flight Air O.P. It was commanded by Major Norman Lane, who had recently applied to the Commander-in-Chief, Middle East, to be married, presumably by the Exceptionally Reverend James Denny, Grenadier Guards.

There was, however, a slight hitch. He was asked when he planned to marry, permission being granted in principle, and where? "Here," he replied. "As soon as my fiancée gets her divorce!" In formal military circles this did not go down too well. What did go down was one of his Auster aeroplanes. This resulted in his replacement by John Cameron-Haye. The incident took place just before we arrived. After a New Year party one or two of the guests were taken up for a gentle flight. The Austers were spotter planes. In that role they preceded the helicopter, but were unable to hover.

The officer flying the machine allowed the engine speed to drop to a level where it stalled. He was flying too low to do anything about it. The Auster plummeted. Pilot and passenger were killed. Five officers were now left in the flight. Momentary consolation was sought at the bar of what was soon to be our shared mess. A bar was not an innovation ever seen in a Brigade of Guards mess. There were mess waiters, but there was no such occupation as a barman, at any rate in the normal run of affairs, in His Majesty's Household Regiments. The barman at Petah Ticvah was a gunner.

The reader may appreciate that, while preparations for the likely imposition of Operation "Elephant" went ahead, while senior officials in the Foreign Office prepared the British referral of the Mandate to the United Nations and the State Department sparred with the White House over the matter, and terrorists threatened dire revenge for those under sentence of death, harnessing their hatred and harbouring their intention of dismantling the Mandate, Brigadier Rodney, and Lewis were determined to dismantle the bar.

On this side of the offending obstacle, our wearing caps in the mess should the whim occur, inflicted pain upon the Royal Artillery. Nor did we discard our leather belts which were worn with service dress. Lewis went a long way not to call them Sam Brownes. These differences mattered much to the traditionally minded and before long I was deputed by Rodney to arrange a divorce.

His brief was simple and direct, in the best form of military orders. I was to tell the extremely courteous officer commanding the Air O.P., now John Cameron-Haye, that the base was big enough for more than one mess. Two would not be stretching the facilities. Soon afterwards, he invited me with great grace to fly with him over Tel Aviv, Petah Ticvah and the neighbourhood.

On 22 February I had military business in Haifa, whither I was driven, accompanied by Bill Tilleard and Geoffrey Bowden, KRRC. We lunched, with Lilli Manheim and Max, at the Astoria. In the evening we dined at the Piccadilly. According to my diary there was a *"tremendous party with Rachel Saphir, the friend of Brigadier Rodney. Geoffrey invites the Hungarian dancer to our table – enormous champagne bill"*.

We stayed in Haifa and met the Brigadier at the Balfour Cellar, then lunched at Edmunds with Ruthe and Rudi Sugarenski before returning to Petah Ticvah. On 25 February I accompanied Rodney when he inspected the 2nd KRRC who were under our command. We then went to Rehovot, turned off the main road and drove for a few hundred yards down a track towards a modest house built in the middle of an orange grove. It was the home of Dr Chaim Weizmann. Here, on 6 July, 1946, he had called a conference of those prominent Jews not rounded up in Operation "Agatha". He had requested, the reader will recall, a postponement of the King David Hotel bombing until after the Zionist Paris conference in August.

Rodney was certainly fully briefed. The house and the man were both modest. He was small by our standards, with narrow eyes and his sight going; his head was large and his nose spatulate. He wore an imperial beard. We were introduced and I stayed only for a moment as Rodney and his host wished to talk over lunch. The driver took me the short distance to Tel Aviv where I had been asked to John Lascelles' farewell lunch at the Pilz.

He was going home, prior to becoming ADC to Louis Mountbatten in India, the last Viceroy. He later wrote to me from Viceregal Lodge. It was a sad letter and he died shortly afterwards: the end of the Raj, the end of an era, the end of the British Empire – regrettably the obsession of the envious imperialist Franklin Roosevelt, whose death precipitated Harry Truman into the White House in 1945 – and the beginning of the oft-underestimated Commonwealth. The end in Palestine was to be the forerunner, as in India, of indigenous bloodshed. Thenceforth, those left behind were engulfed irresistibly in the vortices of their own violence.

CHAPTER NINE

Bombs and Casualties

The terrorist outbreak which police and military intelligence anticipated, following information received from reliable Jewish sources,
took place on 1 March. The most brutal attack was launched
against the Goldsmith Officers' Club in Jerusalem, named after a
generous Jewish sponsor. There thirteen British officers were killed
and sixteen wounded. A further nine British soldiers were killed in
other Irgun activities. Had the jeep carrying Andrew Gibson-Watt,
two guardsmen and myself been better targeted, there would have
been four more to add to the list.

Like last year, Saint David's Day was celebrated in Palestine by
the 1st Battalion Welsh Guards, only this time it was held in
Sarafand and the leeks were presented by the High Commissioner
after he had taken the salute. We had a splendid lunch and were
due to return in the early evening. News of the terrorist murders
reached all headquarters immediately, and the two escort vehicles
sent to Sarafand to bring us back were an obvious alert signal.

I was alert myself, returning to Brigade headquarters, sitting next
to the driver, armed with my cocked Tommy gun. The sky was clear
and the moon in its first quarter. I was aware that the stretch of road
we were approaching, near the camp, before turning off right, had
been the scene of several bomb attacks. It was the mark of the inexact counter-measures taken by the British authorities that the
orange grove on the left of the road, as we approached it, was still
standing. The trees formed three sides of a square around a one-
acre field. This provided an excellent view from behind cover. I
became instinctively aware that something was going to happen, or
could well take place, as we drew nearer.

Behind us was the second jeep, and in front the 15 cwt truck.
Suddenly there was a flash and loud explosion twenty yards ahead,

and behind the truck in front, which stopped. It was immediately obvious the thug who detonated the mine had bogged it, either, as mentioned, by being covetous and craving to destroy two vehicles and their occupants instead of one, or mistiming. I gave orders to switch off all lights, take cover and fire into the orange grove, inevitably inexact, but it established the initiative. My next command would have been to root out and arrest the criminals.

We had the psychological advantage, although we would have had to cross the field to reach them. Being pursued, however, by soldiers with automatic weapons is unenviable, regardless of any small arms the terrorists may have possessed. In the event, as described, all this came to nought when the camp searchlight operator, trained to spotlight anything suspicious, silhouetted us. There were no means of communicating with him. We embussed and returned to camp.

I wrote home shortly afterwards: "*Please don't worry about me, as everything could not be more peaceful. I am acting DAA & QMG. As well as Battalions normally in the Brigade, I have also six line regiments and artillery regiments who are cordoning the zone under martial law. Spent this morning in Jaffa slums finding billets.*"

Indeed Operation "Elephant" was put effortlessly into effect on Sunday 2 March at 0330, when the cordon was completed. At 1315 the civil administration was taken over, amicably, and 300,000 people were placed under martial law. The ten mile by five area included Tel Aviv, Ramat Gan and Petah Ticvah. Cable and wireless communications were cut off; the automatic telephone exchanges in the three towns were shut, under the direction of 1 Division CRS, Lieutenant-Colonel D.M. Rhind. 1st Guards Brigade signals forward wireless net had eighteen stations.

These included the three Guards battalions, 2KRRC, 4th/7th Dragoon Guards, 1 Field Regiment RA, 13 Anti-Tank Regiment RA, 2 Cheshires, 1 DCLI, 2 Foresters, "A" Flight 651 Air OP RA and seven other stations, including the Royal Navy, RAF and the Motor Boat detachment of the RASC, patrolling the coast. The civil Jewish authorities acted closely with the British District Commissioner, McGeagh, himself under military orders. Israel Rokakh, the Mayor of Tel Aviv, bore no rancour and fully understood the need to curb extremists.

No one could enter or leave the area cordoned off without a pass. Business came to a standstill. There was no outside communication. Door-to-door searches were made for terrorists. In many cases Haganah helped discreetly.

Other than one exception the first night was quiet. A Jew, riding a bicycle, was shot by a Coldstream sentry after he had failed to respond to a challenge made three times. There was, however, one unrecorded incident, which was unravelled with a little help from the author. Woody, the AMWD clerk of works at Brigade Head-quarters, was caught napping – or rather no one informed him of the forthcoming event – in that his girl was still inside his camp billet, unable to pass through the cordon. I arranged for the lady to be placed in the back of a 15 cwt truck, with Woody next to the driver, who was ordered to head for Tel Aviv. The mission was accomplished.

The initial house curfew lasted forty-eight hours and, as the cordon was put into place on a Sunday, many wished to leave and others to enter. The Military Liaison Officer was Jack Bowman, second-in-command of the Coldstream. He issued 8000 passes for those wishing to cross the line. The civil authorities cooperated, but bus and funeral services had, however, to be prodded into life.

Jack's impression of Weizmann, whom he saw several times, was acute: "He always greeted us cordially, with a display of some emotion, thanking God we were safe: but I always had the feeling, although he was genuinely relieved we were safe, he was not sorry to hear about Jewish terrorists being active against others." Jack, assumedly, knew nothing about X Command.

On 3 March there was a commanding officers' conference which I attended. Lewis handed over to me the following day when he went on leave. He also wrote my confidential report, which I initialled. It stated that I could do his job in his absence. I thanked him. On the same day the Regimental Lieutenant-Colonel commanding the Grenadiers, Dick Colvin, returned to England by air after attending the funeral of the Grenadier and other soldiers killed by terrorist outrages on the night of 1/2 March, when Andrew and I had our narrow escape.

On most days during the operation I went into Tel Aviv. On 5 March I sent a telegram to Beirut on behalf of Marco Albahari, the band leader at the Pilz, and messages of goodwill to relations of those I knew outside the cordon. Marco Albahari was anxious to obtain a contract at the Saint George Hotel in Beirut. Thanks to my help, he did so. I saw him five years later in Beirut. He had retained his British passport, having had it re-issued in Cyprus to erase any reference to Palestine, but when I greeted him he did not wish to speak. He was passing as an Arab. Maybe Mossad had recruited him, or simply the Saint George Hotel.

On 8 March Citrus House and Sarona were attacked by Jewish terrorists. Four grenades were thrown at Guardsman Stocker, the Coldstream sentry on gate duty at Sarona, around 2045. He died shortly afterwards. A British and an Arab constable of the Palestine

Police were also wounded. The Arab died. In addition to the Coldstream, a company of Grenadiers and Welsh Guards were in the camp and mustered. Mike Stilwell, commanding the Coldstream Support Company, led a carrier patrol to the aid of the Anti-Tank platoon under fire and guarding a house half way between Sarona and Citrus House. He also escaped a roadside mine which exploded prematurely fifteen yards ahead.

Citrus House came under fire shortly after 2100. This was returned. When firing subsided, four terrorists, including a woman, were found dead; fifteen wounded Jews were treated in hospital and a number of suspects were handed over to the police. A six-pounder anti-tank gun was mounted on the roof of Citrus House. In the event, it was never fired.

Operation "Elephant" resulted in the arrest of twenty-four known members of Lehi/Stern and Irgun, with more than thirty-six suspects also detained. No letters were delivered for eleven days: 2300 mail bags were left unopened and valuable parcels, such as raw diamonds, were reckoned to total some £250,000 by insurance companies. The object was not only to arrest terrorists but also to warn the Yishuv that continued passive tolerance of terrorism, or ineffective action against, was inadvisable. On the whole the point was taken, and the following year, after independence, both groups were outlawed by the Israeli government.

Meanwhile, during the current operation, a female Jewish police officer was murdered in her bed by one gang or the other on 9 March. On the following day I visited Jaffa Port. At the same time Brigadier Poole, commanding 3 Brigade, was nearly blown up by two mines at 1100 near Ramat Gan. He lost his staff car, but not his life. My staff car was lent to him.

On 17 March martial law and Operation "Elephant" were lifted at 1300. The next day Rodney Moore took seven Grenadier officers to the Tel Aviv Opera. All were received by the Mayor, Israel Rokakh. None was asked to sing.

At a cabinet meeting on Thursday, 20 March, the government took stock. Recently terrorism had cost thirty lives, including twenty-four British soldiers and one British civilian. It was agreed that the Yishuv would not want martial law reimposed. On the other hand, terrorism was still active and relatively unrestrained. In Acre gaol five Jews were under sentence of death. They were joined by a sixth on 3 April.

21.3.47. My diary entry contained eight words: "*Stern gang blows up the Haifa oil refinery.*" Matters were obviously returning to near normal in the Mandate. The refinery burnt for nearly a month and was still smouldering when four terrorists were hanged on 16 April.

In fact, at this moment everything was smouldering in Palestine.

The death warrants, as mentioned earlier, were signed by the former GOC, General Sir Evelyn Barker, in the course of duty and in strict accordance with the law. Irgun wished to kill him, once again distorting the teaching of the Torah. His name and address were in the telephone book. A former Royal Air Force Officer, Ezer Weizman, nephew of Chaim Weizmann and cousin of Michael Weizmann killed in the RAF, was deputed to mine the road with another agent near the General's house.

Weizman had been recruited by the Irgun intelligence chief, Eli Tavin, who, in 1945, before the formation of X Command and Chaim Weizmann's change of tactics, had been captured by Haganah, held for several months, and was distinctly in poor health when they released him. He lived. On 31 October, 1946, he damaged the British Embassy in Rome with a suitcase bomb. The Vaad Leumi considered it an act of madness.

A year later Ezer Weizman's plans were interrupted by Scotland Yard. An inspector called at Weizman's flat and enquired when he was leaving the country. According to his own account in his book *On Eagles' Wings* and confirmed by Begin's *The Revolt*, he replied, "Within forty-eight hours", to which the inspector replied: " A bloody good idea!"

Ezer Weizman became an Israeli air force general, minister of defence in 1977 and president of Israel in 1993. General Barker observed many years later that his death would have helped no one, although helping others was never the prime motive of either Stern or Irgun. He added that the murder would have been on the conscience of Weizman. No doubt, exceptionally, this would have been the case. Terrorist leaders, otherwise, expressed no regret whatsoever, and never accepted that the Mandatory power was there to rule Jew and Arab equitably. As for the Arabs, the Jewish presence represented the acme of inequality and betrayal from the beginning.

On 27 March I lunched with the Welsh Guards. My old friend and former company commander at Mons and brother officer in Italy, Paul Makins, was now commanding Prince of Wales Company and was acting as second-in-command.

On the next day the execution of Dov Gruner was once again postponed, and the day after Geoffrey Bowden, KRRC, returned to his battalion, but more significantly, a TJFF officer, Sam Whitfield, was shot dead by Jews near Orchard Camp. He was notoriously anti-Jewish and, in the sense of using his horse in the manner of a mounted policeman, had frogmarched Jews during the search of Kefar Geladin in north Galilee last summer when John Lascelles and I were there. No doubt such persuasion had long been translated in the telling to trampling under foot, and one of the terrorist groups dispatched the captain, but spared his horse. In terms of horses, I recorded that Canghoo won the Grand National and Cambridge won the boat race by ten lengths.

Rodney Moore held a Commanding Officers' conference at 1400 on 30 March, at which I was asked to attend. Sadly Billy Malcolm had neither Peter Leuchars, adjutant, nor Ivor Roberts, his quartermaster, to take notes on behalf of the Welsh Guards and the commanding officer's jottings were not comprehensive. This was unfortunate. Shortly afterwards I accompanied the brigadier when he visited the Welsh Guards. There were certain irregularities concerning dress, minor matters about which I have forgotten.

Rodney was not best pleased. I was instructed to write a D.O. (demi official letter) which he would sign. My first draft was rejected: "Not strong enough, Philip!" I then wrote an extremely courteously phrased, major rocket which Rodney signed. I was careful to leave off my initials. Rodney, lynx-eyed in such matters, no doubt noticed, but he made no comment.

The day following the conference, Monday 31, Mr Pilz, the eponymous owner of the restaurant, kindly invited Bill Tilleard and me to dine at his house. I hired a dinner jacket for thirty shillings (£1.50). The manager, Julian Marberg, a jovial, rotund character, too gentle for the cut and thrust of New York, yet complaining of Tel Aviv's comparative provincialism, told me that he was underpaid at £65 per month. The same wage, he added, as the drummer, Louis, who was also by way of being a friend of mine. I pointed out that Louis did not receive tips!

On 2 April the British government referred the Palestine problem to the United Nations. The outcome was going to change the life styles of all the inhabitants of Palestine: in the case of Julian Marberg not so much; in the case of many displacement; and for some death. The referral came twenty-nine years and five months after the Balfour Declaration. Even so most observers, including Bevin and his senior Foreign Office adviser, Harold Beeley, doubted the General Assembly would muster the necessary two-thirds majority for any effective decision.

More locally, on the same day, 1st Guards Brigade went into mourning for King George of the Hellenes, who had spent more time off the throne than on it. Black arm bands were issued. The Brigadier and I had lunch at the Pilz in Tel Aviv. Julian Marberg beamed and bowed as Rodney slipped something appropriate into the palm of his hand – the tax free one. The following day we repeated the performance, this time joined by Rachel Saphir. It was Good Friday.

At this moment I was commanding the headquarters – as distinct from the Brigade! – in the absence of both Lewis, for whom I was acting DAA & QMG, and Bill Gore-Langton, the Brigade Major, who was on leave in Cyprus. Andrew Gibson-Watt was in hospital and Hugh Stanley was in bed sick.

Others gave me a hand, but courts martial were my responsibility. Andrew enjoyed the work. I found it tedious. It was done, nevertheless. Then, having buried King George of Greece, we went into mourning for Christian of Denmark. His grandson, whom I knew later, spoke highly of his gallantry during the War, particularly of his defending Jews.

I spent the Easter weekend at the Villa Melchett on Lake Tiberias. Francis Widdrington, that benign and very big man with a Hogarthian appetite, and Michael Bonn, who was tall but not with the same desire to eat as Francis, were also there. On Easter Monday I was joined by Mary Rosner, dark haired, around twenty, gentle and kind. We spent the afternoon sunbathing on the roof. Mary's sister, Jean, joined us for dinner and I drove them back to Tiberias. The Airborne were now in the Elizabetha Hotel, the former Welsh Guards billet.

After Easter I drove back to Petah Ticvah in two-and-a-half hours, having left at 0615 and passed the KDG convoy en route from Palestine to Benghazi. It was a journey of eighty miles on secondary roads with an average speed of 32 mph. Anyone who has tried to pass a military convoy may agree this was not bad going.

The following week was likely to see the reopening of the hanging season, thanks to continuous terrorist activity and the imposition of the law. In preparation for likely further terrorist attacks in the form of reprisals, commanding officers, civil officials and police representatives were summoned to attend a conference at Brigade. Far-reaching security measures were taken should Dov Gruner and others be executed. Afterwards the Brigadier, Rachel Saphir, Bill Tilleard and I had lunch at the Pilz. Specie and Julian Marberg were harmoniously joined as one.

15.4.47. My diary entry speaks for itself: "*A quiet day. Preparations for Gruner's – and three others' – execution. All ranks confined to camp, except on essential duty.*"

On 16 April Dov Gruner and three other members of the Jewish terrorist groups were hanged within the confines of the grim Acre gaol. We expected widespread retaliation, and indeed some gelignite – enough to blow up the whole building – was found in a ladies' sanctum in the Colonial Office. Elizabeth Hart, a cleaner, noticed a large parcel and called the police. Inside were twenty sticks of gelignite. The fuse had stopped. It had been planted by a

Stern gang member, Yaacov Levstein or Lavstein (Eliav). Later, following the practice of poacher turning gamekeeper, he became a director of an Israeli security firm.

Retributary action in Palestine came rapidly after two condemned men committed suicide by placing hand grenades, which had been smuggled into the gaol inside oranges, against their hearts. They then pulled out the pins. In the early hours of 22 April the Cairo-Haifa train was blown up near Rehovot, disturbing Weizmann. There were eight dead. Trucks were also blown up in daylight near our camp without casualties. The Air O.P.patrolled but found nothing, not surprisingly. The would-be assassins were unlikely to lay out markers.

On the domestic front, the Regimental Lieutenant-Colonel commanding the Coldstream, Colonel Bootle-Wilbraham came to dine at Brigade, together with the commanding officers of the Grenadiers (John Davies), the Coldstream (Billy Steele), the Irish Guards (Michael Gordon-Watson), whose battalion was serving with 6th Airborne, and the Welsh Guards (Billy Malcolm).

Revenge for the suicides was exacted when the Stern gang shot Assistant-Superintendent A.E. Conquest, a remarkably competent CID chief, driving his car in the main street of Haifa. On the same day, 25 April, there was a terrorist attack against Sarona. A post office van stopped at the gates. The passes of the two occupants were in order. They said they had come to repair some telephone lines. The corporal of the guard refused entry. No civilian vehicles were allowed inside Sarona or Citrus House. His sergeant overruled him.

After thirty minutes the two men returned to the gate with a ladder: some wires outside the perimeter needed repairing. They were not seen again. Their van exploded ten minutes later. Four Palestine policemen were killed and sixteen wounded. The telephone exchange was destroyed. The sergeant, to say the least, had made an error.

At the time I was in bed with an unpleasant but superficial affliction which besets inhabitants, permanent or temporary, in the region, namely sandfly fever: a headache, feverish and liverish, caused by the bloodsucking bite of a small female fly. I was seven days in bed and must have run out of sheets as James Denny kindly lent me a pair, while Sammy Stanier, commanding the Regiment, came to see me.

On 30 April, while lobbying in New York at the United Nations was becoming intense, prior to the appointment of the last committee to investigate the Palestine problem – the United Nation Special Committee on Palestine or UNSCOP – I was preparing to take local leave in New York itself and then go on to Canada. My mother's brother and his family lived in Winnipeg, Manitoba. This particular day seemed to evolve around dress: khaki drill replaced winter battle dress and was worn at the Commanding Officers' conference, which I chaired.

It would have been singularly inappropriate to have worn either of my two American-style suits which had just been delivered by Mr Zvern of Tel Aviv, a friend, needless to say, of Julian Marberg's. Mr Zvern had thoughtfully provided a bulge for my shoulder holster, which in fact I did not possess. With dark glasses, fedora and co-respondent shoes, I would have passed for a young *mafioso* soldier or hit man. My semi-automatic pistol shooting with a Luger might have earned me a contract. I considered the price of £84 for the two expensive, but the material was good, even if the jacket nearly came down to my knees.

More conferences followed, both at Brigade and under Jack Sanderson, Scots Guards, AA & QMG at 1st Division. He wrote plays in his spare time. On 2 May the signatory and recipient of my DO departed on leave together; that is to say, Brigadier Rodney Moore and Lieutenant-Colonel Billy Malcolm went off in a car lent by the Jewish Agency for Beirut. They then drove to Damascus. A man for all seasons was Rodney. The Brigade was temporarily commanded by Colonel "Mouse" Gurney, KRRC.

In the absence of the distinguished pair, but presumably with no desire to follow them, on 4 May Irgun dissidents blew a hole in Acre gaol, allowing 214 Arabs and 41 Jews to escape. Eight Jewish terrorists were killed and among those recaptured were three Irgun men who were later tried and condemned to death. Their execution provoked one of the most barbaric acts by Begin and his gang in the whole of Jewish history.

In the meantime Spring Drills were not forgotten at Brigade Headquarters, it being well known that Brigade of Guards discipline is founded upon drill and the square, and had proved its worth in worse situations than that which faced us in Palestine. At midday on the first day of these drills a crisis erupted when orders marked "secret" disappeared. Half an hour later they were found in James Denny's "in" tray. There was nothing particularly secret about James's job as Education Officer, although a mysterious activity as far as I was concerned, but more important for James was Rodney's obsession about empty "in" trays.

A trait which had its charm in James's character was his occasional vagueness. This was, of course, anathema to Rodney. Vagueness was not part of his vocabulary. If, for example, my work load was particularly heavy, my "in" tray was always empty, my desk clear of clutter, but my top drawer would have told a different story, had it been opened by the Brigade commander. It never was: Rodney was no pryer. He simply demanded results, and the result of the unfortunate discovery in James's office was not why he had come into possession of documents which did not concern him – the fault, presumably, of the Chief Clerk – but a crime far more heinous: he had not cleared his "in" tray. D-Day planning was based on such details.

On 15 May the United Nations Special Committee on Palestine was appointed, comprising anti-colonialists with preconceptions from imperial countries, egocentric idealists – the Jimmy Carter complex – and rank incompetents: the usual mixture. It did not absorb the clear warning from Great Britain: produce a practical plan, which, under the circumstances, was probably impractical advice. In any case no one really thought that the necessary two-thirds majority would be mustered. On this score the doubters were proved wrong. Nothing is ever certain in politics.

While UNSCOP was forming, and informing, itself in New York, the Mandatory government, besides dealing with the problem of terrorism, was also coping with illegal immigration. After the basic cause of the problem, the Balfour Declaration, this was the fundamental subject of dispute. It was a particularly emotional matter for the Yishuv and, for different reasons, a singularly emotional matter for the Arabs. Most illegal immigrants tried to come in by the sea. Thus their being stopped was chiefly the concern of the Royal Navy.

As many as thirty ships from Europe attempted to land in Palestine during the eighteen months between July, 1945, and the end of 1946. Small ships stood a better chance of slipping through the patrols. Twelve did so, adding 1225 to the Jewish population. Eighteen, with a total of 17,992, did not. They were interned in Cyprus. The immigration quota was 1500 a month. Nevertheless, the Foreign Office circulated Arab capitals to ask their views on increasing the number to 4000.

Inevitably the reaction was negative: "Palestine was an Arab country; Jewish immigration was a means of obtaining sovereignty; it was yet another example of the dire injustice against all Arabs." This was undoubtedly true. Truth, however, in the propaganda game, ably orchestrated and organized by Haganah and echoed in the American press, was a non-starter, and if it expressed a valid Arab viewpoint, it was drowned in a cacophony of counter-argument conducted with crude success.

More immigrant ships were dispatched and turned back. Camps in Cyprus could only take 7000 more. Haganah were planning to send 25,000. Once again this was the outcome of double dealing by the British government in 1917, which had brought and was to bring untold suffering to both Jew and Arab, whomever might claim to be the victor.

On 30 May double dealing was not the reason for my winning £50 in two poker sessions with four Grenadiers: Jock Rowan, Bubbles Hornsby, Ronnie Ball and Nigel Bromage. I had never wished to learn bridge; whist bored me, as did canasta. My father and I, when I was very young, used to play endless games of bezique. He was a most kind and generous man. He always let me win in a manner which almost convinced me it was merited. The actuarial factor, however, left me with the feeling it was not.

Towards the end of the month I had two lunches with the Brigadier in Tel Aviv: the first with Rachel Saphir and Bill Pease and the second with Bill Tilleard and the Matalon brothers. Rodney had recovered from his "gyppy" tummy and the Matalon brothers were known to us. Eliezer was a member of Irgun, although he was unaware we knew. He was not a very important member and was more use to us outside of prison than in it.

In the afternoon Rodney was having tea with someone who, in 1945, coaxed the djinni of terrorism out of its bottle, when he could, had he wished, have kept it corked: Dr Chaim Weizmann, the future first President of Israel.

CHAPTER TEN

Hanging and Throttling

The summer months of June, July and August, 1947, were a trimester of intensified turbulence and terror, which was only to be expected when murder was on the upturn. The condemned cells in Acre gaol, in consequence, were double-booked. Yet on the whole the Mandatory administration was singularly reluctant to execute Jews – in comparison to the Draconian measures it ladled out during the pre-War Arab revolt – in anything like the proportion it had hanged Arabs.

This statistical point was unlikely to be appreciated by the condemned nor by their adherents in Tel Aviv and New York, however heinous their crimes might have been. Three men in particular – Irgun gang members captured after the Acre raid in which men were killed, Avshalom Haviv, Yaacov Weiss and Meir Nakar – were only a few feet and eight weeks away from their appointment inside the drab and functional execution chamber.

In all executions throughout the British Empire, and in all but five States in America, dispatch was humane and instantaneous: the use of the trap door drop and the imbedding of a metal eyelet in the noose, adjusted tightly beneath the ear, resulted in a fracture of the cervical vertebrae. A white cap was placed over the head of the condemned, who was standing beneath the gallows on a trap door. The hangman adjusted the halter around his neck and pulled a lever which opened the trap. Death was immediate. This was not the case in the revenge killings by Irgun. These took a quarter-of-an-hour, following days of torture.

It was the ironic, if objective, observation of Samuel Johnson, which said a man's mind was concentrated wonderfully when he knew he was to be hanged in a fortnight. In fact, while Begin and his gang were concentrating on issuing dire threats of vengeance if

96

the three were executed, effected with incredible barbarity, my attention was fixed on making the necessary arrangements for my leave in North America, the brief details of which are given in an appendix, in order not to divert the reader's attention from the dramas taking place in the Holy Land and the arrival of UNSCOP.

I required a visa for the United States, a passport and a ticket. The American consul, Mr Cornell, the High Commissioner's office, and Mr Townsend at Thomas Cook's, took care of these matters in Jerusalem. I had had no need of a passport before. My mother was making similar arrangements. It was to be a return trip, for me, of 17,000 miles. In 1947 the flight was hardly direct and jet lag was an unknown phenomenon.

On 2 June, in the same manner as a degree of sadness had descended upon Brigade headquarters when Willy Whitelaw left us, although his successor, Lewis Dawnay, was now very much an integral part of the cast, so too melancholy was apparent when Bill Gore-Langton departed and was replaced by Simon Bolitho, who could well have been described, then, as a right-wing, true-blue Grenadier, which he might have accepted as a compliment. Unlike his Coldstream predecessor – a tall, regular-featured, urbane, intelligent man – he had two arms which he swung nervously when aroused. He was often aroused.

Simon was also tall and Saxon in appearance, although of Cornish stock, with a particular, rather blasphemous phrase which he used frequently and to such an extent that he became known as CABM Bolitho. He was, however, unusually silent when his departing GIII, my contemporary at Mons, David Erskine, Scots Guards, threw a pot at him containing blue ink. There were ink pots in those days. Simon, in fact, did not have the same aura of quietude and competence exuded by his predecessor of whom I wrote that he was a "splendid fellow who had taught me a great deal".

Much later I saw quite a bit of Simon. He was content in civilian life, not least with his family and in his own county of Cornwall. At Brigade he would have been happier serving under the more easy going Eddie Goulburn, rather than the exacting Rodney Moore, and the highly intelligent former Scots Guardsman, George Johnson, who succeeded Rodney in July, 1947. As it was Simon soldiered on and not too much china was broken in the process, nor inkpots.

Lewis returned on 4 June, and on the 9th I went to Jerusalem to collect my passport. I lunched with Michael Pitt-Rivers, "Mac" Reynolds and Richard Mosse all in the Welsh Guards and Robert Heywood-Lonsdale, Grenadiers, in a bad restaurant called the Villa Rosemary. She was absent. The villa was crumbling and the dust was falling into the food. All the good restaurants were out of bounds, and the Holy City was infernally depressing, with barbed wire, barricades and tight security everywhere.

Also on 9 June two Palestine policemen were kidnapped, but under police guidance were discovered by the Grenadiers. This was the result of information received from inside the terrorist gangs. It was also Rodney's forty-second birthday, celebrated in his bungalow in the evening. There were eight guests: Rachel Saphir, someone called Hilda, Colonel Billy Steele, Lewis Dawnay, Simon Bolitho, Bill Pease and myself.

On 11 June, my mother's sixty-first birthday, I lunched with Mark Norman at Citrus House and discovered he was the only member of a celebratory quartet who was not knocked out: the previous day had been George Edwards' twenty-first birthday. He was still under the care of the Medical Officer. Ernie May had not gone to bed and was still tight, as was Peter Spurgin who was flat out on his bed unable to move. Whatever business had taken me to Citrus House could not, in consequence, be completed.

George Edwards' party had begun in the bar of a Tel Aviv restaurant. Mark Norman had earlier achieved a certain success in the individual pistol shooting championships. While in the bar, he was unsure whether the safety catch of the pocket-sized pistol he had been lent worked or not. Having no desire to alarm the civilians present, none of whom looked as if they belonged to either Irgun or Stern, he retired to the gents.

There, in the privacy of this small room, he went through the usual safety precautions, squeezed the trigger while pointing the pistol away from him – and blew the lavatory bowl into fragments. The noise caused his brother officers – at that moment exceptionally sober – to rush to the windows, drawing their guns and seeking the enemy. A most professional waiter calmed everyone present by saying a pile of dishes had been dropped in the kitchen. It may be said that Mark spent a pretty penny in compensation.

The King's Birthday parade was held this year in Jerusalem under the command of Robert Heywood-Lonsdale: four detachments of 36 Other Ranks and a total of five officers took part, coming from the Grenadiers, Coldstream, Irish and Welsh Guards. No one was killed and no one fainted. I took the opportunity to bathe at the Jaffa Officers' Club, which reminded me of Brighton on a Bank Holiday, except I had never been to Brighton, let alone on a Bank Holiday. The date was 12 June, which was also the day Haganah intervened to prevent Irgun blowing up Citrus House. To say the least, we were profoundly grateful.

An explosion was heard by the Coldstream in Citrus House emanating from a building across the road, opposite the gate. The dead body of a man was found near the entrance of a tunnel which began in the basement of the building and led in the direction of Citrus House. It was already, at forty-five feet, half-way there. The Coldstream Regimental History states: "The body was that of a Haganah officer. The IZL had decided to blow up Citrus House. The Haganah visited the tunnel and left a chalked message."

The warning was ignored. Haganah then returned with a lorry-load of cement bags to seal the tunnel. "The Haganah officer suspected there might be a booby-trap. He entered the basement alone and died as a result. All those Coldstreamers who lived in Citrus House at the time owe a debt of gratitude to the Haganah. His name was Zeev Werba. Twenty thousand, including many British, mourned his death and attended his funeral in Tel Aviv."

Terrorist tunnelling had been discounted by those who thought they knew, because the predominant sandy nature of the earth was considered a barrier to any such operation. The report of the Intelligence unit, stationed at Citrus House read: "Among entertaining rumours is one that a tunnel is being dug under Citrus House." A copy was received at Brigade, but it was not sent to Billy Steele, commanding the Coldstream. Orders were given to search all neighbouring houses, and a small factory producing Sten guns was found as well as thousands of magazines.

On Saturday, 14 June, the 1st Division entertainments section arrived for the weekend. Whence they came and where they had been hiding from our appreciative eyes I had no idea. They performed a play of Emlyn Williams, *Night Must Fall*, which was rather a terrifying psychological thriller, written in 1935. It was well acted, but I thought something lighter in Palestine at that moment would have been more appropriate. It was done in the evening, after some of us had taken the cast to the beach and we considered it the minimum of courtesy to watch the play.

After subsequent nightmares, Charles Frederick, Grenadiers, and I took two of the girls, Elizabeth Walton and Judy Whomever, to the Jaffa Club in Charles' car. We had dinner and then a riotous evening in my room at Petah Ticvah, which was, wisely, broken up by Lewis who said we were making so much noise it could be heard at the other end of the camp. This was probably exaggerated: Lewis never went to the other end of the camp but had his own room near to mine. His point, however, was taken. The next day, I was reminded of the Roman phrase: more died from drink than the sword.

This was the day, 16 June, which heralded the arrival of the

United Nations Special Committee on Palestine. This travelling circus, under its self-appointed ringmaster, Jorge García-Granados, a Guatemalan whose country had little to learn about oppressing indigenous peoples, passed five weeks in the Holy Land, adding not a jot to its preconceived ideas. His personal conclusion was that Palestine was a police state, because, thanks to terrorism, it had been forced to spend $2,000,000 a month on security, or £7,010,000 per year. Necessity, the need to support a subjective viewpoint, in this case became the mother of invention.

Eight days after their arrival UNSCOP discovered the limited joys of the Jaffa Club, where they had lunch. They looked rather well fed in their bathing costumes. I went up to Haifa on 27 June and had something to eat at Lilli Manheim's Astoria, only two days before it was shot up by the Irgun. Three officers were killed and Max was cut by flying glass. The Brigade was moving to Camp 22, near Nathanya, in time to be near, and attempt to abort, one of the worst terrorist crimes ever committed. Also, at this time Woody, the Petah Ticvah AMWD Clerk of Works, gave a farewell party at the Park Hotel, Tel Aviv, which was marred more that somewhat by the shooting of three soldiers in the town. The "amber" alert was turning to "red". "Green" meant walking out in fours, armed, until midnight. There was no normal.

On 1 July 3 Brigade moved into Petah Ticvah and we left for the camp near Nathanya. I went to Lydda and took off in a "Skymaster" on the first leg of my journey to New York and then Canada. It was while staying with friends on Long Island that I read of the kidnapping of Sergeants Clifford Martin and Mervyn Paice, both of 252 Field Security Section. Although in an affiliate of the Intelligence Corps, neither was exercising any great intelligence by being unarmed, in civilian clothes and strolling around Nathanya after midnight with a Jewish friend, Weinberg, when they should have been back in camp.

There was a "red" alert because the three IZL members were due to be hanged in Acre gaol and it was obvious Irgun would be seeking hostages. At 0045 on 12 July Martin and Paice were bludgeoned, chloroformed and pushed into a car. Weinberg was bound and then dumped by the side of the road. At 0400 he freed himself and gave the alarm. Martin and Paice had, meanwhile, been entombed in a cell of twelve square feet and less than six feet high. It had been dug underneath a diamond factory floor, with a thick layer of sand on top.

The cell was soundproofed, airtight and with only a small, insulated entrance hatch. Amihai Faglin, the Irgun operations chief, was in charge. He allotted the minimum needs to keep the kidnapped sergeants alive: some food, two oxygen cylinders which they were instructed to regulate in order to survive, and a canvas bucket. There was no light, sound, or fresh air for seventeen, terrorful, death-presaging days. At certain intervals they were taken out and pushed back at great speed. The bucket was changed, some fresh air let into the cell and food replenished.

Brigadier George Johnson summoned the Mayor of Nathanya, Oved Ben Ami. He warned him the Army would take action. The *Palestine Post* quoted the Mayor as saying the kidnapping was provocative and would discourage any prerogative of mercy by the High Commissioner. On 12 July 1st Guards Brigade and troops from the 4th/7th Dragoon Guards, 15th/19th Hussars, 59 Field Regiment RA, 23 Field Squadron RE, 2nd Warwicks, 2nd Middlesex and 1st Suffolks with a considerable number of the Haganah, cordoned and began to search Nathanya. The operation was code named "Tiger".

This time the place was combed from top to bottom: tunnels were dug, floors were ripped up, but, incredibly, no search was permitted on premises being used by the diamond trade, in case of theft. On 27 July the search was called off. Several wanted terrorists had been arrested. The sergeants, barbarously buried in their underground prison, waiting every second for deliverance, were not found.

29.7.47. The three convicted terrorists were hanged in Acre gaol. They had risked their lives in committing themselves to terrorism and, as they had taken the lives of others, so, too, they lost their own. On the following day Amihai Faglin drove to Nathanya with his accomplices. The first sergeant was extracted. A hood was placed over his head. He was bound and placed on a chair. A rope was strung round his neck. He asked if they were going to kill him. Could he leave a message? There was no time. The chair was kicked from under him. He was slowly throttled; the rope compressed his windpipe. After fifteen minutes he was dead.

Half an hour later the second sergeant was pulled out and murdered in the same brutal manner. The bodies were dumped in a jeep. Three miles away, in the early hours of 31 July, at Tel Zur, they were strung up on the branches of two trees, still hooded. A mine was placed underneath. Irgun then fretted that the bodies might be discovered by Haganah and, after Citrus House, another or several, of their number killed. Were this to happen, Haganah would make short shrift of Irgun, as they did eleven months later, who, together with Stern, they considered to be the acme of crazed amorality and evident defective dregs of the Yishuv.

Irgun, apprehensive of the outcome, then telephoned the

Mayor's office and gave a map reference. A Haganah patrol found the bodies early on Thursday, 31 July. They reported their discovery to 1st Guards Brigade. Captain D.H. Galetti, Royal Engineers, led a section of sappers with mine detectors through the grove of trees where the bodies were said to be. Behind were police, civilian officials, more troops and the Haganah. The bodies were discovered. The area was declared safe, a little prematurely. Photographs were taken and appeared worldwide. Captain Galetti then tied a knife to a long pole and cut the rope.

As the body fell, he jumped clear. The corpse landed on the mine. It was blown to pieces. The explosion also uprooted the tree from which the second body was hanging. Galetti was slightly injured in the shoulder and face.

The Jewish Agency and the Vaad Leumi called the crime " a dastardly murder of two innocent men by a set of criminals". The extremes of terrorism, as practised by psychopaths, had now stirred the feelings of even more horror than those which followed the King David Hotel murders and Weizmann must have reflected on the wisdom and fruits of his policy. In New York Ben Hecht was asked whether Irgun bestiality induced a little holiday in his heart. This assumed he had one.

The strangulation of the two sergeants was certainly no propaganda victory for Irgun: the *Daily Express* description of "medieval barbarism" and that of *The Times* comparing it to the worst of Nazi crimes was echoed worldwide, not least in the Jewish press which reflected the horror of its readership.

31.7.47. Discipline was definitely loosened among certain elements in the police and Army: five Jews were killed in Tel Aviv, four by bullets and one by a grenade. No one was identified in the enquiry; barrels had been cleaned and the ammunition replaced. Divulgence was not forthcoming from those who could have helped with enquiries. This was sometimes the same barrier of silence erected by the Yishuv when questioned about acts of terrorism, however much horror might be expressed after the event.

The High Commissioner reported to London: "Such conduct cannot be excused; but most of them have had to work in an atmosphere of constant danger, and increasing tension, fraught with insult, vilification and treachery." All this might, however, have been avoided if, following the kidnapping and murder in the first place, diamond trade premises had not been placed out of bounds.

The appalling events which had taken place in Palestine, although covered worldwide, did not provoke the same violent anti-Jewish reactions as those which then occurred in Great Britain. Under the circumstances these would have been immeasurably worse had the details of the incarceration been known. Even so, it was no *Kristallnacht* (the organized Nazi anti-Jewish riots in Germany in 1938) but a few shop windows were broken. In Birkenhead slaughterhouse men would not handle kosher butchering and a synagogue was burnt in Derby. After a few days it died down and was condemned by both police and public.

On 1 August, 1947, the Mayor of Nathanya wrote to George Johnson: "My dear Brigadier," he began, "This is a grim and melancholy letter for me to write". He ended by saying: "We stand ashamed and disgraced and we can say no more. Yours very sincerely, Ben Ami."

Thirty years later, on the well-tried principle of poacher turning gamekeeper, Amihai Faglin, certainly one of the most brutal of the psychopaths, was appointed by his unrepentant terrorist boss, Menachem Begin, in 1977, when the latter was leader of the Likud Party and prime minister, as the Israeli government's anti-terrorist adviser. He was killed within a few months in a motorcar accident. It is possible that a former member of Haganah loosened the steering wheel. The British Secret Service, on the whole, did not indulge in vengeance.

CHAPTER ELEVEN

Introitus and Exodus

The year 1947 was the turning point in the Mandate's affairs. In the House of Commons Ernest Bevin stated baldly, "Balfour is dead". That is to say, there was no point in trying to discuss the meaning of the Balfour Declaration as it might relate to resolving the current dilemmas. Even Arthur Balfour would have been hard put to describe what he meant by a Jewish national home, following the Arab revolt, foreseen so clearly by Curzon, and the insoluble question of immigration, desired passionately by Zionists and evoking unbending Arab hostility.

Winston Churchill, as Colonial Secretary, had elaborated the Declaration in 1922, establishing Transjordan as Arab territory and stating that there was to be a national home *in* Palestine with immigration permitted up to "economic absorptive capacity". This was to be judged by Great Britain. President Truman's aforementioned request for the admittance of 100,000 Jewish refugees ran contrary to this policy and wholly ignored the legitimate Arab position.

Truman had inherited Franklin Roosevelt's sympathetic attitude towards a Jewish national home; for whatever reasons, both may have fundamentally held such views. On the other hand, he wished to take no action which could be considered hostile to the Arabs, but this was tempered by the fact he was on record as saying, "I have to answer to hundreds of thousands who are anxious for the success of Zionism. I do not have hundreds of thousands of Arabs among my constituents."

The State Department and the Joint Chiefs of Staff, however, were well aware of (a) the importance of a British base in the Middle East and (b) the importance of oil, and the imperative need not to alienate the Arabs; equally (c) for strategic reasons, when (d) relations with the Soviet Union were deteriorating. They were not, however, prepared to send troops into the area, although their Mediterranean 6th Fleet was strengthened.

At the same time, for reasons of economy, the British withdrew their advisers and forces from Greece, which until then they had buttressed against communist aggression. British advisers were also withdrawn from Turkey. Nevertheless, support for the British position was particularly strong when General George Marshall became Secretary of State in January, 1947. He followed the general lines of Dean Acheson, then Under Secretary and later his successor, not to rock the British man-of-war, and wrote to the Colonial Secretary, Arthur Creech Jones: "The British have been the victims of an impossible situation and considerable unjust criticism." As a former head of the Joint Chiefs of Staff, he was especially aware of the military question.

Truman did not have the same mastery over the Palestine situation within his government as did Attlee, who left the spadework to Ernest Bevin and Arthur Creech Jones, as well as the Imperial General Staff, under Field Marshal Montgomery. There was no inter-departmental committee in the United States to give permanent attention to the problem. Nor was there any delegation. The State Department, with Acheson in charge of such coordination as existed, presided over policy by trying to reconcile the pro-Zionist views of the White House staff – votes – with the contrary view of his own Department; policy was based on the majority view of any given country, democratically inclined, but inclination in this case was limited to the Mandatory power, not to its Mandate, a situation insouciantly supported by both Truman and the Zionists.

Acheson was thus caught between his Department's Middle East experts, joined by the Pentagon, and the President's political advisers. As far back as 1945 the State Department summed up its viewpoint: "The active support by the government of the United States of a policy favouring the setting up of a Jewish State in Palestine would be contrary to the policy which the United States has always followed of respecting the wishes of a large majority of the local inhabitants with respect to their form of government." In 1945 there were 1,200,000 Arabs in Palestine and 560,000 Jews: 69% against 31%, small minorities excepted. Democracy was not practised in Palestine.

On 27 January, 1947, the London Conference opened. No agreement was reached. Bevin, meanwhile, was being pressed by Churchill, leading the Opposition, to rule or get out. Our relationship with the United States, said Churchill, was being politically damaged. Why not return the Mandate to the United Nations?

Bevin now had four options: imposing partition on the Arabs and

sacrificing the United Kingdom's wider imperial interests; ruthlessly suppressing Jewish claims to independent statehood, which
would risk an American political reaction and possible loss of financial support, then urgently needed, not least during a run on the
pound (in 1803, in contrast, the London bankers, Barings, under-
wrote the United States purchase of the Louisiana territory from
Napoleon for $11¼ million, making $2 million on the deal);
thirdly, refer the matter to the United Nations; or fourthly, declare
a democracy and put the future of Palestine to the vote of its people.

The fourth option would have caused an uproar in the democratically elected White House, dismay among Zionists, disbelief
among Arabs who had never experienced it, and derision within the
Foreign Office. British public opinion supported the UN option,
and on 18 February this was done, without surrendering the Mandate. It was proposed the UN should find a solution, imposable by
the Mandatory power. The inauguration of the United Nations
Special Committee on Palestine was the outcome. It arrived, as we
know, in mid-June, and spent six weeks jotting down its impres-
sions of a heavenly country made into a living hell by disingenuous
politicians and elemental passions.

Meanwhile there had been a second incident in the Mandate
which had further distanced British public opinion concerning the
continuation of the British presence. The first, already covered, was
the murder of Sergeants Martin and Paice; the second concerned
the arrival in Palestine waters of the 320-foot-long Chesapeake Bay
ferry boat, known as the *President Warfield* and re-named *Exodus
1947*. *Introitus 1947* would have been more exact; at any rate until
the vessel was turned back.

The boat was specially fitted with two metal pipes circumscrib-
ing the hull. One was connected with the boilers and could deter
boarders by hosing them with hot steam; the other was joined to
the fuel supply which enabled boiling oil, as of old, to be doused
upon intruders. An alternative wheelhouse was constructed below
decks, various other anti-boarding devices were incorporated and
the technical overcrowding – 4500 passengers in the 1814-ton four-
deck steamer – was covered by the construction of bunks with 24"
headroom: about the space allotted in 2nd Class European railway
sleepers.

It was a propaganda exercise well organized by Haganah and Palmach. The passengers travelled from refugee camps in Germany to
Marseilles, using false names but genuine papers. They were en
route for Colombia, and Palmach had bought the documents from
Colombian officials. On 12 June, to recede chronologically, the
date of the King's Birthday Parade, most Haganah and Palmach

internees were amnestied. The Jewish Agency flew the Union Jack next to the Star of David outside their building, and Haganah expressed its thanks by blowing up an Irgun arms dump.

Reconciliation between Haganah and the Mandatory power spread to New York, where the reputable Jewish organizations turned on the supporters of terrorism, such as Ben Hecht and the Irgun US agent, Peter Bergson (Hillel Cook) who hid behind the presumptuous "American League for a Free Palestine". On the other hand the smuggling of arms and immigrants was regarded as sacrosanct and could not be abandoned, no matter how amicable the new *rapprochement*.

14.6.47. Ike Aranne, commanding the renamed *Exodus*, and his crew arrived in the small harbour of Port-de-Bouc, near Marseilles. They took on 315 tons of fuel oil. On 9 July the ship entered the fishing boat harbour of Sète, some 65 miles to the west. Following British protests – the ship's certificate of seaworthiness, issued in Baltimore, stated it could sail in *fine* weather; passengers were *not* permitted – the French authorities detained the vessel. On 11 July, during the evening, the guards were entertained liberally with whisky, the passengers were on board, and at 0600, without the pilot who failed to turn up, despite being paid one million old French francs (£1000), they managed to cut their cables and slip out to sea.

The Royal Navy and the Royal Air Force were hovering, respectively, nearby and overhead. Ernest Bevin, who was visiting France at the time, expressed his strong disapproval to both the French prime minister, Paul Ramadier, and to the foreign minister, Georges Bidault. He informed them that he would return the ship to France and they agreed to accept it. Meanwhile the vessel was being shadowed throughout its voyage by the Royal Navy and the RAF – then under command of Air Commodore, later Air Chief Marshal, "Tubby" Dawson, Air Officer Commanding Levant – and, when it entered territorial waters, was boarded. Resistance was considerable, thanks to the additional infrastructure and the desperation of the defenders, but it was overcome.

The would-be immigrants were transferred to British ships and returned to France on 19 July. The French government – very much an unreliable Fourth Republic ensemble – went back on its word and legal obligations and refused disembarkation. The refugees were then shipped to the British zone of Germany and landed there, a propaganda gift to all anti-Mandatory exponents who were in no way concerned about governing Palestine and injustice towards its Arab population. The sand, however, in the horologe which gauged time in Palestine was running out. In ten months as many immigrants as could be shipped onto the beaches could land whenever they wished.

At the time, however, UNSCOP was still *in situ*. Its members returned to New York at the end of July and later made their report to the General Assembly. It recommended the end of the Mandate, the partition of Palestine, the British administration to continue for two years, after which Jewish and Arab states would be independent. Jewish immigration, to the tune of 150,000, was to be increased immediately. Jerusalem was to be under United Nations control.

Ernest Bevin had made Britain's position clear: if a solution acceptable to both sides was not found – and, with it, a sensible plan to implement it – Britain would withdraw. In the event the Soviet Union supported the Zionists, despite its rabid anti-Judaism – destabilizing the Middle East was paramount – and the American executive put maximum economic pressure upon the smaller states in the General Assembly to vote for partition. Great Britain abstained.

After the vote on 29 November Bevin stated that British troops would withdraw with their vast tonnage of military stores and equipment by 1 August, 1948. The Mandate would end on 15 May. Other than 100,000 British troops in Palestine, plus the Palestine Police, there were 5200 British subjects in the civil administration. The cost of running the Mandate, exclusive of military expenditure, was then £40 million per year, some of which was recouped in taxation. In comparison to the Palestine figures, and exemplifying the difference between a sound and an unsound political basis, until 15 August, 1947, 60 British Indian Civil Servants ruled 28 million people in the Punjab. When they left ¼ million died in religious riots.

The Economist wrote "Partition now is not [advocated] primarily because it is in the best interests of the Jews or Arabs: it is simply because it is in the best interests of the long suffering British, before they remove themselves."

One fact was firmly established and confirmed by both Israeli and United States sources. Indeed it is still prevalent: the United States legislature and executive were both blatantly prone to pressure from ethnic and special interest lobbying. This did not, however, change one iota the fundamental flaw introduced by Lloyd George's government in 1917, when they promised a national home for the Jews in Palestine, a year after they had solemnly agreed in writing to full independence for all Arabs then under the Turkish yoke. Where, too, stood democracy?

Leaving the cloud-enshrouded peaks of politics and diplomacy, as well as the low depths of terrorism and the covenanted floating ark *Exodus*, together with other would-be immigrant barques, for the median level of my life in the Holy Land, I arrived at Lydda airport on 16 October, after flying from New York. Unlike today's procedure, I was waved through customs, and after collecting my luggage was driven to Brigade in my staff car. Our headquarters were now back at Petah Ticvah, after the traumas of Nathanya and Camp 22. James Denny had seen the plane land and most kindly telephoned Lydda to check I was on board.

Rodney Moore had left. George Johnson, was now commanding. Rodney's LO"P", Bill Pease, had also gone and was replaced by Johnny Cobbold, Welsh Guards. Tony Samuelson, Irish Guards, was the Camp Commandant. He and James Denny had each bought a boxer dog from a local breeder. Readers with an attachment to man's most faithful friend will be interested to know that James's dog was called "Spike" of whom I have fond memories: useless as a guard dog and with a habit of disappearing, particularly in the desert. "Spike! Come here!" Spike went anywhere. He was, however, affectionate.

This could not be said of Tony Samuelson's dog. Like brothers in the Bible, Tony's boxer was different. It felt, particularly, that its master's position entitled it to wreak mortal havoc with its snap-clamp bite. Only two hours had passed after the arrival of this animal when it was considered the camp had been cleared of cats, three at least falling on the field of feline honour, and that two small dogs were dispatched as a form of digestive after the cat chase. The dog itself was removed by an angry guardsman with the aid of one rifle and a bullet. The Camp Commandant was dissuaded from taking disciplinary action.

22.10.47. Simon Bolitho, James Denny and I, with Spike, left for Transjordan. We were embarked on another Divisional exercise, calling 1st Guards Brigade across the river, while lobbying at the United Nations was approaching the frenetic in anticipatory manoeuvring. The fate of Palestine, at that moment, was unpredictable.

As for the exercise, it lasted until 11 December, fifty days of freedom from the dramas which had long beset the Mandate and which were to grow a good deal worse before the end, although much more for the indigenous population than the Army.

This time we remembered to tell King Abdullah we were coming. He honoured us again with his presence at lunch. We had the flag the right way up. The cheese – Jewish, but called Stilton – was excellent and much appreciated.

James and I shared a tent: Spike heard the Bedouin in his sleep.

After they had crawled away, empty-handed, Spike regained consciousness and began to bark. This did not please Simon Bolitho who blamed the bark on James. Furthermore, he expressed total disinterest, perhaps even antagonism, in helping James to return to London for the wedding of their mutual Grenadier Colonel, Princess Elizabeth, to Prince Philip of Greece. Likewise, Lewis Dawnay was equally adamant in his indifference. It became obvious that only Spike and I had sufficient pull or clout to fix it.

First, James obtained leave due to him. The Brigadier was not unsympathetic. The next step was a free return air passage on the right dates on a flight to be undertaken by the Royal Air Force. On this matter my friend at Division, Peter Nicholson, Royal Army Service Corps, spoke to Headquarters, MELF, where James's performance was recalled as the Married Woman's Property Act. A seat, or canvas chair, was obtained on the right aircraft. James arrived on time: 0930 for 1130, Westminster Abbey, bride's side, 20 November. There was, thus, no need to postpone the ceremony. He returned five days later.

Meanwhile, on 15 and 26 November, I went to Azraq, the Jordanian outpost and marsh mentioned earlier, on the first and second of three trips to shoot there, respectively with Andrew Gibson-Watt, and then with Nigel Kearsley and Hugh Stanley. These initial trips were meagre in terms of the bag – duck and snipe – compared to the third with Dick Chaplin. On the second, Nigel nearly overturned his 15 cwt truck and trailer on the treacherous salt flats. In sunlight, not least when driving due west with the sun in our eyes, everything, both sand and salt, shimmered. He drove onto them without warning.

I reflected at the time that I, on the other hand, had managed to overturn a light P.U. (Public Utility) vehicle while driving uphill from Tiberias to Nazareth in 1946. This might have had something to do with the fact I had dined with my Regiment, or it could have been a question of the altitude and that there were many bends, or all three. I climbed out first and the Irish Guards sergeant, momentarily underneath me, followed. We righted the vehicle in a trice. He suggested he drove, not the first time this suggestion has been made to me. In similar circumstances in Italy, driving after dinner, a Military Policeman of the United States Army had most courteously put forward the same proposition. In neither case had any damage occurred to either vehicle or occupants. The non-commissioned officer then made a cardinal error: he reported the matter to the Brigade Major, Bill Gore-Langton. In the Army tails do not wag dogs, however shaggy. He was confined to camp and then sent back to England, where rationing, drill sergeants and drizzle were lying in wait. Soon afterwards, in the inscrutable ways of God, I was made Brigade Transport Officer.

Meanwhile, in Transjordan, other than the birds we bagged at Azraq, we also went to Qasr El Hallabut, 25 miles north-east of Amman, to shoot dove or wild pigeon. It was an ancient site, an outpost of the Roman and Ottoman empires, beyond which was the desert and Bedouin tribes. One observed walls and a deep well, inside which the birds roosted. A stone thrown inside brought them out and we brought them down. This reduced the pecking order and provided a change of food for our dinner. I pondered as I glanced around the place: "Go to Hallabut!" must have been a terrible phrase to hear. It was certain death, not least from boredom.

In Transjordan, at this moment, were two journalists, a married couple, Alexander Clifford, the *Daily Mail* chief foreign correspondent and former war reporter, and his wife, Jenny Nicholson, the daughter of Robert Graves and an early victim of women's rights in that her mother, Nancy Nicholson, insisted that her daughters took her name. Nancy's brother was Ben, the painter, and their father was Sir William Nicholson, also a well known painter. Her uncle, Richard Graves, was the last British Mayor of Jerusalem. His ultimate successor was the renowned Teddy Kollek.

On 29 November, twelve days before our return across the Jordan, my diary entry made note of two events which the reader may consider of unequal importance: I attended a party given by the Coldstream and heard on the wireless in a broadcast relayed by the British Forces Network from the BBC that the United Nations General Assembly had voted for the partition of Palestine. Jerusalem was to be under United Nations control.

There, in the Holy City, the Jews rejoiced while the Arabs rioted. Richard Graves, an exemplar of empirical administration and fairmindedness, was appalled by what he saw. Worse was to follow: soon riots and rejoicing were replaced, first by inter-racial terrorism and bestiality on both sides, and secondly, by war and the mass exodus of Arabs.

The United Nations vote was not what Bevin and the British Foreign Office had foreseen, but, on the other hand, the vote put a definitive end to their sipping the contents of the poisoned cup, concocted in 1917 and passed to them by the original alchemists.

CHAPTER TWELVE

Terrorism Merges With War

After some reflection, and rioting, the predominant Arab view after the United Nations' decision was that it was a blessing in disguise; the Almighty had presented them with a cast-iron reason to attack and exterminate the Jews. In short, to cast them into the sea, any sea. Thus the removal of the embryonic Jewish state was taken as a *sine qua non*. How could such a puny, outnumbered, unmilitary people resist the full force of the united Arab armies?

The Jews were certainly outnumbered, but they were neither puny nor unmilitary. Their first need was arms. On the Arab side the more difficult question was who among them would obtain the larger slice of the cake, or, even more specifically, grab the whole? Thus, from the beginning they were never united, although their initial more or less concerted efforts in the field were both deleterious and, at moments, highly dangerous. Never for one second did the Jews underestimate them.

Among the Arabs, the Grand Mufti, Haj Amin el-Husseini, considered himself to be the rightful heir. Outside his family, and those whom he could influence, few trusted him, and all treated him with considerable circumspection. He was, nevertheless, a contender, who had, in passing moments, the backing of King Farouk of Egypt, who hated the British as much as the Mufti, an irrelevancy under the circumstances, and of some sycophantic functionaries in the Arab League, benefiting from his spasmodic largesse.

His rival, the Arab Liberation Army leader, Fawzi el-Kaoukji Bey, saw himself as the latter-day Saladin without either the force of arms, character or *nomenclatura* to back it up. As he told the author: Palestine was to be his by right of conquest.

King Abdullah of Transjordan on the other hand, who had both character and armed forces, never abandoned his desire to reign over a Greater Syria, and could not envisage anyone other than himself as ruler of Palestine. Furthermore, he was on good terms with the Jews and well understood their undoubted qualities and enterprise, expressed not only in his admiration for their cheese. Abdullah also knew he possessed the only professional force worthy of the name in the region: the British-trained and led Arab Legion.

The Lebanese and Syrians had no particular objectives other than to stop the others, particularly Abdullah. The Iraqis, territorially, were not directly concerned – their borders did not march with Palestine – but they sent troops and their king was the great-nephew of Abdullah. Egypt, on the other hand, with memories of conquests under Amun and the hawk-god Horus, now monotheistically clad following more recent revelations, had a firm and imperial eye on large slices of southern Palestine, including the Gaza strip and points north, as well as most of the Negev.

Meanwhile, various unofficial meetings were held, during which anything other than peaceful Jewish acquiescence to Arab proposals was met with a degree of incomprehension: the Jews had no chance to defend themselves. Why not be pragmatic and do a deal which would exclude the others? An exception was the meeting in London, two months before the UN decision, between David Harrowwitz and Aubrey (Abba) Eban, both of the Jewish Agency, and the Secretary General of the Arab League, Abdul Rahman Azzam Pasha, in his suite at the Savoy Hotel, London. He proposed no deal. In an hour's conversation he expressed his deepest regrets that only war was possible, given the emotional nature of Arabs: "We have only one test: the test of strength".

A more positive and practical meeting took place when Chaim Weizmann persuaded a hesitant President Truman, on 19 November, to support the assignment of the Negev and the site of the future port of Elat to the Jews. In the event it was assigned, but the new state of Israel had to fight for it, as they had to fight for every square inch of land they were awarded.

Two days before the UN decision, on 27 November, the Grand Mufti proposed a meeting with the Jewish Agency to consider a compromise, involving *his* assumed role and rule, which was supported by Syria. The Agency replied that it would meet anyone but him. Indeed on this day Goldie Myerson (Golda Meir) met King Abdullah at Naharayia on the Jordan, where, if nothing else was agreed, it was clearly established that the Mufti was their common enemy. Abdullah proposed a Hebrew republic within the Transjordanian monarchy. This was rejected; but Transjordanian control of the West Bank was accepted.

Four months further on, in late March, 1948, Yoshua Palmon

of the Jewish Agency listened to the same ideas. It was proposed that Palestine become a federal state under Fawzi, to the exclusion of the Mufti and King Abdullah. This was what psychiatrists would term an exposition of inflation. Nevertheless, it was agreed, not unusually, that the Mufti was the common foe. Abdullah was held in a more kindly light.

Darkness, however, came early on 29 November, both in the sky and upon the land. Immediately the United Nations' decision was announced fighting followed the rioting. In Allenby Square, centre of the New City, Arabs ran amuck on 2 December, while their frenzy was beheld with deep sorrow by Richard Graves. Jewish shops were burnt and, when British troops intervened to stop the Arabs breaking into and destroying the Warsaw Synagogue, they were fired on by the Arabs.

The UN had also proposed an economic union between the two separate states, as well as establishing a UN trusteeship within and around Jerusalem. The UN representative of this idea, Count Folke Bernadotte, was shot dead by Stern a year later; David's City belonged to none other than the Jews, and certainly not the UN. The Jews had received 55% of the land, including the Negev, within which area the 568,000 Jews represented 58% of the population. Some 32% were largely Arab. The 1,200,000 Arabs had been awarded 45% of the land which was 99% Arab populated.

11.12.47. British troops were positioned between the Jewish and Arab quarters in the Old City. The Jews, surrounded by Arabs, were in a precarious situation. On the same day 1st Guards Brigade returned from Transjordan and was again stationed at Nathanya, under Brigadier George Johnson and under canvas. I shared a tent with Bill Tilleard. In a very bad storm, it held its own. Not so that of our neighbour, Tony Samuelson, whose tent was unpegged. He was exposed, on his camp bed, to the elements.

Two days after our return Arabs raided Ramleh police station. The Coldstream – the 3rd Battalion gradually handing over to the 1st Battalion – had been detailed to guard the Jerusalem-Tel Aviv road. Some of the Arabs involved in the attack were returning to their base when they ran into a Coldstream roadblock commanded by Richard Leventhorpe. Their truck was captured, as was another which followed, as well as a car.

In the fracas which followed an Arab was killed, seven captured, many arms and much ammunition recovered. The next day a carrier patrol under David Watts found more arms in a farm, captured an Arab and discovered a cache of ammunition: 70,000 rounds, 160 rifles, four Brens, fifteen Stens and a shotgun which belonged to the Police Inspector at Ramleh.

On 17 December, as forecast by its Secretary General, the Arab League stated it would stop any division of Palestine by force. Henceforth, following the riots, the Arabs became increasingly cock-a-hoop and felt it was only a matter of time before the Jews were annihilated. It then became the primary duty of the British Army to protect, as best it could, Jews and Jewish settlements against Arab attack.

28.12.47. The Arabs attacked the Jewish settlement of Kefar Yavetz, seven miles south-west of Tulkarm, and ten miles south-east of Nathanya. The Welsh Guards intervened and the Arabs withdrew. Nevertheless, in the irredeemably schizophrenic psyches of the Irgun and Stern gang members, the British were to blame for the deaths of the Jews at Arab hands. Soon Jewish terrorism, counter-attacking Arab terrorism, would result in an ethnic purge involving 58% of the Arab population in Palestine – 700,000 refugees.

Meanwhile, in what were becoming British military cantonments, the Army passed a comparatively quiet Christmas. Major General Horatius Murray, who had commanded 6th Armoured Division in Italy and Austria, was now commanding 1st Division, having replaced Windy Gale. I wrote home: "*He was interested to hear I had been with the 3rd Battalion, and discussed all sorts of things with me, except I spoke as a platoon commander and he as a divisional commander!*" I do remember saluting him when he visited the front.

Football, rugby and leave in Cyprus were available diversions for all ranks, if desired and granted. Shooting could still be had in the Huleh. If the hunt continued, I have no record of attending it, but there was riding and I was invited by Mark Norman and David Somerset to exercise an animal they provided, before having dinner with them. The horse had been fed on amphetamines and had not been saddled for two or three days. There appeared, it seemed to me immediately, to be some mischievous intent to unseat the Staff Captain.

My hosts were disappointed. The animal bucked and did its best to bolt – I sawed on the bit – tossed its head wildly, bucked again and then settled for a gallop, more or less under control. We developed an understanding, but I declined a suggestion by David that we clear a wide ditch, as a form of short cut, saving thirty seconds and as many yards, since I strongly suspected that the animal would be disinclined to take it. A week later I returned their hospitality, dismounted. Hugh Stanley was my co-host.

On 2 January my diary refers to appalling outrages by both Jews and Arabs, and I add, with some prescience perhaps, "This country will never be peaceful without some great power looking after it." On 7 January an Irgun pamphlet called us Nazi British: Arabs killing Jews, as stated, were our responsibility. On this day Lionel Harrod, who later became a Major General, kindly asked me to dine at the Grenadier mess.

It was there that I recognized a former Lance Sergeant in my platoon in Italy who was now in charge of the officers' mess, with access to cash. The Lance Sergeant had told me, while we were under heavy fire in Italy, as a very vague form of confession and *mea culpa*, that he had served eighteen months at His Majesty's pleasure, after being found guilty of transferring £15,000 from a customer's account to his own. He was a bank clerk. It was, he said, considerably diluting his contrition, extremely bad luck that the customer, an old lady, should have come into the bank before she died.

Furthermore, on the proceeds of money obtained from German prisoners of war, in exchange for cigarettes and other NAAFI goods, he ran a book on the first Derby held after the War in 1945. The German money, completely worthless, was handed in by me to the Banca di Venezia. Then, under a benevolent Allied decree, it was changed into a meaningful medium of exchange, collected by a brother officer, and distributed to the depositors. I was foolish enough to place £20 on a horse which he said was running – and lost.

It was without any feeling of a *quid pro quo* – the reader may believe me or not – that I mentioned the facts to the adjutant, who later became a much experienced Brigadier. I felt, I said, that funds and the Lance Sergeant were best kept apart. He, Alan Breitmeyer, acted on my advice.

On 9 January I went with the Grenadier Commanding Officer, John Davies, and one of his officers, Geoffrey Sewell, to 3rd Brigade Headquarters, then on to the Manshiva quarter of Tel Aviv where the Grenadiers were finding two companies. There was much terrorist sniping there, which was hardly helpful when the Army was trying to defend the Jews against Arab attack.

Indeed, on the same day two hundred Arab Liberation Army men crossed the Syrian border and attacked Dan and Kefar Szold. General Sir Gordon MacMillan sent a troop of armoured cars and the Irish Guards to defend them. The Arabs fled. The British Ambassador in Damascus protested to the Syrian government. Also, on this same Friday, several hundred of the Arab Liberation Army, a ragbag of volunteers under lacklustre leadership, arrived at the Transjordan frontier.

Glubb Pasha, Sir Alec Kirkbride, the British resident minister, and King Abdullah himself all opposed their crossing, but Abdullah had agreed to the establishment of a volunteer force. His good faith would be questioned by other Arab leaders if he refused passage. Finally, they were allowed to pass during the night and entered Palestine via the Allenby Bridge, then made for the hills near Nablus.

MacMillan was disturbed when told of the ALA presence. He signalled HQ MELF in the Suez Canal Zone and was told by General Sir John Crocker, Commander-in-Chief, to expel them. Then the Secretary of State for War, Emanuel Shinwell – who, in passing, exceeded the real age of Methuselah by living to 102 – ordered no involvement with either Jew or Arab unless the withdrawal of British troops, which had already begun, was being blocked or threatened. The religious faith of Shinwell was Jewish.

10.1.48. I wrote home: "*The situation is deteriorating daily.*" This is indicative of how tight the military grip had been on the situation, despite continual terrorist attacks. Now, after the General Assembly vote, we were pulling out. A vacuum had to be filled and, inevitably, it was with blood. According to my diary, a Grenadier Guardsman was killed in Tel Aviv on this day.

On 14 January the war between Arabs and Jews became more serious. A thousand Arabs attacked the Kefar Etzion settlement, lying in the hills 12½ miles south of Jerusalem and 13½ miles north of Hebron. One hundred and thirty Arabs were killed. Ammunition within the settlement was low. Jewish reinforcements left during the following night, but they were too late to arrive before dawn. The whole relief force of thirty-five were massacred. Two days later British troops brought in the dead, brutally mutilated.

The mutilation of the dead was a particularly revolting Arab custom in what was now fast developing into a nasty ethnic war. Meanwhile, with hideous atrocities let loose, the heavens, in turn, had loosed a deluge of rain and storms upon us: torrential downpours and biting wind had beset us since our return from Transjordan. Suddenly and rather early this changed.

19.1.48. "*The weather is getting very hot,*" I wrote in my diary. The heat may also have contributed to the disequilibrium of a frenzied dog which bit the BEME after it had torn round his tent yelping and frothing, a sign of rabies. Arthur Butler's tent was next to mine. I saw him pick it up. It bit him. He threw it out. After a final convulsion, it died. It was then forked into a nearby dustbin.

I reported the incident to the Senior Medical Officer, a Lieutenant-Colonel, and confirmed the conversation in writing. Anyone infected with rabies had to be, *post hoc* and posthaste, injected. Prolongation could involve a massive counter-dose, in 1948 injected through the stomach. This was both painful and unpleasant, although better than death. The SMO agreed immediately to collect the dead dog for a post mortem. We then both broke a golden rule: neither of us checked if his instructions had been carried out, or, on my side, if he had given any.

I looked into the bin two days later. Luckily the carcass was still there. The Arabs, whose job it was to collect the rubbish, were never punctual at the best of times. Now shooting off rifles, frequently at Jews, offered more satisfaction and, momentarily, more pay. I went once more through the same procedure. Again inertia was evident. I asked the Brigadier to intervene. The dog was collected. The post mortem revealed death from poisoning, probably taking a chunk out of the "in-tray" cat which had disappeared.

This feral feline had sought refuge, when I was out, in my in-tray, as a haven from raving dogs. It must have been caught napping, but the biter was bit, if my guess was correct. There was no rabies, but the Senior Medical Officer was sacked.

On 20 January I lunched with my old friend Peter Nicholson at Division and learnt that we would be going to Tripoli, North Africa, as we called it – that is to say, Libya – when we left Palestine. This was not to be for a further six months. Another old friend, Christopher Thursby-Pelham, came to dinner. We had served together in the 3rd Battalion, Welsh Guards, in Italy. He later became a Brigadier and commanded British troops in the Gulf before armies were required to stop invaders from the north. He had survived an Irgun terrorist train attack near Lydda: the Jewish engine driver was killed. The two murderers were fired on, arrested by police and later hanged. The following day other would-be invaders crossed the border into Palestine from Syria: twenty lorries carrying over 700 men, bearing Syrian licence plates, under Safr Bek, a senior Syrian officer, joined the Arab Liberation Army.

Forty-eight hours later, Dick Chaplin and I went in the opposite direction, and left for Transjordan, where, as described earlier, we stayed with Colonel Shan Hackett and his wife, and then went on to Azraq. We were joined by two TJFF officers late of the 9th Lancers, Dick Koenig and Otto Thwaites, and three Micks serving with the 1st Battalion, Irish Guards, then at Rosh Pinna and Safad in North Galilee: Angus McCall, Ted Whitley and Peter Talbot-Wilcox.

The bag per gun was large: low-flying big duck, probably mallard, and many snipe. We returned via Jerusalem, where we lunched and found a singularly sinister atmosphere permeating the place: a strong presence of Jewish terrorists on one side, with many Arabs on the other. The ring was being held precariously by the British Army.

25.1.48 Fawzi el-Kaoukji passed through Amman and crossed the

Jordan into Palestine, disguised as a bedouin. MacMillan sent the District Commissioner, John Pollack, still functioning officially, to see Kaoukji at Tubas, his headquarters near Nablus. Kaoukji promised not to attack the Jews until the Mandate ended in four-and-a-half months' time. Within as many days he had broken his word, not to anyone's surprise. Our intelligence estimated there were now four thousand ALA in Palestine, divided into four regiments, largely led by Syrian officers.

On the Regimental front, two days later, Colonel Sammy Stanier dined at Brigade. He was a most conscientious visitor to this troublous spot. On the following morning I left early for Nablus police station to supervise the handover of part of the building to the Arabs. I returned with Ivor Roberts, the Welsh Guards quartermaster, in the staff car and we lunched at the Battalion. All battalions at this time were engaged in flag marches, or flag drives, to impress upon the Arabs the imprudence of causing trouble.

On one occasion the Coldstream found their road impassable: the drive had been planned at Brigade by Simon Bolitho and ended in a goat track. They claimed that it was a staff bog. The Brigade Major maintained that the Coldstream could not read their maps. I took a disinterested position, but this was not the case when an inept and insubordinate Arab attempted to hold me up at gun point, with a view to obtaining both my jeep and my arms and those of my companions, perhaps even our lives. He was carrying a Sten gun and waving his arms spasmodically, as if trying to semaphore.

This excited, keffiyed creature leapt frenetically onto the crown of the road, a safe distance ahead of the jeep, which contained the driver, two others and myself. We were all armed with automatic weapons. It appeared he wished us to stop. Either we ran him down or we stopped. Many would have chosen the first. I did not. Hitting him might have overturned the jeep, and it was unlikely he was alone.

He was full of bravado. We cocked our guns, assuming an azimuth defence. It was up to him to approach. He did. I smiled and listened. His men, meanwhile, emerged from their coverts. His English was good and my Arabic non-existent, which was important: that he understood. I told him two things: first, my gun was aimed at his midriff and I was not in the habit of having my way blocked. I was quite prepared to clear it. Secondly, as it happened, I was on my way to see his commander-in-chief, Fawzi el-Kaoukji, who would be displeased by the interruption.

This was not true, but I also added that he was my friend, as was Nabolsi Bey, the Mayor of Nablus, whom I had met more than once. Name dropping in this case had an electric effect. Bravado, already waning, was replaced by equally traditional salaams. An offer was made to take me to the presence. In the event he was absent. I was to meet him, however, before too long. We returned to Nathanya unmolested.

The same could not be said for the *Palestine Post* offices, which were blown up on 1 February. One person was killed and twenty injured. The attack was organized by Abd el-Kader el-Husseini, an anti-Zionist anti-British agitator who had been imprisoned for five years after the pro-Axis revolt in Iraq had been crushed during the War. A deputy, Abdel Nur Khalil Janho, led the operation, with two mercenary British deserters in tow, to help pass through British roadblocks.

Two vehicles were stopped at the Nablus Gate, Jerusalem. Identity cards were asked for and produced. The car and five-ton lorry were waved through into the New City, where they also passed, without difficulty, a Haganah checkpoint. Two barrels of TNT were in the lorry which drove slowly to Hassolel Street, where it parked outside the *Post* offices. The car drove to a nearby street. Abdel Nur Khalil Janho lit a long fuse, joined the others in the car and returned without incident through the same two roadblocks.

The linotype operator, sitting nearest to the street and the explosion, was killed outright. The building, as well as two neighbouring offices, was partly destroyed. The *Palestine Post* produced a much abridged version of its journal: "The truth is louder than TNT and burns brighter than the flames of arson." It was a momentary Arab victory in terms of boosting morale. It was to be followed by a further Arab-inspired outrage three weeks later.

On the same day as the *Post* bombing four officers from Brigade went to Haifa on military matters – Simon Bolitho, Lewis Dawnay, Bill Tilleard and myself – in order to meet Major General Hugh Stockwell, who was now commanding North Sector. This covered a wider area than North Palestine District, commanded by Brigadier Rathbone, the brother of a then well known stage and film actor, Basil Rathbone. We lunched at Pross' Restaurant, looked after by Dorothy George. Bill stayed in Haifa to study his new job as G2 Intelligence, North Sector.

On 2 February we had the full details of the *Post* bombing. Nevertheless, entertainment was offered at Brigade to Paul Freyberg, Grenadiers, who came for a drink. He was the son of the commander of the II New Zealand Corps in Italy, heavily engaged in the Cassino battles, Lieutenant-General Sir Bernard Freyberg, later Lord Freyberg and Governor General of New Zealand. Paul had escaped as a prisoner-of-war and spent some time hidden in the Vatican before rejoining his regiment. In the evening Bill

Gore-Langton, Dick Chaplin and Lionel Harrod came to dinner.

On 4 February we were issued with our Palestine medals and clasp, which we duly added to those already possessed, putting them up with the help of Regimental tailors. There was no medal, sadly for Corporal T. Jones, Irish Guards Regimental Band, who was killed taking part in an expedition to Bethlehem under the spiritual guidance of Father Murphy.

The group was escorted by thirty men of No 2 Company, 1st Battalion Coldstream Guards, under Ronnie Cooper. It had been decided to visit Solomon's Pools which lay two miles south of Bethlehem. The Palestine Police had said the route was clear. It was not. Arabs, thinking they had caught a Jewish convoy, opened fire. A roadblock had been set up. The Coldstream fixed bayonets. The Arabs fled. The convoy proceeded, but after half a mile there was another roadblock. Obviously Solomon's Pools were not going to be seen. There was more firing from the Arabs. Jones was killed, three musicians and one Coldstream Guardsman were wounded. Ronnie Cooper waited until nightfall, which came early in February. As he began to withdraw, a platoon of the Sussex Regiment arrived. The withdrawal was completed without further incidents.

On the same day the Irish Guards were also attacked by Arab irregulars, near Tiberias, who myopically thought they were Jews. This was a serious mistake. They were beaten off in a trice with casualties, and several Syrians were rounded up and captured. The Irish Guards suffered more casualties in Palestine, however, than any other Brigade of Guards regiment: ten were killed, of whom eight were in action and two from vehicle accidents.

Aggression was not limited to the Arabs. Ten days after the mistaken attack on the Irish Guards, in the same area of North Galilee, the Haganah raided the Arab village of Sasa, seven miles north east of Safad, and well inside Arab-controlled territory, near the Lebanese border, to prove penetration of this kind was not suicidal. Thirty-five houses were destroyed and more than sixty Arabs killed.

16.2.48. Arab forces returned the compliment and attacked the Jewish settlement of Tirat Zvi. British troops arrived from Beisan, but not before forty Arabs had been killed for the loss of one Jew. Fawzi el-Kaoukji, hardly mindful of his word to the District Commissioner, felt he ought to do better.

Not, however, before he suffered a further blow in North Galilee. Acting on a tip-off, Palmach ambushed a bus from the Lebanon. On board was a senior ALA officer. The roadside explosives failed to detonate, after torrential rain, but small-arms fire killed sixteen, including the senior officer. This was achieved, remarkably, by one woman armed with a rifle. This formidable female, an Amazon Sabra born and bred metaphorically in Kefar Scythia, went on to further glory a short time later in Safad. Her name was Netiva Ben-Yehuda.

Meanwhile, after Irgun had bombed the Damascus Gate in Jerusalem and Stern had destroyed Arab property in Jaffa, the Grand Mufti, supported by Egypt, Fawzi el-Kaoukji, supported by Syria, and King Abdullah, supported by his own Arab Legion, were competing for the largest slice of the Palestine cake as they could grab militarily. After much manoeuvring, Kaoukji was given command in the north, with central Palestine under the Mufti's men. An Iraqi, General Ismail Safwat Pasha, was appointed by the Arab League as Commander-in-Chief of all Arab forces in Palestine, including the Egyptians in the south, but his writ did not run much beyond his headquarters in Damascus.

At the time a power in the Arab heartland of Nablus was the local Arab dignitary, Radi Bey Nabolsi. I had met him with Bill Tilleard when he was Brigade Intelligence Officer and before he left for Haifa. Bill invited me to join them for lunch. As befitted his generation and education, Nabolsi spoke little English, but was fluent in Arabic, Turkish and French. We settled for French. There was, in consequence, a *tour d'horizon* which largely comprised Nabolsi's plans for the Jewish exodus. As the reader will be aware, it did not turn out exactly as he hoped.

In celebration of this event, before the piastre dropped and reality arrived, he was planning a naughty *nuit rouge* to which we were invited: the flying in of a troupe of Egyptian belly dancers, whose abdominal undulations were to be the *hors d'oeuvre* before more succulent fare. The scene was a little off-putting, and we left unimpressed. I was to meet him again, twice.

Before the first of these two meetings Paul Freyberg and Windy Hackett-Payne asked me to dine in the Grenadier mess. The senior major, second-in-command of the 1st Battalion, Grenadiers, Pat Robertson, was there. Like the Coldstream, the 1st Battalion was relieving the 3rd, due to return to England.

21.2.48. *"A very big luncheon indeed with Nabolsi Bey, the notable – and mayor – of Nablus, near Tulkarm. Almost in no-man's land!"* My diary also mentions a large number of personal bodyguards, presumably armed, and towards the end of the meal, when arak was going to the heads of our fellow guests, they produced precious weapons which they began firing into the air. Sitting next to me was George Leeds, a large, rather rotund, red-faced and moustached officer – that is to say, no catamite he – who, in the perverse taste of a Syrian doctor, attracted unwelcome, amorous attentions.

We had sufficiently recovered from both shock and arak to drive to Haifa the next day in Hugh Stanley's Sunbeam Talbot – a rather pointless, even dangerous, accessory, it always seemed to me, which was in fact shot up on a later occasion – accompanied by Philip Duncombe and Dicky Birch-Reyardson, both Grenadiers. The intention was to meet big drafts of the 1st Battalions of the Grenadiers and Coldstream, which was carried out. We lunched, rather inevitably, at Lilli Manheim's Astoria Restaurant, despite its being the recent killing ground of terrorist murders. We had tea at Nathanya, sparing a thought for Sergeants Martin and Paice.

While we were in Haifa events in Jerusalem took a particularly brutal turn when the Atlantic Hotel was blown up by Arab terrorists. The attack was again organized by Abd el-Kader el-Husseini. A police armoured car led three British Army vehicles in convoy, coming from the west towards Jerusalem. They were stopped at a Haganah roadblock. A man dressed as a Palestine policeman in the armoured car vouched for the others and said they were running supplies into the city. After a cursory inspection of the first vehicle, the convoy passed through and headed for Ben Yehuda Street, via the Jaffa Road.

The time was around 0615. Six men – four British deserters, including two from the *Palestine Post* outrage, and two British-looking Arabs – got out and lit the fuses. One deserter dropped a pistol which went off. The adjoining Palestine Discount Bank's night watchman emerged to see what was going on. He was shot dead. The six men then clambered into the armoured car and made their getaway along the route they had used to enter. A Bren gun was pointed at the men manning the Haganah roadblock. The armoured car raced through and headed for the Judaean hills. Forty-seven people died and one hundred and thirty were injured in the subsequent explosion.

The murders gave a momentary boost to Arab morale, unable to distinguish between a single, from their viewpoint, successful outrage and overall victory. The Jews were equally shaken. For the first time Jewish terrorists could reflect on the efficacy of their own tutelage; the sorcerers' apprentices were now fully fledged guild members. Rejoicing in Nablus had, however, quietened when I arrived two days later to pay a visit to Henry Coombe-Tennant and Support Company, Welsh Guards, stationed in the town police station.

The countryside was looking refreshed and smelt fragrant after the rain of the last few days. Wild flowers were beginning to bloom and the central hills were looking more green than brown, the colour associated with them throughout most of the year. There were several Arab roadblocks on the way, but no repetition of the earlier encounter with the volatile and vexatious malefactor in the middle of the road.

On 25 February the IZL announced that they were going to renew their attacks – we were unaware of any cessation – against the Mandatory power and all its minions. With only two-and-a-half months left of this unfortunate régime the threat seemed more like the conditioned reflex of Pavlov's dog than a serious menace. That their madness and venom were truly rabid, however, was proved four days later. More peacefully, at Brigade Headquarters, three Grenadiers dined with us: Pat Robertson, Tim Bradley and Vere Eliot. All lived to see happier days beyond the borders of Palestine.

Rugby football had not been neglected meanwhile, and on Thursday, 26 February, I went with three other Welsh Guardsmen, Billy Malcolm, Luke Dinsdale and Jerry Spencer-Smith, to support the Battalion team playing against the Royal Irish Fusiliers. My diary records that we won quite easily but does not mention the score. The event was the Divisional Cup and we lunched at the Division "A" mess, itself in mourning for the death that day of the Chief Signals Officer, Colonel "Cheesy" Rhind, who had been blown up in his jeep.

27.2.48. "My twenty-third birthday. No celebration. Bill Tilleard leaves for Haifa. We cut down the orange grove where Colonel Cheesy Rhind was blown up to prevent it being used again as cover."

This was by no means an automatic response on our part, as indicated earlier. The Roman practice correctly anticipated trouble in recently captured territory: all cover for the distance of an arrow flight, on both sides of the road, was removed and cut down. They would then cut down anyone who opposed them. In Palestine there was always some reluctance to make the probably innocent horticulturist suffer for the deeds of terrorists. On the other hand, if his orange grove offered cover for these gangs, the logical action was to remove the cover. Logic, however, was not always a predominant factor in Palestinian affairs.

The entry for 28 February mentioned a further exciting match on the rugby field. This time the Welsh Guards won against a REME Base Workshops team. Our opponents claimed the refereeing of Ivor Roberts was biased. This might well have been an understatement, but it appeared that the better team won after a slow start, with a final score of 13-10. I went to bed early and read the *Decameron* by Giovanni Boccaccio, a fourteenth century friend of Petrarch and first lecturer on Dante. He began his great work in 1348 and took ten years to complete it. His fables, based scenically in Tuscany, but written in Naples, were far removed from the reality of our own surroundings at this time.

Yet for those of us who had served in this same 1st Guards Brigade, and thousands in scores of other formations in Italy during the War, Tuscany evoked memories of both peace in Florence and behind the lines, but also of the front, fraught with its inevitable scenes of anguish and human suffering. Indeed, for the last commanding officer of the 3rd Battalion Welsh Guards in Italy and Austria, Robin Rose-Price, and our brother officer, Andrew Gibson-Watt, Nemesis was thwarted by the failure of a bomb to explode beneath their railway carriage while they were having breakfast.

CHAPTER THIRTEEN

More Bombs While Fawzi Bey Boasts

Saint David may or may not recognize leap years. Either way, the leap day, 29 February, 1948, was exactly one year after Andrew Gibson-Watt, our companions and I had nearly suffered the fate, on 1 March, 1947, of the recently murdered Colonel Cheesy Rhind. Exactly one year later, for Andrew, it was a coincidental second near miss he could well have done without, however divinely protected.

Andrew was returning from leave on board the Cairo-Haifa train. Also travelling was Robin Rose-Price, holding a staff job at O2E, Haifa Staff College. Just north of Rehovot Station three bombs, planted by Irgun, exploded underneath the train, killing thirty soldiers. A fourth bomb, beneath the carriage where they were breakfasting, failed to explode.

I am able to say that Weizmann did not spill his coffee; he was in London. Had he been there, he would have heard the huge explosion. Andrew wrote: "I did my best to get some people out. There was no panic. The men were marvellous. An Army camp was nearby and help arrived quickly. So many soldiers were killed or hurt. I remember the incident with horror."

Irgun and its collaborators remembered it with satisfaction. Their need for blood was insatiable and well beyond the control of either Weizmann or Ben-Gurion. This was no political gesture or counter-demonstration. The British were leaving the Mandate in which Lloyd George's government had promised a homeland for the Jews; it was simply a form of blood sport as practised by psychopaths who were threatening to turn their assumed patrimony into gangland.

1.3.48. "Saint David's Day. The High Commissioner, Sir Alan Cunningham, takes the salute and presents the leeks."

12.3.48. Abd el-Kader el-Husseini executed his third bomb out-rage. This time his target was the Jewish Agency and its occupants. He was approached by a Christian Arab chauffeur of the American Consul General in Jerusalem, Mr Cornell, whom I had seen last year. For a considerable award, including cash and tickets for his family and himself to Central America, he would drive the con-sulate green Ford car into the compound. Inside the vehicle would be packed with explosives.

His name was Abu Daoud and on 12 March he was sent on an errand to the Jewish Agency. He went via the Old City where, in front of a certain store, he stopped. There Arabs loaded boxes into the boot of the car and demonstrated how to detonate the bombs. At the Jewish Agency gates the guards recognized him, were informed he was delivering a message – true – and allowed him to park his car in front of the building.

Above were the offices of Ben-Gurion and other Jewish leaders. Abu Daoud lit the fuse which ran from the boot to the front seats. He then got out of the car and walked up the steps, entered the building and made a quick exit by the back door. He had, however, left the keys in the car. A Jewish security man, seeing the car was blocking the entrance, leapt in and drove it to the left wing, which housed the Jewish Foundation Fund offices.

As the guard was leaving the car it blew up. The explosion was considerable. It killed the guard, as well as thirteen Foundation Fund officials. Forty others in the building were injured. No one found the Stars and Stripes flag, under which banner, misrepre-sented and betrayed, the bombing had taken place. None of the Jewish leaders, against whom the attack was aimed, was harmed. Israel was to need their skills to defend the territory awarded them by the UN, and to administer the antitoxin against terrorism, which continued internally, like a spastic convulsion, after independence.

The next day, in the more peaceful surroundings of the rugby field, the Welsh Guards won the Command final against 2nd/3rd Parachute Battalion at Sarafand, with a score of 6-3. This time Ivor Roberts was not refereeing. The Jews, meanwhile, buried their dead. Simultaneously Irgun and Stern plotted revenge.

15.3.48. Amid the growing confusion and terrorist acts, which as far as Irgun and Stern were concerned, were aimed indiscriminately – Stern would have said discriminately – at both the British and the Arabs, the latter being far from reticent in perpetrating their own atrocities, the Brigade of Guards began Spring Drills. Staff officers were not exempt. As I wrote home: "*That perennial event so loved by Drill Sergeants* (a rank above company sergeant major but below regimental sergeant major, whose extra pay was found from

Household funds) *and those officers who have not to attend.*"

Hugh Stanley so hated the idea that he drank too much and fell into a ditch. It was considered better to leave him there and hope his failure to attend would not be noticed. He was not missed and, afterwards, we put him to bed. He was quite heavy was Fat Stan.

Three days after we had borne Hugh Stanley to bed a few thousand miles away in Washington Chaim Weizmann obtained an interview with president Truman. This had not been easy: zealous pressure upon the President had been counterproductive. It took the intervention of his former haberdashery partner, Eddie Jacobson, to persuade him to see Weizmann.

At the end of their discussion the President promised support for partition – and a Jewish state, including the Negev – which was now beginning to be questioned. It seemed to many, including the State Department officials concerned, that it was not feasible. The idea of a United Nations trusteeship, the new word for Mandate, was returning.

Truman's support for the partition plan was not made immediately clear to his subordinates. The American ambassador to the United Nations, Warren Austin, stated that his government would propose the partition plan be suspended and a temporary Palestine trusteeship be instituted. Consequently United States recognition of the Jewish state – Israel was not known as such until 14 May, 1948, when Ben-Gurion revealed it in Tel Aviv – remained in doubt until the last minute. In practice a reversal would have been chaotic.

In Palestine, meanwhile, we were unaware, as was most of the world, of the dramas taking place within the United States administration and the Jewish Agency. At our local level, Johnny Cobbold had left us as L.O."P" to George Johnson. One of his main duties had been to follow his brigadier with a jam jar, while the commander netted butterflies; he was a leading lepidopterist. His successor was Nicholas Rivett-Carnac, Scots Guards, who arrived on the same day as Headquarters, 1st Battalion Grenadier Guards and the Apostolic Delegation. If coincidental, it was also sacramental: absolution was offered to all, albeit conditionally.

A little later, Nicholas took a Very Important General, whom he had been deputed to meet at Lydda airport, half way to Jerusalem. Instead of turning left, as briefed, and heading north, he allowed the driver to go straight ahead. I had obviously over-briefed him. We all liked Nicholas, a rather short, fair young man. The VIG forgave him. I forget who he was.

On 25 March matters once more took a serious turn when a Jewish convoy from Nahariya in the north, on its way to Yehi'am, eight miles inland and isolated in the western hills of Galilee near the

Lebanese border, was ambushed. All forty-six Jews in the convoy were killed. Seven weeks before the end of the Mandate the writ of the British Army no longer ran in that part of Palestine.

Good Friday fell on 26 March. Possibly in a mood of remorse, Lewis Dawnay showed me my confidential report, which I was obliged to initial. It was unduly flattering and I wondered if it was either an act of contrition or whether he had had a touch of the sun, although, unlike mad dogs and most Englishmen, he never went out at midday and a bathing costume was certainly not part of his accoutrement.

Two of Lewis's fellow Coldstreamers, Matthew Page-Wood and Victor Lefanu, had dinner with us and on Easter Sunday Colonel Peter Deakin (later a Major-General commanding the Territorial Army), Alec Gregory-Hood, commanding King's Company, and Ronnie Taylor, all Grenadiers, came for a drink and departed without their Easter eggs.

Easter Monday, 27 March, saw no respite in terms of Arab aggression: Abd el-Kader el-Husseini once again organized an attack against the Jews. This time a large Jewish convoy had left Jerusalem for Kefar Etzion, the scene, two-and-a-half months earlier, of a repulsed Arab attack, followed by the annihilation of a Jewish relief column and British intervention, which comprised nineteen armoured cars, a roadblock buster, thirty-three armoured lorries and buses, plus two hundred drivers and soldiers. The settlement was supplied with ammunition, guns, food and fuel. On the way south the convoy had been unmolested. The return journey was to be a different story.

Initially, roadblocks were demolished, but at the seventh, just when the pile of large rocks was almost cleared, the bulldozer or buster slid into a ditch. The convoy was now blocked at both ends. It sought refuge in a nearby building, which the Haganah commander ordered to be surrounded by the armoured vehicles. None of this could take place in an instant. The Arabs began firing mortars and machine guns. The ominous crunch of the first and the steady rat-tat-tat of the second continued until nightfall. Haganah headquarters in Jerusalem were radioed that the position was serious.

The British were asked to intervene and did so. In the subsequent negotiations – shooting and dispersing the Arabs would have cost lives, not least Jewish – it was agreed that all Jewish equipment was to be handed over to the Arabs in return for the Jews being escorted to Jerusalem. Not everything had gone in favour of the Arabs. Kefar Etzion had been restocked and the Arab dead numbered 135 against Jewish losses of twelve, a ratio of more than 11:1.

On 30 March, after nearly two-and-a-half years in Palestine the 1st Battatlion Welsh Guards set sail for home in His Majesty's Troopship *Scythia*. They had been due to sail the day before and I had gone to Haifa to see them off, but the sea had been too rough to leave harbour.

31.3.48. Another Jewish convoy, *intent on breaking the Arab blockade of Jerusalem*, was partly destroyed, just before leaving Hulda, five miles south-west of Rehovot, on its way to Bab el-Wad. Roads were also cut by Arabs in Galilee and the Negev.

Two days later Brigade headquarters received a telephone call, via the Nablus police station, suggesting that one or two officers, including myself might like to meet Radi Bey Nabolsi who would then take us to Tubas, where he would introduce us to Fawzi el-Kaoukji, or Fawzi Bey, although it was unclear which Arab monarch had bestowed the Bey upon him, even if in Turkey it was then used more or less as esquire. This fine point was not at the front of our minds when we met him.

He was a man of close-cropped, grey hair, even features, medium height and clean-shaven. He was dressed in a drab-coloured track suit, but wore leather shoes. At this moment he was not running anywhere. In our party were Donald Marsh, Coldstream, Bill Tilleard's successor as BIO, Alistair Morrison, the Intelligence Officer of the 4th/7th and our drivers.

After we met Nabolsi Bey in Nablus we went to Tubas, some twelve miles to the north-east, accompanied by some Syrian officers. Also present were Issan Bek, commander of the Circassian Arab Liberation Army, Mahmoud Bey, an Arab Legion Captain, and Doctor Khouri from Nablus. We listened to their plans. They reckoned to be in Tel Aviv within a week of launching their attack. They were vague about tactics and the direction their thrusts were going to take.

More predominantly, there was talk of Jewish mistresses, three each, and the rewards the gallantry of the Arab Liberation Army would reap in a few weeks' time. We said nothing about the Jewish airstrip being built not too far from Nathanya. After coffee and the conference, if it were that, which we attended in Fawzi Bey's tent, we were asked to watch the parade laid on for us. A long column marched past and I had a suspicion that the same three hundred men, in columns of three, made the circuit three times to impress us with their numbers.

There was no sign of the reported four thousand who were supposed to be in the region, nor were there any heavy weapons, at any rate on show, nor armoured vehicles. Our photographs were taken, alternatively, by the Intelligence Officers. We did not send copies to either Damascus or Tel Aviv, although we might have sent one to Nabolsi. He certainly entertained us for luncheon later, in a most hospitable and traditional manner.

Towards the end he confessed he had found, already using the past tense, the administration of British justice both confusing and expensive. Under the Turks, he said, you bribed the judge and you knew the result beforehand. Under the British, you paid fees to lawyers and never knew the outcome. I sympathized.

As we said goodbye, it went through my mind, no doubt, too, through the minds of the Haganah commanders, that the distance from Arab-held Tulkarm, fifteen miles north-north-west of Nablus, to the Mediterranean Sea at Nathanya was less than ten miles. A successful push there would divide the Jewish-held part of Palestine in two. It seemed also to have occurred to the Arabs and Radi Bey Nabolsi. He was quite a tall man, clean-shaven, wearing a suit, collar and tie, his head crowned with a red fez and tassel. He held both my hands: "*Mon Capitaine*, may I ask you to undertake a most discreet and delicate mission on my behalf?" I did not wish to become too involved in the wiles and wishes of Nabolsi, who later became, for a short time, prime minister of Jordan, so I asked him cautiously what had he in mind. He had always a humorous twinkle in his eyes, but I think he was serious.

"You know," he said, "my very close friend and confidant is Oved Ben Ami, the Mayor of Nathanya. We have land near his town. Tell him, when we attack, and I don't know the date, the battle will be on the left-hand side of the road, where my cousin's orange groves are situated, and not on the right where mine are!"

Perhaps this was a bey's eye view of contemporary combat, like fixing the judge before the verdict.

CHAPTER FOURTEEN

Mass Murder as Mandate Ends

The State Department's proposition of 19 March, 1948, that partition be suspended was in practice as much out of touch as Truman's request for the entry of 100,000 Jews into Palestine three years earlier. The growing lawlessness in what was still the Mandate reflected British withdrawal, and with it the reduced capacity of the Army to intervene, although it did so, notably in Jaffa, two weeks before the end.

On 1 April Ben-Gurion launched an offensive operation by Haganah, the first objective of which was to clear the Jerusalem-Tel Aviv road of Arabs. As a preliminary, two days later, the assault wing of Haganah, Palmach, attacked and took Kastel, a Roman fort three miles outside Jerusalem, which dominated the road and neighbouring villages in all directions.

On 4 April, sixty miles further north, Fawzi el-Kaoukji's forces attacked the Mishmar Ha'emek kibbutz, which was strategically situated on a ridge astride the Haifa-Jenin road. The kibbutz was sixteen miles from Haifa harbour and twelve-and-a-half from the sea. Its military importance was obvious, and not far from the jugular which even I, and greater strategists, recognized as being the weakest point in terms of Jewish defensive depth.

Fawzi's ALA forces surrounded the kibbutz: 1000 men, supported by 3" mortars, armoured cars and a battery of 75mm and 105mm guns, formed the attacking force. The outcome ought to have been a foregone conclusion, but an estimate of this kind discounted Jewish courage and resourcefulness, combined with a degree of incompetence then associated with Arab assaults. The defenders, numbering 300 men, women and children, possessed a heavy machine gun, two light machine guns, a 3" mortar, two 2" mortars, fifty rifles and some grenades. They had fortified the kibbutz to the extent that there were connecting trenches, barbed wire fences surrounding the settlement, and a concrete kindergarten or baby bunker. Fawzi el-Kaoukji had cut the telephone lines, and the kibbutz radio transmitter was out of order; these things always happen at the worst moments. The ALA opened fire at 1700 hours and killed a mother and child. Tragic as this was, it was equally miraculous that they were the only casualties.

The next day telephone lines this time played a positive role, when the tapping of the Afula-Jenin-Nablus line alerted Haganah, listening in to Arab conversations. Immediately reinforcements were sent and arrived at Mishmar Ha'emek from Afula, in the Jezreel Valley. They were deliberately allowed through by the Arab commander to increase the number of those he considered surrounded and trapped. The ALA began closing in when the 3rd Hussars, stationed nearby, intervened. The Arab commander agreed to a cease fire under threat of attack.

Two days later the British again intervened. A further cease fire was arranged directly with Fawzi el-Kaoukji. Then, on 8 April, a four-day battle started when the cease fire was broken again. In the end, after more Jewish reinforcements arrived, Haganah defeated Fawzi Bey's forces in and around the kibbutz. He then abandoned his objectives on this front, basically vital for any successful push towards the sea or Tel Aviv, and became the recipient of abuse from King Abdullah, who called him a "dog", while the Syrian president, Kuwatly, reduced his support. The Lebanon looked more kindly upon him.

Meanwhile, on the day the Arab Liberation Army attacked Mishmar Ha'emek, some of us, including myself, passed quite close to the scene of action when we went to Haifa to say goodbye to the 3rd Grenadiers who were leaving for England. Johnny Johnson, the adjutant of the 1st Grenadiers, and Colin Dalrymple, Scots Guards, a brother officer on the staff, joined our party at the Astoria. I saw Bill Tilleard and arranged two good rooms for Andrew and me in our new billets on Mount Carmel.

Around this time, 5 April, Haganah agents were active in Italy, when they sank the Italian ship *Lino* carrying 6000 rifles, 8 million rounds of ammunition, explosives and hand grenades bound for Beirut, in Bari harbour, with the connivance of the Italian authorities. At the same time, and from the same source, Czechoslovakia, the Haganah bought 10,000 rifles, 4500 submachine guns and complementary military necessities. This was a considerable increase on the 200 Bren guns, 1500 rifles and 400 submachine guns which had slipped through British customs.

Arms were now being flown in at night, using the airstrip near

Nathanya, and all available means were used to transship guns and equipment, sometimes via Panama, to the Palestine coast. None of this would have been possible without Jewish–American support and exemplary Haganah organization. Nevertheless, the heavy weaponry required would not arrive until much later: a tank could have dominated the battlefield, as it did in subsequent Arab-Israeli wars – plus the Israeli Air Force.

On 6 April, in the middle of the Mishmar Ha'emek battle, which provoked the 3rd Hussars to intervene more than once, Brigade Headquarters moved to Haifa from Nathanya. I wrote that I was in a very comfortable room in the requisitioned house: "*big balcony facing the sea. Also a bath, basin in my room, and electric light. The mess, too, is very comfortable, and appreciated by the Major-General* (Commanding Brigade of Guards) *John Marriott, who came to dinner.*"

On the next day, 7 April, the Arab terrorist, Abd el-Kader el-Husseini, informed of the fall of Kastel, near Jerusalem, returned to the scene from Damascus. Fawzi Bey sent a token force, as a symbol of Arab brotherhood, but otherwise left the action to el-Kader, who led the attack to capture Kastel. He was killed. Nevertheless, the place fell to the Arabs, who left 50 men to guard it, while the rest went off to bury their leader in Jerusalem. Three days later Kastel fell to a Palmach platoon of 30 men, while, on the same day, a Moslem Brotherhood attack against Kfar Darom, a Jewish settlement in the Negev, was repulsed.

As far as we were concerned, our move to Haifa was the beginning of a coordinated withdrawal: Jerusalem and the southern coastal strip, including Gaza, to the Canal Zone; then, six weeks later, Haifa to Cyprus and Libya. The Beys of Nablus and the surrounding region were left to act or not, as their whims came and went. Meanwhile Nabolsi's orange groves and those of his cousin remained unstained by the blood of battle, and Fawzi had not yet been fitted with running shoes. Spring flowers were blooming. Hillsides were red with scarlet anemones, the wind-flower of ancient Greece, while white narcissi, the mistranslated rose of Sharon, which is, in fact, a creeping shrub with large yellow flowers, as well as orange and yellow narcissi, grew by the roadside, where Jewish terrorists still planted their bombs.

9.4.48. On this date Irgun and Stern razed the village of Deir Yassin near Jerusalem by dynamiting the houses of the inhabitants, while men, women and children were inside. Some 250 people were killed in many hours of slaughter. The Haganah commander in Jerusalem, David Shaltiel, formerly Haganah head of intelligence "viewed the Irgunists and Sternists as straightforward thugs and murderers". He was unable to stop them, but specifically warned them, in writing, not to blow up buildings or kill the inhabitants.

As with the King David Hotel bombing, orders given to these people had no point or meaning. Both Irgun and Stern went ahead. The direct result of this appalling massacre – Haganah were horrified when they arrived on the scene – was the flight of 700,000 Arabs from Palestine. Three days after the massacre the High Commissioner, Sir Alan Cunningham, wrote to the Colonial Secretary, Arthur Creech Jones: "This village is still in the hands of the Jews as I write. I wanted the soldiers to attack it, if necessary, with all the power they can produce and turn out the Jews. But I am told they are not in a position to do so, or indeed do anything which may provoke general conflict with either side, as their troops are already fully committed. This is only one example out of many where the Civil Government has to stand idle while its authority is flouted in all directions." (Cunningham papers)

The United States government, meanwhile, gliding high above the ground and reality like its own symbolic American eagle, was still flirting with the idea of a trusteeship – but by whom? The theoretical idea was to replace the British Mandate "until such times as the Jews and Arabs could work out a *modus vivendi*". Like the aphorism concerning the Bourbons who had learnt nothing and had forgotten nothing, this musing aloud by Dean Rusk, then head of the American Office for United Nations Affairs, was remarkable to hear.

The Arabs and Jews had failed to work out a *modus vivendi* in thirty years of virtually constant conflict and neither side saw any reason why they should: their views were diametrically opposed and would always remain so. It was Dean Acheson who later observed that the British had lost an empire but had not yet found a role. In the case of Palestine the UN and USA had lost an umpire but had not yet found *their* role.

Rusk's ideas were pie in the sky of the eagle. The CIA put it more succinctly: "Such a plan cannot be implemented without Arab cooperation; and it is inconceivable the Arabs will abandon their violent opposition to partition. Nor (can they) be forced to acquiesce to a Western-sponsored movement which they believe is threatening the twentieth century renascence of their indigenous civilization."

The United States Joint Chiefs of Staff estimated, interestingly enough, that a *minimum* force of 104,000 would be needed to keep the peace. Also, they asked, was the United States government going to forbid the effectively independent, if beleaguered, Jewish Agency from declaring the establishment of their State on 15 May?

How could it implement such a policy? Conversely, if, *in extremis*, the Jews were being pushed into the sea, either as a people or as a State, or both, what would be the role of the military? In the end Truman kept his word to Weizmann and recognized the State of Israel. The subsequent, theoretical scenario did not take place in practice.

10.4.48. Dr Jacques de Reynier, Red Cross representative in Palestine, arrived at Deir Yassin, and found two women and a ten-year-old girl still alive amid the ruins. Forty of the hundred or so terrorists involved in the attack were killed or wounded: the villagers had put up a desperate resistance.

Four days later a Jewish convoy conveying supplies from the New City to the Hadassah Hospital on Mount Scopus was ambushed as it passed through the Arab quarter of Sheik Jarrah. Out of 104, only 28 survived, 76 being killed. British forces under Brigadier Charles Jones, commanding troops in Jerusalem, arrived late in the day. The Arabs were driven back by mortar and machine-gun fire.

At this time I travelled the sixty-five miles by road from Haifa to Lake Huleh, to stay with the Irish Guards. I saw an old friend, Charles Tottenham, with whom I had served as an officer at the Guards Depot. The battalion was commanded by Lieutenant-Colonel Michael Gordon-Watson, who later became a brigadier, with considerable staff responsibilities in the British Army of the Rhine. His second-in-command was Basil Eugster, later a lieutenant-general. The adjutant was Will Berridge.

This was my last visit to the Huleh. A few weeks hence, after initial Arab successes, the muktar and his clan fled; the whole of Galilee was conquered by Haganah, against considerable odds, later the marshes were drained and the aquatic birds migrated. On 16 April the Irish Guards left Safad. The Arabs occupied the town in strength, leaving the Jews in a weak position, but in the end from their weakness grew strength and the Arabs departed.

Also on 16 April, I visited the Athlit ammunition depot near Haifa. We had a Royal Artillery rocket troop there, commanded by Norman Lane who was worried about the behaviour of his neighbours, all Stern detainees under 18B emergency regulations. The next day Headquarters, North Palestine, gave a cocktail party, not uncommon in the British Army, and General Hugh Stockwell, implying his intentions, indicated that he would concentrate on guarding Haifa port and the approaches to Mount Carmel, while allowing the Jews and Arabs to face one another in the central part of the town.

The following day a Jewish friend, Peter Wolf, telephoned me about guards for the flour mill, which I organized, but they were not required for long, as the reader will see. Meanwhile, on 19 April, King Abdullah sent thirty lorries to evacuate the women and children from Tiberias, but the men fled too: Abu Abd el-Tabari, the local mufti, and his fellow Arab notables who attended the King's Birthday Parade, when Prince Talal took the salute, all climbed aboard, abandoning homes and livelihoods. They were either mindful of the town massacre on 2 October, 1937, of twenty Jews, or they had a dread fear of another Deir Yassin.

The Haganah in Tiberias were not responsible for this slaughter, but this might have been too fine a point for the Arabs. A Jew was a Jew and they had killed them before the War. Tiberias was too small a town for the two communities not to intermingle in the market place, as I witnessed during the months I spent there. On 19 April the British Army withdrew from Tiberias. Further south the Arabs ambushed yet another Jewish convoy near Bab el-Wad, on 20 April, comprising 350 vehicles, bound for Jerusalem. Only six were lost, but the heights nearby, dominating the road, were captured by the Arabs. The convoy arrived safely in Jerusalem.

In Haifa, meanwhile, the clashes between the evenly matched Arab and Jewish forces, about 600 fighters on both sides, which had continued for several weeks, and had caused concern to Hugh Stockwell, came to a head. Haganah proposed to clear the town, awarded to the Jews by the United Nations, in a matter of 48 hours. In fact, the Haganah commander, Mordechai Makleff, made a bet with the General that he would do so, against Stockwell's estimate of a week.

The primary concern of the British commander was the protection of his troops, and an unimpeded evacuation via Carmel Avenue and the port area. A Jewish victory would stop the sniping, simplify the manoeuvre and avoid casualties. On 22 April I wrote home: "*I expect it will all be over by this evening.*" Indeed it was, and a bottle of whisky was presented to Mordechai Makleff.

Operation "Scissors", which took Haifa for the Jews, was considerably helped by a precipitous drop in Arab morale. Mohammed Hamad al-Huneiti, formerly with the Arab Legion in Transjordan, was their charismatic leader, but he had been killed in an ambush a month previously. After that, nine out of eleven convoys were intercepted, following details being divulged by an Arab League official – at a going rate of £50 per convoy. Captain Amin Izzedin succeeded al-Huneiti, but, in the event, he led his men from Damascus, whither he maintained he had gone to seek reinforcements.

Our withdrawing the 1st Coldstream from the centre of the town, the likely no-man's-land between the opposing forces, prompted the Arabs to accuse us of leaving them open to Jewish attack, but they were of similar numbers, and it was the Arabs who had begun attacking the Jews, when 41 Jews were murdered in December, 1947, by Arabs working in the oil refinery.

In the two days of fighting 100 Arabs were killed and 18 Jews. After the battle 40,000 Arabs fled, 10,000 remained and we arrested their appointed head for corruption. There were then 80,000 Jews in Haifa out of a total population, pre-battle, of 146,000. The Arab exodus went largely to the Lebanon. The Jews, to their credit, pleaded with Arab leaders, in Hugh Stockwell's presence, to stay. They fled. The rest followed.

"The Jews have won easily. So provided the Haganah control the terrorists, there ought to be peace in Haifa", I wrote home. Indeed, Haganah did control both Irgun and Stern. Only the desperate need for unity, and the use of every man to fight the Arabs, postponed Haganah and the Jewish Agency, later the government of Israel, outlawing both organizations and locking up their leaders. The personal animosity between Ben-Gurion and Begin was extreme and, to the best of my knowledge, Galilee and Haifa were no-go areas for terrorists. X Command had long ceased to function, and both Ben-Gurion and Weizmann must have regretted the initiative.

26.4.48 "Life here," I wrote, *"is very busy evacuating Arabs from Haifa, but otherwise completely quiet. General Stockwell and Brigadier George Johnson seem to have sufficient time to join the Yacht Club and attend a meeting."* The Yacht Club no doubt continued after our departure. There was, however, a certain air of dressing for dinner on the *Titanic* as the ship sunk slowly and the band played on when I joined the Haifa Club eight days earlier. I think I proposed and seconded myself.

Maybe I was the last to join. It had a library stocked with such thrillers as Buchan's *The Thirty Nine Steps*. I have to say some of my fellow members looked as if they preferred to take a lift. It had a bar – anathema to my friend Lewis Dawnay – so my joining was one of the better kept secrets in Haifa at the time. The Club stocked good whisky and had the advantage of being equidistant between my room and the flat of Fay Rachman, to whom I had been introduced by Rachel Saphir.

Fay was tall, intelligent and svelte, a dark haired American who spoke English with an attractive East coast intonation. We soon became fairly constant companions. I had lost touch with my gentle friend, Mary Rosner, whom I had last seen in Tel Aviv, staying in the flat, during a rare moment of peace, with a close friend, Sioma Schiff. At an earlier date Sioma had collected me in Tel Aviv, where, at that juncture of curfews, I should not have been, a little ahead, I have always assumed, of either Irgun or Lehi. The drummer at the Pilz, Louis, had telephoned him. My appreciation remains undimmed towards both.

On 26 April, as mentioned above, I had written home that everything was quiet in Haifa. This was not the case elsewhere. On the same day Palmach attacked Nebi Samuel, 3½ miles north-west of Jerusalem, to relieve the seige of Nevi Yaakov, 3½ miles to the east. It failed, but an attack to take the Sheik Jarrah quarter in Jerusalem succeeded. The British Army, however, ordered the Haganah, through the Jewish Agency – Ben-Gurion arrived in the convoy of 20 April – to leave. The quarter was on the Army evacuation route. It would be handed back to the Jews when the Army evacuated Jerusalem. This was done.

Also on this day a third Jewish attack was launched in southern Jerusalem against the Katamon quarter, inhabited by rich Arabs. More to the point, an Iraqi unit of the Arab Liberation Army was ensconced in the large Greek Orthodox monastery of Saint Simon which overlooked the whole area. Half the Jewish force was killed, but the objective was taken and the Arab counter-attack failed. Also Arab communications and the sending of reinforcements were blocked by Etzion Bloc settlers, south of Jerusalem and north of Hebron. Telephone lines were cut and bridges blown.

Jaffa was also attacked on 26 April. This time six hundred Irgun under the principal murderer of the two sergeants in Nathanya, Amihai Faglin, assaulted the town. The IZL were given a pep talk by Begin beforehand, his contorted features camouflaged behind a beard. Soon fierce fighting broke out between the attacking force and the Arabs. After three days the first of 70,000 began to flee from Jaffa. The Life Guards were ordered to provide an armoured-car troop to halt the fighting.

Derek Cooper, with whom I had lunched three weeks earlier in Haifa, commanded Headquarter Squadron, and was the force commander. He told me that Ernest Bevin was determined Jaffa would remain Arab while the Mandate lasted. This policy was contrary to that of his cabinet colleague, Emanuel Shinwell. Derek Cooper was supported by the Royal Navy, the Royal Artillery and the Royal Air Force, and his success was immediate, but the two sides could not be kept apart for long.

The remaining Arabs were left to fight it out before fleeing. Symptomatically, Begin claimed he had not only defeated the Arabs, but also the British Navy, Army and Air Force, a pathetic rejoinder to the number of occasions the Life Guards had shot up his adherents. In one such encounter Trooper Mulgrew of "A" Squadron had put a 2-pounder shell into a scout car, stolen by

Irgun, when they were trying to drive it away near Jerusalem. The Jewish Agency were asked to clean the car out, which they did. Irgun had recently informed Haganah they were not grave diggers when told to bury those they had murdered at Deir Yassin. They said they were soldiers, which illustrates how much they knew about soldiering and how removed they were from basically civilized behaviour.

The Life Guards had served in Palestine previously. In the summer of 1941 1st Household Cavalry Regiment, a composite Regiment of The Life Guards and The Blues, were in 1st Cavalry Division in Palestine when it was mechanized. We used some of their mounts for hunting. They were then sent to fight the Vichy French in Syria and the Iraqi rebels investing the RAF base at Habbaniya. Their mission was accomplished.

In 1948 the Life Guards were under the command of Lieutenant-Colonel Ferris St George. They spent a year in Palestine, from May, 1947, until the end of the Mandate, and escorted the High Commissioner, Sir Alan Cunningham, from Jerusalem to Kalandia airstrip on 14 May. They were based at Khassa, half way between Jaffa and Gaza. They lost three men, two by terrorist attacks and one killed in a scout car accident. The Regiment was under direct command of 1st Division.

28.4.48. "Irish Guards leave Rosh Pinnar (near Safad in Galilee). *The Haganah take over."*

There were sixteen days to go before the end of the Mandate and the death toll was mounting. In five months of fighting since the United Nations decision and the British statement to quit, 10,000 Arabs and Jews had been killed, and many more were to die before the year was out. Since 1945 338 British subjects had been killed by Jewish terrorists and thirty British policemen were killed between 1 December and mid-May.

More cheerfully, the two and a half months spent in Haifa were certainly the most relaxed and positively active of the two and a half years I spent in Palestine. Certainly Haganah must take its share of the credit. It was the forerunner of the Israeli Defence Force, a citizens' army which soon became professional. They were soldiers, as were their worthy opponents, the Transjordan Arab Legion. The bestiality of the hoodlum gangs, who initially tried to be a law unto themselves, until they fell foul of Israeli legal authority, made them anathema to their mortified compatriots.

30.4.48. "Guardsman Howlett, Grenadiers, and Sergeant Dimitriadis, interpreter, killed and Lance-Sergeant Allen, Grenadier Intelligence Sergeant, wounded by Arabs while taking a Jew – also killed – to Nahariya." An act of goodwill which went sadly awry.

In the Haifa enclave, meanwhile, Lewis Dawnay and I were kept particularly busy with loading schedules and movement orders. Troops under command included the Grenadiers on the north side in the Acre Bay area. In the docks were 40 Commando, Royal Marines, and in Peninsular Barracks, as well as being spread over the town, were the Coldstream. The Irish Guards were between the south end of Haifa and Athlit, and were also in a camp in the middle of Carmel.

The 6th Field Regiment, Royal Artillery, were guarding the southern extremity at Athlit, sharing the area, as mentioned earlier, with about 400 members of the Stern gang who were imprisoned there, presumably not for much longer. I never discovered how they were fed and who was supposed to be guarding them. At any rate, it was not my responsibility, and presumably the Royal Artillery would have been aware if they had been forgotten by the soon to be disbanded Palestine Police.

The castle ruin at Athlit, with its huge stone blocks and colossal derelict surroundings, was a trading town which clustered around the walls of the fortress during the time of the Crusades. It was a base camp and in 1218 the main bastion of the Knights Templar. It was the last to fall, its cavernous vaults, store rooms, armouries, chapels, great halls and ramparts now crumbling. Recently its Arab inhabitants had fled. We bathed off the beach.

In the town 35 Field Ambulance and 7 Company Royal Army Service Corps were stationed. 1st Guards Brigade Workshops, under Ronnie Sutcliffe, were in the same camp as the Grenadiers. Our Headquarters was on the top of Mount Carmel, as were Headquarters North Palestine District and North Sector until their dissolution, leaving 1st Guards Brigade Group until 30 June, the ultimate date of departure.

Further out were the 4th/7th who had moved into the Ramat David airstrip, 15 miles south-west of Haifa in the northern sector of the Esdraelon Plain. Half way between Ramat David and Haifa was Jalama, where the 17th/21st were stationed. Headquarters, Palestine, had moved into the old Divisional Headquarters at Stella Maris on Mount Carmel, but there was a surfeit of headquarters and soon three of them were to disappear.

The RAF at Ramat David could also use the Haifa airport. The Royal Navy was in some strength off-shore, including the light fleet carrier HMS *Ocean*. In effect, we were there until the end of the Mandate on 15 May. After that date our main reason was to guard and evacuate the enormous ordnance stores accumulated in Palestine. In some cases certain officers and NCOs, largely of the RAOC and other corps concerned principally with technical matters, were tempted to set up shop and sell government property.

Those caught – and there were a few, including a lieutenant-colonel, a captain and quite a number of quartermaster-sergeants – were dealt with by Andrew as Staff Captain "A". The immediate higher formations were in Egypt. Thus he was very much in charge, under Lewis, who, with me, was mostly concerned with other matters, although our days were far from monotonous.

In a letter home at this time I enquired after my second cousin, Michael Bankier, who had served with the 3rd Battalion, Welsh Guards, in Italy, lost his twin brother and been wounded. His half-brother, Bertie, was Lieutenant-Colonel Commanding the Regiment at the time and Sammy Stanier's predecessor. I asked my mother, certainly rhetorically, how he was enjoying his honeymoon? One thing being certain – she had not accompanied the momentarily happy couple.

The bride was the first of Michael's four marital endeavours, a war widow, born in Middle Europe, who had inherited the shares of her late husband. The shares, however, were those of a private company, and as such unquoted and deliberately kept below par, which was soon the value she placed upon poor Michael. First she threw his silver hair brushes out of the window, a form of inanimate defenestration, shortly followed by Michael.

Next, for her, came an Austrian gentleman with a title and a line in ancestry. She gave him a Bentley, and he gave her a considerable amount of jewellery – and the bill. She gave him the push. She then married, after her shares were quoted publicly, an impecunious prince, exiled, but certainly royal. "Ah!" said Michael, "Now my beloved has the crown on her luggage she will stick with that!" She did. Michael later married three Americans, in sequence. He died in a car crash as a passenger.

There were no passengers in the Kefar Etzion bloc lying between Hebron and Jerusalem. All within its perimeter were on constant alert against Arab assaults. These were renewed on 4 May when the Arab Legion attacked. Artillery (25 pounders) and armoured cars, backed by local infantry, let loose the most intense bombardment of the war. The Russian monastery was taken, but other Jewish positions held. At nightfall the Arabs abandoned the monastery. The Jews lost 42 men and women out of a fighting force of 400. An appeal to Jerusalem for help could only elicit the classic reply when nothing else could be done: stand firm and hold on at all costs. The lull in the fighting lasted a week.

Meanwhile, in Haifa, at the suggestion of Brigadier George Johnson, I located the Forces' broadcasting studios. We had heard the announcement every day: "This is your British Forces Network,

Haifa, broadcasting to you from our studios on Mount Carmel." The question put to me by the brigadier was simple: "Where are the studios, and how many of the staff are on our strength?"

Neither Lewis nor I had any idea. I was sent to find out. Like all good policemen, I patrolled on foot. After one or two false trails, I came across a small tented site, with a large collection of aerials. I went inside. A young man, whom I assumed correctly to be an officer, was lying in a languid and indolent manner, his feet propped on a canvas chair, putting on records. It was he who relayed the news from London, and implied as near as he dare that he was running an organization far larger than that which, I could see, was liable to be dismantled by the first storm blowing in his direction.

In an agony of unusual exercise, he unfastened his headphones and stood up. I introduced myself and indicated the possibility of there being an inspection of his hideaway by the Brigade commander. I detected a slight hint of alarm in his eyes. He put the studios on automatic pilot, raced to a barber's shop and polished his shoes for the first time since purchase. He practised his salute, after finding his cap, and I had his clothes sent to the dhobi.

In fact, the dhobi was soon to leave us. He enquired where and when we were going. It was no longer a secret. I said Tripoli in a couple of months. He replied, "I be there Captain before you!" He was. The distance is 400 miles to Alexandria and then another 1000 to Tripoli. Some time later he departed with his team in a ramshackle truck with a canvas top and mobile big end. Most remarkably he encountered no problems en route, either mechanical or military, but which route he took out of Palestine I am unable to say. He kindly offered me three rather low-quality silk shirts.

Earlier, Charles Lambton, in the Coldstream, had taken a fairly similar route home, travelling along the coast road of North Africa to Tangier and then crossing to Gibraltar. He had bought a Rolls-Royce from an Arab sheik in Jaffa for £50. It was probably the same vehicle offered to Nigel Kearsley for £25. It had had little maintenance and required even less on the way.

On 9 May I had lunch with Buster Luard who was acting commanding officer of the 1st Coldstream in the absence of John Chandos-Pole who had been hit by a Jewish sniper during the battle. John had been leading an ambulance convoy at the time, so his being wounded would seem to have been an unnecessary act of aggression, no doubt in the heat of the moment.

Also on this day a party of 1st Grenadiers, under Pat Robertson, were due to leave on *HMS Striker*. There was a muddle in the docks. I had gone to bed, but got up and went down to sort it out.

I returned to bed at 0030. Those leaving for Tripoli did not go to bed at all.

The following day there was two-way traffic across the Jordan. Glubb Pasha drove to Hebron to sort out the chaos accompanying the assaults against the Kefar Etzion bloc and organized a further attack. He then returned to Amman and ordered the dispatch of more armoured cars and artillery, together with Bren carriers. He had no tanks. The ill-assorted local infantry force was augmented.

On the same day, 10 May, Goldie Myerson (Golda Meir) and Ezra Danin, both members of the Jewish Agency, drove from Naharayim to Amman, disguised as Arabs, to meet King Abdullah at his invitation. Abdullah proposed postponement of the Jewish State being set up, the creation of a joint Parliament and Cabinet. The alternative, he said, with considerable sadness, was war. His proposals were courteously declined.

Also on this eventful 10 May Palmach, Haganah's shock troops, took Safad amid the usual Jewish gallantry and equally gallant Arab defence, but accompanied by needless muddle. The Arab commanders had left to seek help. The remainder fought well, but in vain. In the end every Arab remaining in Safad fled, plus those in the Taggart position on the summit of nearby Mount Har Kenna'an. Nor had the Arabs been able to capture Ramot Naftali, besieged for weeks, nine miles north of Safad, and two-and-a-half from the Lebanon.

These Jewish victories signalled the end of Arab rule in northern Galilee, although a central stretch southwards remained in the hands of the Arab Liberation Army under Fawzi el-Kaoukji, who must have realized that his dreams of conquest were now wholly imaginary. King Abdullah's latest epigram expressed the view he was a *dirty* dog.

On 11 May, while the Arabs attacked Kefar Etzion yet again without success – in sixteen hours they failed to achieve any objective – the Arab League met in Amman and decided to invade Palestine in four days, the date of the end of the Mandate. None, other than those already *in situ* – the Grand Mufti and Fawzi in particular – were particularly keen to do so, despite earlier bravado and tentative ambitions.

The Egyptians were aware their regular army was served by ill-equipped fellaheen and ineffectual officers. Sudanese mercenaries were the only stiffening force. As for King Abdullah, he neither wished to fight the Jews – *pace* Kefar Etzion – nor to have his fellow Arabs meddling within his sphere of influence.

As far as he was concerned both the Mufti and Fawzi were equally unattractive and incompetent schemers. The others, Syria,

Lebanon, Iraq and Saudi Arabia, effectively sent token forces, although most of the officer corps in the ALA was Syrian, comparatively ill-prepared and ill-equipped. Nevertheless, combined with Palestine irregulars, the numerical menace to the nascent State of Israel was acute.

On 13 May the British Army left the Old City of Jerusalem. On the same day Glubb Pasha sent Colonel Abdullah Tel, the commander of the Arab Legion, Jerusalem area, to take over command of the attack against the Kefar Etzion bloc. This time the attack succeeded. The slaughter by the Arabs of the Jews was horrific. Almost all the defenders were killed. Those few who were taken prisoner were sent across the sanctified river to Transjordan under Legion auspices. They were released at the end of the war, a few months hence.

14.5.48. On the same day as the Jewish prisoners were being transported across the Jordan General Sir Alan Cunningham left Jerusalem in a bullet-proof Daimler, used by King George VI during the War, and lent by him to the High Commissioner. He, in turn, passed it on for a short while to General Sir Gordon MacMillan. The Highland Light Infantry provided the guard of honour. Palestine Police outriders escorted him to Kalandia airstrip, as did the Life Guards in armoured cars. Overhead was the Royal Air Force, in one of whose planes he was flown to Haifa. I wrote home: "*Today the High Commissioner embarked in one of the ships belonging to the Mediterranean Fleet* (HMS Euryalus). *The Royal Navy fired a salute. The King's Company Grenadiers were the guard of honour. The Irish Guards provided pipers. The Royal Air Force flew overhead. So ended the British Mandate over Palestine – or rather it will at midnight.*"

Meanwhile, it was a busy day in the office and in the docks. We were hardly concerned with the ceremonies, other than having organized them. In the evening I had a drink with Rachel Saphir and Fay Rachman. Whatever Rachel's role had been in the past, her mission was finished and maybe, or maybe not, accomplished. Within a few hours she was about to become a citizen of a new state, exchanging, if she wished, her British passport for an Israeli one, the name of the country only being revealed at 1600 in Tel Aviv.

I felt it diplomatic to leave my friends to celebrate their new dawn at midnight. I returned to the mess, at the entrance of which the mezuzah or piece of parchment inscribed with scriptural passages remained fixed to the doorpost, respected or unnoticed. In six weeks the house would be returned to its rightful owners and de-requisitioned.

Our discussions over dinner were detached, in so far as we

touched at all upon the subject matter of the Mandate's end. As soldiers, the operation for us was completed, although there was still a considerable amount of work involved in evacuating men, stores and equipment. The political factors and the origins of the fiasco had been discussed in the past *ad nauseam*. There was nothing more to say; the harvest of tares and turnips was being reaped by those who followed the sowers who had scattered their seed with abandon thirty years earlier.

As for the future, we were not haruspices; there were no entrails we wished to examine, nor would we have divined much had we done so. Perhaps our personal thoughts, unexpressed, reflected the fact we seemed to have survived the relatively unimportant and minor perils of running Palestine, with due respect to those who fell, in comparison to those of fighting the War, with memories of enemy shells and mortars exploding in our midst, the disturbing cry of "stretcher bearers!", the staccato bursts of machine-gun fire and the crack-thump of small arms.

We may have remembered, too, the eerie silence of patrols between the lines, so often mined by our opponents, whose diligence in such matters we never doubted; the air raids and the more direct menace of dive bombing; all the wearing tautness of war, which stretched the nerves and tore the flesh, and which not all our compatriots and comrades either in the War or in Palestine had survived. Nor, to date, in Palestine had thousands of Jews and Arabs: the price of Zionism in human lives was becoming high and would, we reckoned, continue to rise. This was not, of course, a prophecy, only a logical conclusion.

CHAPTER FIFTEEN

Israel Fights for its Existence

David Ben-Gurion had been in the convoy of 350 vehicles bound for Jerusalem on 20 April which the Arabs, with only limited success, ambushed en route. He then returned to Tel Aviv and convened the National Council of Thirteen which he had created to replace the Jewish Agency Executive. The question which faced them on 12 May was whether to declare independence or not in two days' time. They decided to do so.

14.5.48. On the day and at the time the High Commissioner went on board HMS *Euryalus* and the Jewish prisoners were crossing the Jordan Ben-Gurion entered the Tel Aviv museum in Rothschild Boulevard and stated, "I hereby proclaim the establishment of the Jewish State in Palestine, to be called the State of Israel." Chaim Weizmann was named as president and Ben-Gurion the prime minister and minister of defence.

The Jewish State *in* Palestine, thirty years and six months after the Balfour Declaration, used the same terminology as its forerunner: "the establishment *in* Palestine of a national home for the Jewish people". Half a loaf had been attained. The Arabs were now determined to devour it, even at the risk of indigestion.

14.5.48. King Abdullah authorized the Arab Legion to enter the Old City of Jerusalem. The Egyptian air force mistakenly shot up the Life Guards as they moved in convoy across the Sinai. In a more serious error – for them – they attacked the RAF on the ground at Ramat David. Not so many of the Egyptian pilots lived to return to base once the RAF took to the air. The Life Guards suffered only light casualties.

On the same day the GOC Palestine, Lieutenant-General Sir Gordon MacMillan, with his chief of staff, Brigadier J.M. Kirkman, were preparing to leave. The general, nonetheless, read a proclamation in the Town Hall, Haifa, to Jewish leaders and those of the Arabs who had not fled. He hoped for peace; we were there to evacuate our equipment and would then leave. The 1st Battalion Grenadiers provided a guard of honour; there were no incidents.

15.5.48. On the first day of Israeli Independence the Egyptian army advanced in a two-pronged attack sixty miles south of Tel Aviv and 115 miles south of Haifa, first along the coast, where they soon occupied Gaza, Ashkelon, Ashdod and Yavneh, 12½ miles south of Tel Aviv, taking Jewish settlements on their way; secondly via Beersheba, towards Hebron, later reaching southern Jerusalem, including the kibbutz of Ramat-Rahel.

The Jordanians and Iraqis took the West Bank and the Jordanians occupied Lydda (Lod) which had been allotted to the Arabs under the Partition. It was only 6½ miles from Tel Aviv. They also took the Jewish settlements north-east and south of Jerusalem. The Iraqis, further north, awfully near to Radi Bey Nabolsi's orange groves, tried to cut the Haifa-Tel Aviv road, but failed.

The Syrians invaded south of the Sea of Galilee and attacked the kibbutz of Degania, but this also failed. Meanwhile, the Lebanese and Fawzi el-Kaoukji's Arab Liberation Army occupied west central Galilee, including Nazareth, the largely Christian Arab town where 1st Guards Brigade had spent several months. Much had happened since, and with the departure of the High Commissioner, the GOC Palestine, the officers commanding North Palestine District, North Sector and 1st Division Headquarters, 1st Guards Brigade Group in Haifa were left as the rearguard to evacuate the remaining stores and themselves within reasonable time.

On the second day of this unfolding drama Israel may have been fighting for its life, but the British Army had withdrawn from all involvement and my diary records: "*Entertained Chief Broadcasting Officer in the Middle East*". Presumably he had come to collect our friend down the road, who polished his shoes for the second time. As far as I know he embarked with his kit and sailed to wherever he was bound.

Andrew Gibson-Watt, as I have mentioned earlier, was much engaged with those who disposed of kit which did not belong to them. There was, nevertheless, an authorized motorcar and jeep dump. My first visit on 11 May is marked in my diary as being "*rather fruitless*". My intention had been to buy a jeep. Quite obviously, my uniform and naivety told against me; better prices could be obtained elsewhere. In fact, if I recall correctly, I was told blandly there was nothing available. Here, the RAOC officer concerned went too far. I thanked him, made one or two enquiries, and acquired one, either for nothing or a nominal sum. I obtained a British licence in Tripoli and sold it to my friend and predecessor in the Irish Guards, Micky Boyd – who had been joined by his wife and two-year-old son – for £25, when I left. (Micky later retired from his Regiment, farmed in Ireland, then joined the Oman Scouts. He was gored and drowned while shooting wild boar and duck in the Iraqi marshes.)

Michael Gordon-Watson was more ambitious; he obtained a large motorcar. He neglected, however, to look after the dockers. After the flight of the Arabs these were Jews. The car was lifted majestically from the quayside. Michael watched with some well earned, and presumably well spent, satisfaction. It was swung high in the air, lowered gently and exactly over and above the deck of the ship. It was then, as accidents can happen, dropped twenty feet. The Royal Marine Commandos were guarding the docks, but dockers who dropped motorcars on decks inadvertently were not within their control. The vehicle was a write-off.

On 19 May Moshe Carmel, the Haganah commander in the north, attacked Acre. The capture of the police station lowered Arab morale, always mercurial, who surrendered the following day. Further north, Nahariya had been allotted to the Arabs under Partition. The mayor reminded Carmel and his successor, Mordechai Makleff, of this fact and formally asked them to annex the town to the Jewish State of Israel. They obliged.

British Intelligence estimated at this point, accurately, that the Jews had a force of 30,000 Haganah, including 3000 Palmach assault troops. There were also many thousands of back-up para-military settlers in the kibbutzim, plus around 3000 ill-disciplined and virtually untrained terrorists within the Stern and Irgun milieux which were being integrated, with considerable agony, into the Israeli army.

In Haifa, meanwhile, John Chandos-Pole was recovering from his bullet wound in the arm, but an Arab sniper had earlier shot Guardsman Porter, and the same 1st Battalion Coldstream lost one other, Guardsman Bissex, from drowning. We normally bathed off Athlit, but the Palestine coast was treacherous and had to be watched for undercurrents. Some beaches were safe; others, adjoining, were not.

In Peninsular Barracks the Coldstream stationed there were taking it in turn to do company duty in the town, which after the Arab defeat was considered safe, except for the menace of rogue terrorism from either community. There was a cinema for all ranks, otherwise entertainment for the officers was largely restricted to dining in each others' messes. It seems I once gave a memorable cocktail party on our balcony. Compared, I suppose, to the heat and asphalt of the town, the view from Carmel, a soft breeze and strong drink made a pleasing contrast.

Cocktail parties were in abeyance, as far as David Ben-Gurion was concerned. Israel's prime minister and minister of defence had to face the military realities on the ground and do something effective or else be pushed into the water. The strategic options open to him and his commanders – now controlling nine Brigades with a nominal strength of 2750 each, plus a reserve – was either to hold on to every scrap of land they possessed, which meant their forces being dispersed, or to concentrate their strength along the coastal strip and retain a foothold in Jerusalem, forcing a corridor of communication.

In fact he accepted the status quo as he found it on 15 May. The Kefar Etzion loss was a bitter blow and there could well be more, but the Beisan Valley, near Afula, was secure and the road network in the Negev, which linked some 27 settlements, was more or less open. The Jewish area of Jerusalem was holding. He considered the Egyptians would make initial progress, but the forces to be challenged and defeated had to be the Arab Legion, the most professional and well led of his opponents.

In practice, the correct strategic decision to destroy the enemy's forces on the ground, as distinct from capturing territory, began badly and may be summed up in one word: Latrun. This was an Arab village, said to have been the home of the Good Thief, crucified with Christ – "Verily, I say unto thee, today shalt thou be with me in paradise" – and was certainly the temporary home of the not so good terrorist detainees during the Mandate.

It lay amid the hills dominating the Tel Aviv-Jerusalem road, where another road forks off to Ramallah, which in turn lay on the northern Transjordan-Jerusalem supply route. Latrun dominated the Valley of Ayalon and had been the scene of many battles from those of Joshua, David, the Philistines, Crusaders and Saracens. A Crusader castle was still there, its ruins standing starkly against the skyline. More to the point, the British had built a solid, stone-walled police station on the western ridge.

A further stone artillery bastion, Gun Hill, 1300 feet up, was on the eastern side. In addition there were strongpoints and connecting trenches near the Trappist monastery and the Arab village lying close to the fortress.

Reinforcing his aim of destroying some of the enemy forces, Ben-Gurion also insisted that Latrun must be taken to clear the road to Jerusalem and relieve the Jews besieged in the New City. It would then forestall a link up between the Arab Legion and the Egyptian army pushing up from the south.

25.5.48. Latrun was defended by two battalions of Arab Legion. Their supporting weapons were 2" and 3" mortars, as well as 6-pounder and 25-pounder artillery. The first Jewish attack by a quickly assembled 7th Brigade of recently arrived immigrants, with no supporting fire, was a failure with 140 dead.

On the other hand it had drawn off Legion units from attacking Jerusalem, but this had not been the primary objective. Ben-Gurion then appointed Brigadier General Michael David Marcus, known as Stone to conceal his American identity, to command three brigades and select whom he wished for the second attack which was to be, like the first, a frontal assault, but backed by armoured cars and half-tracks.

On 30 May Jewish assault troops blew open the gate leading to the Latrun police station and entered the courtyard. They were not, however, backed up. New recruits in an infantry battalion were badly led, failed to attain their objectives, and in playing safe, lost only two men. Other sectors involved lost men but did not gain ground. It was the second failure.

Meanwhile, up to a point, out of these setbacks there came a certain amount of progress for the Israelis. The two Arab Legion battalions centred on Latrun were also spread out along a 70-mile front and had suffered casualties – around 20% of their strength, enough to dampen enthusiasm for the war in Amman, although not with the military. The Jordanians would require a third battalion to stop or disrupt work on the second positive point – the construction of a secondary road to Jerusalem.

On the day after the second failure at Latrun senior Jewish officers investigated the possibility of building a nine-mile road south of the bastion from Deir Muchsen via Beitz Jiz, Beit Susin and Beit Mahzin, joining the Jerusalem road at Saris. It was completed in five days. Wire netting was ground into the surface and at one point there was a drop of 400 feet into the wadi below. This required very careful driving. The Arab Legion were aware of this undertaking – known as the Burmah Road – but had not the men on the ground to stop it.

On 11 June the American Jewish commander, Marcus, was shot stone dead by one of his own sentries when he failed to answer the challenge and give the password – in Hebrew. Marcus/Stone was in his underclothes, wrapped in a blanket, and had probably been relieving himself, outside the camp perimeter. He had been drinking fairly heavily before going to bed. The sentry was totally exonerated. It was probably a mistake on Ben-Gurion's part to have taken him on. Few Israelis held him professionally in much esteem.

On the day of his death a ceasefire was arranged by the United

Nations, brokered by Count Folke Bernadotte of Sweden, between the Arab armies and the Jews. An obvious breathing space was accorded the Jews, allowing time to build up reinforcements and obtain heavier weapons. On the other hand, ostensibly it appeared that the Arabs were winning the war. The Egyptians had occupied parts of the Negev and both the Jordanians and the Egyptians were within a day's march of Tel Aviv.

The occupation of land, as already mentioned, was not the only factor involved in war. On the Arab side there was now a crucial ammunition shortage; the United Arab Command had collapsed from discord and heatstroke in Damascus; the Jordanians and the Egyptians were now bogged down, unable to advance for a variety of reasons; while the Iraqis marked time on their large front, not wishing to push beyond Jenin, a wish with which the Israelis concurred. Fawzi Bey passed the time in Nazareth. The Syrians alone were keen to continue.

Also on 11 June two events occurred which affected both sides of the conflict. In Amman Glubb Pasha was informed by the Jordanian prime minister, Tawfiq Pasha that there would be no more war and no money for new recruits to replace Legion casualties. Two shiploads of arms bound for Amman had been pirated by the Egyptians and sold to the highest bidders. Thus, effectively, in one month the combined strength – the test of strength as the Secretary General of the Arab League had called it in London – of the invading forces had failed to crush the Israelis.

These forces numbered 10,000 Egyptians, 4500 Jordanians, 3000 Iraqis, 3000 Syrians, 2000 Arab Liberation Volunteers, 1000 Lebanese, and 500 Saudis. Thus, despite a combined Arab population of 40 million, only 0.06% – 24,000 men – turned out to attack.

The second event took place nearly 1900 miles away by sea, on the French Mediterranean coast at Port au Bouc. There the LST *Altalena* weighed anchor with the acquiescence of the French government and set sail for Israel. On board were 5000 rifles, 300 Bren guns, 150 Spandaus, 5 armoured cars, 4 million rounds of ammunition and 900 recruits for the Irgun Zvai Leumi, whose adherents, other than those in Jerusalem, had with difficulty been integrated into the Israeli army.

Ben-Gurion had no time and less need for private armies. He also detested Menachem Begin who now had two new enemies: the Israeli government and the United Nations observers supervising the truce which forbade the delivery of arms to any of the belligerents. Ben-Gurion wished – and had – to break the ban discreetly and at night.

Meanwhile, the BBC announced the departure of the *Altalena*, giving details of its crew, cargo and passenger list.

15.6.48. "Say goodbye to Rachel Saphir, Fay Rachman and my friends the Shapiros." Regardless of the traumas and tragedies of the past two and a half years, I was very sorry to leave, not least because day-to-day living conditions had changed dramatically. Canvas tents and roadside bombs and the blowing up of buildings were now in the past, and the last months in Haifa had been both busy and relaxing, thanks to the absence of conflict and terrorism. My requisitioned room and balcony, facing due west, enabled me to observe that only 25 seconds elapsed between the sun touching the visible horizon and then sinking beyond our sight. Conflict may be prolonged in the region, but dawn and dusk were not.

16.6.48. "Lewis and I exceptionally busy in the docks. LST Messina *taking Brigade Headquarters transport and equipment to Tripoli."* It was also taking me. At the last minute George Johnson ordered the officers' mess 3-tonner to be loaded. This caused problems – until dawn the following day. Other vehicles had to be manoeuvred within the extremely restricted confines of the already tightly packed tank or vehicle deck.

On board, when Lewis and I arrived at dusk, were the Captain – we shall call him Lieutenant-Commander Thomas RNVR – the First Lieutenant, Michael Barker RN, and his Number Two, Lieutenant John Gordon-Nixon RN. There were also two RAOC officers. Lewis appointed me Officer Commanding Troops. The Captain later invited me to join him in his cabin for a glass of whisky. He observed I was in the Welsh Guards and mentioned he came from Cardiff, the capital of the Principality, he added.

The escape of water as the motive force for measuring time was replaced on board the LST *Messina* by the whisky bottle. By dawn its contents had escaped down our throats – certainly more down the Captain's than mine – and, after inspecting the men's quarters, I spent most of the night, at my host's behest, in his cabin, listening to his life in the Merchant and Royal Navies. The point being that the ship could not sail until the 3-ton truck had been accommodated and the bow doors closed.

At 0700, after what some call a white night – no bed and no sleep – I joined John Gordon-Nixon, who was standing on deck, immediately above the bow doors. He was leaning over, speaking on his intercom, having just reported his part of the ship ready for sea, although, in fact, the doors were not quite closed. Nevertheless, we could proceed. The Captain was presumed to be on the bridge, conning the ship. Physically this was correct.

He gave order to let go. We went astern for a short distance in preparation for leaving harbour. The ship then suddenly vibrated with noticeable force in response to his order, "Full ahead!" I was a few paces behind John Gordon-Nixon whence it soon became obvious we were not heading for the gap between the harbour walls, but rather towards Pross' restaurant, via the jetty.

As the ship gathered speed it became even more evident that this was not a sophisticated naval ploy being executed with skill and aplomb, but a potential disaster in which the men's breakfasts being prepared below could well, for some, be their last. I felt it was a bad start for inter-service relations to point out to the Number Two that we were heading fast for the harbour wall. In any case, by the time I had said it, he would have been hurled overboard, with me close behind.

I stepped forward and coughed loudly in his ear. He was startled, looked up, saw the wall was now within yards of the ship, and screamed into the intercom, "Full astern! Port 30!" His orders were executed immediately, a remarkable tribute to naval training and discipline. The ship shuddered and swung to port. Seconds afterwards we felt and heard the starboard side of the ship scraping the wall, making a harsh grinding noise, as well as shaking all and everything on board.

The LST then lay stopped for inspection. A twenty-five foot gash had been torn in the side, only just above the water line. It was considered safe to proceed, not least because the ship was compartmentalized. Once more we let go, at 0730, and, after we were safely through the gap in the harbour wall, we went ahead for our destination in North Africa which we reached after six and a half days at sea. Our speed was much reduced to avoid taking in water.

The rhumb line distance is about 1300 miles, the equivalent to 1130 sea miles in 156 hours, an average speed of 7½ knots. We would not have won the Haifa Cup, but at least we were not paddling. On arrival the RAOC officers on board kindly offered the services of the RAOC workshops; they would repair the damage. This combined operation was less successful, although they did a superb job. Paint work matched and the steel work was impeccable.

The ship, however, after returning again to Haifa to embark the rearguard of 1st Guards Brigade Group, had hardly passed the entrance to Valetta harbour when the Dockyard shipwrights noticed the riveting: "That's Pongo (Army) work!" Naval rivets were hammered in a different pattern. A court of enquiry followed automatically. The inevitable outcome was, nevertheless, better than it would have been had the Captain conned his ship head-on into the harbour wall.

Indeed, if the formula *mass x whisky* = *collision* be accepted as correct, then this Captain's cough saved considerable damage being done to the ship, and may also have saved lives. Meanwhile, as I had had problems with an outgoing ship, the Prime Minister of Israel was soon to have far greater problems with an LST coming in – the aforementioned *Altalena* and its sponsors. In this case there were casualties: Jew killing Jew.

CHAPTER SIXTEEN

Guards leave. Israel Survives.
Bernadotte Shot.

The LST *Altalena*, sailing in the opposite direction to that of the LST *Messina*, was nearing Israeli waters when David Ben-Gurion was informed of its approach, and Begin's demanding 20% of the cargo for his men in Jerusalem, and that it land in Tel Aviv.

18.6.48. Ben-Gurion ordered the arms to be unloaded at Kefar Vitkin, near Nathanya, a place offering solid support for the prime minister. Irgun then demanded the arms be stored in their warehouses. The next day the *Altalena* was told to land at Kefar Vitkin at night. Some of the arms were unloaded. The ship then lay offshore, some fifty miles from the coast during the day.

On 20 June the LST returned to unload after dark. Meanwhile Ben-Gurion had ordered 600 soldiers to surround the area and contain the Irgun gang inside it. In the early hours of 21 June the Irgun man in charge, Faglin, the principal co-murderer of the two sergeants, on hearing of the Haganah presence, ordered the arms to be reloaded with a view to unloading them at Tel Aviv.

Begin was on board the LST and relieved Faglin of his command. The Haganah then delivered an ultimatum: hand over all arms or face the consequences. At 1800 they opened fire. Begin, shouting and kicking, was dragged on board by the captain and the *Altalena* headed for Tel Aviv. At this moment two Israeli corvettes intervened and they, in turn, opened fire. This was returned. The LST was, however, able to make Tel Aviv harbour, with casualties on board. There, near to shore, it became wedged on a submerged wreck.

22.6.48. Ben-Gurion, faced with an Irgun rebellion led by Begin, with Faglin on shore ready to shoot his way to power and oust Ben-Gurion if necessary, ordered Tel Aviv harbour to be surrounded. In the ensuing fight six Irgun members were killed and eighteen wounded. The Haganah lost two dead and six wounded. There were then more casualties when Haganah opened fire on the motor-boat, landing weapons; and also on the LST *Altalena*.

At 1600 the ship was shelled and Begin, this time, was thrown overboard by the obliging captain, who then jumped. There were now 83 Irgun casualties, including fourteen dead. Ben-Gurion ordered the arrest of all the Irgun gang who could be found. Not for the first time Begin went into hiding. Under a 1948 Israeli law, emulating the British, the IZL/Irgun were proscribed as terrorists and branded by their own compatriots as criminals.

A week later, 55 miles further north in Haifa, on 29 June, thirty-five hours before 1st Guards Brigade Group left Palestine, there was a degree of drama. I quote from the 1st Battalion Grenadier Guards Quarterly report, signed by the senior major, Pat Robertson :

> "At 0130 hours, three tanks were started up simultaneously and within seconds dashed across the (Haifa) airfield (guarded by King's Company, under the command of Major Alec Gregory-Hood) and broke through the fence at the north-eastern side. All the tanks had been demobilised, as usual, the previous evening. On investigation the remaining (fourth) tank proved to be re-mobilised, and it is presumed attempts were made to make off with all four tanks.
> "The tanks were not followed beyond the perimeter wire, as the remaining tank could not have operated in the dark. Local recce patrols were sent out at once and a force would follow the tank tracks at first light. One tank was recovered, having skidded off the road. It appeared the two sentries of the 4th/7th Royal Dragoon Guards deserted with their tanks and invited one Jew in to take the third. He was apparently inexperienced."

The report further states that the Commanding Officer, Colonel Peter Deakin, asked for air action at first light. This was decided against. The rocket firing Sea Fires from HMS *Ocean* might attack the pursuit force in error, known as friendly fire. At 0530 a troop of the 4th/7th arrived at the airport from Peninsular Barracks. They began the pursuit under the command of the Commanding Officer and the commander of King's Company.

The tracks were followed north to Qiryat Motzkin. There they turned east and joined the Afula road. The pursuit continued for two miles but was called off. The Air OP reported the tracks had joined the main route south at Zikhron Ya'aqov; also the pursuit force was going outside the enclave established by 1st Guards Brigade Group. Further action was left to the RAF, but the tank tracks were lost on the outskirts of Tel Aviv. The average speed of the tanks must have been around 16 mph.

Sergeants Michael Flanagan and Harry MacDonald, according to their account recorded in *Genesis 1948*, had been engaged in flogging equipment and petrol to Haganah agents since their arrival in Haifa. It was the job of Haganah to encourage them. It was the duty of both NCOs to fall into as little temptation as possible. Sadly, they fell for it, hook, line and tank. The operation, however, as indicated by the Grenadier Report, was only 50% successful: Haganah wanted four tanks, but there were only two miserable deserters and, thus, only two tank drivers. The NCOs did not risk trying to suborn their colleagues.

Consequently Flanagan and MacDonald set about instructing two Israeli drivers. The intricacies of driving a Cromwell tank, however, are not so easily assimilated by using bar furniture as a substitute for the interior mechanism, no matter how often the furniture be arranged and re-arranged in the backroom placed at their disposal. Undaunted, five men were squeezed into a small aircraft which landed at Haifa airport. Two men emerged. Their papers were in order. The plane was not searched. Three men remained on board.

At midnight the sergeants are quoted as saying they used their seniority as NCOs to take over guard duty: "Everyone should do a stint". Or it may have been their turn, although unusual for two sergeants to be on guard duty at the same time. Either way, as confirmed by the Grenadier report, at 0130 they started up the tanks and crashed out of camp. According to the account in *Genesis*, two of the three men hiding in the aeroplane were postgraduates of the backroom, bar furniture school for driving tanks. The third was detailed to cover them.

Neither would-be driver distinguished himself. The first could not find the ignition switch, considered in all schools of driving to be a basic factor. The second, obviously a muscular member of Haganah, overcame the first hurdle but managed to break the gear handle. The tank slewed off the road where it was found by the Grenadier patrol. All three Jews involved escaped.

At dawn, four hours after the deserters absconded, which gave them sufficient time to reach Tel Aviv, the Royal Navy, Royal Artillery and the RAF were all on stand-by to shoot. At 1st Guards Brigade, the GIII, Nigel Kearsley, Welsh Guards, went up in an Air OP spotter plane which found the tracks twenty miles south at Zikhron Ya'aqov. The aerobatics involved did not improve his eyesight, but the pilot's observations were accurate.

Flanagan and MacDonald were required to fight. They and their tanks joined the Commando Battalion of 8th Armoured Brigade, the nucleus of the Israeli Armoured Corps. Flanagan married an Israeli called Ruth. They retired to a kibbutz. These two deserters were joined by two others: Sergeant-Major Desmond Rutledge had met Miriam, a Yemeni serving in the sergeants' mess. Love, in this case, was the initial motivation. He later changed his name to Zvi Rimer and became a professional in the Israeli Defence Force. Rutledge was joined by Sergeant "Tex" Stern. They were both stationed at Tel Hashomer, just outside Tel Aviv. Sergeant Stern was relieved of his armoured car. The Jews who took it suggested he might like to join them. He did.

There were, of course, courts of enquiry. No one jumps for joy under such circumstances. The commanding officer of the 4th/7th RDG, although in Tripoli at the time, felt it was a matter of regimental honour to resign. Luckily for the Grenadiers, the provenance of the two Jewish drivers was not questioned and the matter of guard duty is not within the author's capabilities to judge.

The Grenadiers could not be blamed for the desertion and treachery within the perimeter of their responsibilities. Alec Gregory-Hood was later promoted to Lieutenant-Colonel and commanded a Grenadier battalion. Peter Deakin became a Major-General. Of course, if the tank keys were kept in the guardroom, then there was yet another reason for the deserters to "do their stint". Yet, they could well have had them copied.

The day following the events described above 1st Guards Brigade Group embarked in a military exercise, as distinct from anything remotely ceremonial, on board LSTs moored alongside the quays in Haifa harbour. The Royal Navy was lying offshore. At 12.38 the Union Jack flying over Haifa dock was lowered. Some thirty years earlier the first British troops had arrived under Allenby's command. A glorious military victory had been turned immediately into an inglorious political mess, certainly for the British.

The Arabs were profoundly affected, and the Israelis were by no means assured of an enlightened future – *beulah* in Hebrew: land of rest and peace. Eleven days later, however, what might also have been a disastrous political and military mess for Ben-Gurion and his compatriots was turned into near victory, for which he deserves full credit.

11.7.48. Under Ben-Gurion's direction, the Israelis attacked on the central and northern fronts. Heavy weapons had been brought in at night during the truce, recruits had been given rudimentary training and within ten days Lydda and Ramleh had been taken and the roads to Jerusalem were reopened. Western Galilee was conquered, while the Lebanese and Arab Liberation Army under Fawzi el-Kaoukji lost ground. The Jordanians, however, still clung to Latrun, but the Jews were closing in.

In the south the Egyptians attacked in the Negev, but, despite superior weapons and a numerical superiority, their attack on their principal objective, Negba, failed. The Jews then counter-attacked, taking the Arab village of Karatiya which lay on the east-west road from the coast to Hebron. The assault was led by Moshe Dayan's 89th Commando Battalion. Then, at 1745 on 18 July, a second ceasefire came into effect and Count Folke Bernadotte, based in his United Nations headquarters on the island of Rhodes, prepared to visit the area,

The basic mistake, on a personal level, which Count Bernadotte made in acting for the UN peacekeeping mission in Palestine was to become involved in the first place. It was no job for a gentleman. As the British, who had created the problem in 1917, learnt to their cost, no proposition could or would satisfy both sides, and many propositions had proved to be particularly lethal. Bernadotte's ideas of a neutral, internationalized Jerusalem, and the Negev in Arab – i.e. British – hands in exchange for all of Galilee, was anathema to Jews, whose extremists decided he had signed his own death warrant.

The same Stern gang triumvirate who sat in judgement on Lord Moyne, and killed him, now reassembled and passed sentence of death on the ill-meaning, in their eyes, and unwelcome Swede, who personified an unpardonable intrusion, at the highest international level, into the realm of their temporal and religious ambitions. The Central Committee of the Stern gang met in Tel Aviv.

10.9.48. Present were Israel Sheib, Nathan Friedman-Yellin and Yitzhak Yizernitzky (Shamir) recently released from not exactly arduous imprisonment in Eritrea, although he might have done better in the alternative paradisiac prison in the Seychelles. Their philosophy in killing this man was that they could change the course of history. It was, in fact, a philosophy inapplicable to any of their murders. In this case, details were left to Sheib, in command of the Jerusalem branch of the gang, and his chief executioner, Yehoshua Zetler.

19.9.48 A week after the Stern Central Committee had decided to kill Count Folke Bernadotte the UN mediator himself landed at Kalandia from Damascus. Escorted by an armoured car, he drove with his compatriot and chief of staff, General Aage Lundstrom, to

Jerusalem. The party had a scheduled meeting in the afternoon with Dov Joseph, the Jewish Military Governor of the New City, under David Shaltiel, the Haganah commander.

After lunch at the YWCA in the Jewish sector, Bernadotte, Lundstrom and Colonel Serot, chief United Nations observer in Jerusalem, with others, crossed the neutral Red Cross zone to look at the former British Government House, as a possible UN head-quarters. They then visited the Jewish Agricultural School and started on their way back to UN observer headquarters at the YWCA.

Meanwhile, the Stern gang, who had dumped barrels and boulders by the side of the routes along which Bernadotte might travel and which could quickly be turned into semi-road blocks, were losing the scent of their quarry, after the meeting with Dov Joseph at 1630 had been put back two hours to 1830. They began to quarrel. Stanley Goldfoot, a South African Jew, and an ardent adherent of apartheid, accused Zetler of bungling. He then drove to the Jewish press office where he heard, surreptitiously, by putting his ear to the deserted press office door – it was a Friday, eve of the Sabbath – an amplifier announcement that Bernadotte would cross into the New City around 1700 by a route near the Stern gang base.

Soon afterwards four men in a jeep, dressed in khaki, erected a barricade which would allow single-line traffic, but could be blocked by a vehicle. Zetler and Goldfoot watched from the sidelines. Zetler's deputy, Joshua Cohen, was detailed to be the principal hit man. The four men, in the meantime, stayed in their jeep.

Just before 1700 the three-car convoy returned to the New City. The neutral zone was crossed quickly. It then passed two Israeli checkpoints, the second being in the Katamon Quarter. At 1703 the convoy was forced to stop at a barrier where a jeep driver, with three other men aboard, was trying inexpertly to turn his vehicle around. A Jewish liaison officer, Captain Hillman, shouted in Hebrew that it was a United Nations convoy and was to be let through.

Three men then approached: Joshua Cohen on the left, his two fellow assassins on the right. They walked slowly at first towards the rear vehicle where Count Bernadotte, General Lundstrom and Colonel Serot were sitting in the back seat. The two men on the right continued to saunter, but Cohen ran past the first two vehicles and peered through the open rear window of the last car.

The occupants reached for their passes – they were unarmed at the wish of the principal victim – but these were not required. Cohen fired a short burst at point blank range. Count Bernadotte was killed instantly and either Cohen or his co-killers shot Colonel Serot, they said later by mistake. Lundstrom, sitting in the middle, was unscathed. The hit men then backed away, shooting at the tyres and radiators.

The two men on the right jumped into the jeep, which raced off, leaving Cohen to fend for himself. Colonel Begley, the United Nations security chief, tried to grab him, but was badly burnt in the face by a gun flash. Cohen fled on foot and escaped. Colonel Begley's injuries were better than being killed; but in terms of security, his unarmed escort – largely at Bernadotte's insistence – and his restricted but overheard broadcast of the UN mediator's movements did not place his organization too high in the professional ratings for his job.

The announcement in Tel Aviv that the assassination was the work of the "Fatherland Front" did not deceive anyone, and certainly not David Ben-Gurion. He ordered the immediate arrest of all known members of the Stern gang, proscribed their organization, as he had done with Irgun, imprisoned them and charged some, but released them a year later. *De facto*, it became a matter of *nolle prosequi*. Friedman-Yellin was elected to the first Israeli Knesset in 1949. Yizernitzky (Shamir) postponed his joining for a decade, having had his undoubted flair for cold blooded mayhem recognized by Mossad, the Israeli intelligence arm.

Dean Rusk, speaking on behalf of the United States government, immediately demanded assurances that the Israeli government was more than a junta and that it could rule the country, bringing to justice those of its electorate who perpetrated such crimes. Ben-Gurion, serious and furious at first, initially went through the motions. But he had other matters, military matters, on his mind.

He had, equally, no intention of allowing the Bernadotte Plan of a neutralized Jerusalem and a nominally Arab Negev, with all Galilee as compensation, to be implemented. Thus, in no way was the course of history diverted by the bullets pumped into Bernadotte's chest. Had he lived, the path of events in Palestine, as Ben-Gurion intended, would have dictated, and did dictate, the course of history.

In the interval afforded him by the three-month truce Ben-Gurion organized the now nascent Israeli Defence Force into four commands: Jerusalem and its route to the sea, south, centre and north. Palmach as an independent formation was dissolved, as had been Irgun and Stern, under very different circumstances. Ranks in the defence Force were clearly defined. The chief of staff was to be a brigadier, commanders of the four fronts were colonels, brigade commanders were lieutenant-colonels.

There was no inflation, such as generals galore, except in numerical strength and equipment: an army of 50,000 men at the start of the first truce was increased to 90,000. Immigrants from Europe and Cyprus plus oversea volunteers swelled the ranks. Armaments had poured in from Czechoslovakia and other sources, mostly during the night, despite the UN ban. The Arabs, on the other hand, had not replenished their arsenals.

Meanwhile, in the Negev Egyptian breaches of the truce were providing an excuse for the Israelis to attack. It was particularly important that the principle of possession being nine-tenths of the law be employed, otherwise the so far aborted Bernadotte ideas at the United Nations might still be applied. The State Department continued to waver, and the British remained keen to obtain the Negev through Jordanian proxy.

15.10.48. The ceasefire ended. Beersheba was taken. The seige of the Negev was broken. A week later, on 22 October, another truce with Egypt was declared, but Fawzi el-Kaoukji's forces attacked in Galilee. The Israelis responded with a four-brigade counter-attack. Eight days later, on 30 October, Fawzi Bey put on his running shoes. He and his Arab Liberation Army were driven out of Galilee into the Lebanon and Syria. Fawzi Bey ended his days in Beirut.

Six weeks later, on 14 December, David Ben-Gurion and the Israeli government moved to Jerusalem, thus *de facto*, ignoring the United Nations' proposal that the city be internationalized. The New City alone was in Jewish hands. The Old City was a Jordanian possession, as was Latrun and the West Bank. The situation in the Negev was still, however, not wholly resolved.

On 25 December, with a view to settling the matter in the south, the Israeli Christmas present to the Egyptians was to send them home by force. Soon they were driven out of the Negev entirely. A few remained in the Gaza strip. A third Egyptian army was trapped and the Egyptians asked the UN to arrange a final ceasefire. Before Israel agreed, its Defence Force took the remaining areas of the Negev, including Eilat, on the Gulf of Aqaba. Soon afterwards Lebanon, Syria and Jordan also requested a ceasefire.

Unquestionably this was a most remarkable achievement, both in terms of courageous military skill and indomitable morale, to which post-Mandate terrorism had contributed not one iota. The 1948 war was the longest of the Arab-Israeli conflicts, the remainder lying in the future. One per cent of the Yishuv, 6000 Jews, were killed. Some 4000 were wounded. These figures may be compared with a loss of 800 in the 1967 Six Day War out of a population of 2.5 million.

On the Arab side casualty figures may be described as high. In terms of Palestinians, 58% of the total Arab population fled after Deir Yassin, namely 700,000 people. Some 200,000, however, remained in the State of Israel.

Alone of the Arab lands, Palestinians regarded and regard themselves as being robbed of their promised independence after the First World War. Worse was to follow in 1948. In attacking the British-placed cuckoo in their nest, as they perceived it, they lost their nest. More than half of them fled; they and their descendants still living in camps, 338,000 in the Lebanon alone, their homes occupied by permanent squatters, their land and livings sequestered; deprived of their birthright, all have been either displaced, subjected or absorbed, in the name of a religious tenet to which, in no way whatsoever, do they subscribe.

Now, nearing fifty years after Israeli independence, both Jew and Arab may well ask one another "*Quo vadis?*" Or, as one Welshman put it, "What is the answer? That is the question!"

Epilogue

I left Tripoli and my job as Staff Captain 1st Guards Brigade on 16 October, 1948, four months after leaving Palestine in the LST *Messina*, and just after Golda Meir and members of the Israeli diplomatic mission had returned from Moscow. Their visit had engendered a profound enthusiasm among Muscovite Jews, and a consequent disillusionment within the Politburo concerning Israel, described below. Meanwhile, my return journey to Wellington Barracks, London, to rejoin the 1st Battalion Welsh Guards, was not without its adventures.

The flight was from Tripoli to Malta, and thence to Catania, Sicily. I sat next to a former adjutant of the 1st Battalion, Coldstream Guards – in the First World War. He was then approaching 52, and died in 1993, aged 96, one of the oldest, if not the oldest, member of the House of Lords. His name was Jeffrey Amherst, whose eponymous antecedent, Governor-General of British North America and Commander-in-Chief of the British Army, gave his name to the American college to which my neighbour on this flight presented the family portraits.

We approached Catania in the midst of a particularly violent electric storm. Each flash lightened the darkness within the cabin, but without it failed to penetrate the carbon black cloud ahead of us enveloping Mount Etna. We assumed the pilot was being mindful of the mountain. Soon the plane was sucked up and down like a puppet on Jove's celestial strings and then rocked almost uncontrollably as the wings flipped, but held to the fuselage. We were grateful for that. We then landed more or less blind, it being doubtful whether Catania possessed radar.

We flew on to Rome. I stayed with my friends the Sorbellos in the country, then went to Portofino, where the Cliffords, Alex and

Jenny, whom I had met in Transjordan, had invited me to stay. The railway line between Chiávari and Rapallo, however, was cut by floods. My fellow passengers and I descended onto the track, walked in darkness through a tunnel, dangerously near collapse, and negotiated the remains of the bridge which had been washed away. On the other side our train waited.

The Cliffords' Castelletto was built on the promontory, called Il Capo, above the port. Nearby was a modest chapel where a relic of Saint George was said to be preserved. He is the patron saint of Genoa, Aragon, Portugal, Beirut, England and, as it happens, skin diseases. As well as the Castelletto, Alex also owned a long-bodied Hispano-Suiza, a magnificent model, painted yellow, beautifully designed, its bonnet hinged, its studs shining and, underneath, a powerful engine.

In late October we set forth for Paris. I was wedged in the back with the luggage. We did not go very far. The road had many bends, with alternate stretches of light and shadow. I noticed the flickering streams of burning paint above the yellow bonnet. "The car," I said quietly, "is on fire." I was disbelieved. We were then in sunlight, and drove for another hundred yards until the next stretch of shadow.

The flames were higher. We stopped. I had, meanwhile, resigned myself to a rather blazing departure from this world, perhaps saving me from a similar welcome in the next. I reckoned the fire would spread from the carburettor to the tank at the back which contained thirty gallons. I was above it. To get out probably took half a minute. It seemed like half an hour. Alex dampened the flames with his overcoat, which left the problem inside unresolved. Then, perhaps through the intervention of Saint George, help arrived.

A convoy of nine trucks came into view. They had just been offloaded at Genoa and were part of United Nations relief. All were equipped with fire extinguishers. Only one was needed. We returned to the Castelletto, but before this potentially disastrous fire had interrupted my thoughts my mind had returned to Palestine. Israel had survived its birth. This was no surprise to British soldiers who knew both sides well. Equally, it was a fact that the Mosque of al Aksa and the Dome of the Rock were no Third Temple. One of the litanies chanted at the Wailing Wall expressed and expresses this knowledge:

For the palace that lies desolate
We sit in solitude and mourn;
For the Temple that is destroyed
We sit in solitude and mourn;

For the walls that are overthrown
We sit in solitude and mourn;
For the majesty departed
We sit in solitude and mourn.

There has certainly been more tragedy than triumph in Jewish national history. The claim to be the Chosen Race and the Zionist claim to Palestine, or part of it, regardless of who may be occupying the place at the time is biblical and remains exclusively Judaic. No Jew would disagree that this sets him apart from the rest of the world, since, in his view, few have been chosen, currently around thirteen million.

Historically, in the short term, the actions of the Jewish leaders at the time of the Crucifixion – correctly fearing that rebellion against Rome would lead to the destruction of Israel – appeared prudent. Sadly, within thirty-seven years their worst fears materialized. The Diaspora followed soon afterwards, and with it two millennia of anti-Judaism, a psychological explanation of which is provided by Carl Jung, who stated that the symbol of Christ became an archetype of the collective unconscious which was inherited by all inhabitants of Christendom. In which case Christ crucified symbolized an attack upon the Self, arousing both unconscious antagonism and fear, as well as guilt. The church, until recently, did little to follow Christ's word from the Cross: "Father forgive them; for they know not what they do." The High Priest and the Sanhedrin were not going to kill the Messiah had they recognized Him. The fact that they were blind, despite the raising of Lazarus and other well-witnessed affirmations of Christ's divinity, is one of God's mysteries, prophesied by Isaiah: "He has blinded their eyes, he has hardened their heart, for fear they should see with their eyes and understand with their heart and turn to me for healing."

Outside Christendom the Moslem world, to a greater degree, is anti-Zionist and, by extension, within the ranks of fundamentalists, anti-Judaic. This inevitably affects all Jews whether they be Zionists or not, and is the sequel to the Balfour Declaration, the establishment of Israel and its consequences, which were certainly foreseen by the founders whose convictions carried them forward.

Zionism arose from the Christian-generated pogroms in Russia (a Russian word, via the Yiddish meaning destruction : po (like) + grom (thunder)) and in their authoritative book *KGB* by Christopher Andrew and Oleg Gordievsky, the authors reveal that the notorious Protocols of the Elders of Zion, purporting to describe a Jewish plot for world domination, was probably forged by Pyotr

Rachkovsky, head of the Russian Foreign Intelligence Agency in Paris from 1884-1902.

When Czar Nicholas II was informed they were a forgery, he is said to have observed, "They have fouled the pure cause of anti-semitism." Around the same time, the Czar's fellow monarch, Kaiser Wilhelm II remarked. "Jews and mosqitoes are a nuisance that humanity must be rid of. I believe the best solution would be gas." The Nazis put this odious and unregal rumination into practice. After the Dreyfus trial, Theodor Herzl convened the first Zionist conference in 1897. Is it surprising, living under such European jurisdiction, that Jews sought dignity within their own state? The problem was at whose expense, their own or somebody else's? Negotiations with the Kaiser, of all people, Abd-ul-Hamid II, the Turkish Sultan, the Russian prime minister, Joseph Chamberlain and the Rothschilds proved unproductive. Twenty years later the White Knight from Wales, suitably accoutred and provisioned, entered the lists on their behalf.

The anti-semitism, or anti-Judaism, which Stalin inherited from an otherwise divisive ideological line soon emerged when his plans for a Soviet-dominated Israel came to nought. He had hoped, at the time of the UN vote, that the extreme left-wing Mapam party, from which Ben-Gurion had split in 1944 when he founded and led Mapai, would unfurl the red banner. Mapam called itself "an inseparable part of the world revolutionary camp headed by the USSR". Stalin organized the immigration of Soviet Jews to act as agents. A Russian KGB resident, Lieutenant-Colonel (later General) Vladimir Vertiporokh, was appointed in 1948.

Emigrants were selected in the Soviet Union by Colonel (later General) Aleksandr Mikhailovich Korotkov who had a Jewish wife. On 4 October, 1948, however, when Golda Meir visited a Moscow synagogue she was mobbed by 30,000 enthusiastic Jews, who obviously preferred their religion and Israel to communism. Soon Jewish state theatres were closed, the Jewish Anti-Fascist Committee was dissolved, and its president, Mikhailovich Mikhoels, was thrown under the wheels of a lorry. Zhemchuzhina Molotov, the Jewish wife of Vyacheslav Molotov, Foreign Minister, was sent into internal exile. By 1950 the volte face, motivated also by the evident founding links between Israel and the United States, was complete. The Soviet UN vote had been based on an obvious false premise.

In territorial terms, as distinct from religious, no part of the inhabited globe, with the exception of Iceland and some other islands, has been occupied by man with the prior consent of the indigenous population. Thus the complementary factors to Israeli biblical claims to Palestine, or part of it, are acquisition and conquest. The first facts, therefore, are that the Jews are there and that they will stay. Secondly, there have been throughout history four options open to any acquirer or conqueror wishing to remain in hostile territory and contain the indigenous people: absorption, annihilation, expulsion and subjection.

The first option was practised with success in Israel after the 1948 war. It could not be repeated in the Occupied Territories, although executed provisionally in East Jerusalem. The second was never applied. The third option was much in mind when Begin's IZL and the Stern gang massacred the Deir Yassin Arabs. It was effective in clearing Jaffa of Arabs and, indirectly, Haifa and Galilee. As mentioned, 58% of the Arab population fled. Some 200,000 remained in Israel, where Arabic is the second official language and is used in the courts and in the Knesset.

The fourth option, subjection, applied to the Occupied Territories. It could not work. Future peace required its elimination and self-rule. In fact, international law forbids the settlement of occupied territories by the occupiers. The brutal formula of might being right could not apply long-term. As it was, the Jewish settlements and settlers such as Gush Emmim, or Bloc of the Faithful, were subject to Israeli *civil* law, but Arabs to *military* law and the full force of Shin Bet, the Israeli security service. Jews adjudge the 155,000 Arabs living in East Jerusalem, in which 160,000 Jews now also live, as abiding in Israel. Some 5,300 acres of Arab land worth $1 billion have been confiscated on which 60,000 homes for Jews have been built, but none for Arabs. The decision not to confiscate 133 acres of wasteland in East Jerusalem in 1994 thus represented 2.5% of the total.

The Syrian Golan Heights have formed a basic Israeli defence line and have been partly settled. In the former Occupied Territories, and in Israel, the press is under a chief military censor. In consequence, some journalists refer to Israel as the Garrison State. Yeshayahu Leibowitz, Israel's most esteemed philosopher, warned in 1967, that the occupation of Arab territory could spell the downfall of the State.

In terms of demographic details Israel now has a population of 5.50 millions, of whom 800,000 are Muslim Arabs, 150,000 Christian Arabs, and 100,000 Druses – a minorities' total of 1,050,000, or nearly 19% of the whole, none of whom jump for joy on hearing the Zionist national anthem, the Hatikva, whose composer, Herz Imber, stayed only six years in Palestine, went to India and became a Christian.

In the former Occupied Territories, whence a further 700,000 fled during the Six Day War, although a few returned, there are 1.8

million Arabs and 130,000 Jews in 144 communities. Edward Said in his book *The Politics of Dispossession* writes that 220 settlements have been established and more than 55% of the land expropriated, or designated, to maintain and support the settlements.

These were encouraged initially by the two Likud party prime ministers, better known to the reader as terrorist leaders, respectively of the Irgun and Stern gangs: Menachem Begin and Yitzhak Shamir. There are 750,000 Arabs in the Gaza strip and 3000 Jews. There still remain thousands of Arabs in Israeli prisons, charged – or not– under military law. There are, too, hundreds of thousands of refugees waiting to return to homes and land they left in Israel.

Yasser Arafat, chairman of the Palestine National Authority, now resides in Gaza with a secondary base in Jericho. He has, within limits, control over his fellow Arabs but none at all over Jewish settlers, for whom the time to be evacuated and compensated, at the beginning of the peace process, whether by force or persuasion, has long passed. A Likud government would reinforce their presence, turning a process into an abscess: Arab revolt would intensify and so would Jewish zealotry. This would lead, in turn, to more repression and more revolt.

Fifty years ago the broadsheet of the Stern gang was named *Hamaas* (see Appendix 1, page 182). In Hebrew a rallying cry, a denunciation, or simply enough! It is, therefore, not without irony that their Arab successors should use virtually the same word in Arabic – *Hamas* – which means agitation or revolution. That is to say, it also means rallying cry, but this time it is against the Jews. Their actions may or may not abate in terms of violence. There is no such question mark attached to the Iranian-financed Hezbollah – Party of God – nor is there in relation to Islamic Jihad, whose leader was shot by Mossad in Malta in October, 1995.

Other than the inflammable mixture of politics and religion, there is also the question of hydrology: fire and water. The whole region is dependent on four rivers, the Jordan, Baniyas, Hasbani and Tarmuk, all rising in Arab territory. The desert blooms in Israel, but there is increasing aridity in the densely populated Gaza strip. The scarcity of water in the whole catchment area increases the likelihood of diverting more water, already growing in salinity, from agricultural to industrial and domestic use. Hydrologists wonder whence it will come.

The demographic and hydrologic aspects were not considered when Robert Lovett, American Under Secretary of State, told Sir Oliver Franks, British Ambassador to the United States, in January, 1949, "The State of Israel (will) be the most dynamic, efficient and vigorous government in the Near East in future." There is no doubt whatsoever that this has been borne out, even though the competition is hardly keen, and the United States government continues its annual subvention, currently three billion United States dollars.

As for Jerusalem, Saint Matthew's gospel records the words of Christ: "O Jerusalem, Jerusalem, thou that killest the prophets and stonest them that are sent unto thee, how often would I have gathered thy children together, even as a hen gathereth her chickens under her wings, and ye would not! Behold, your house is left unto you desolate."

Understandably, the Arabs do not wish to be the chickens under the wings of an Israeli hen. Christians concentrate more on the heavenly Jerusalem: " My kingdom is not of this world."

Thus, the dangers to peace remain both internal and external, whether manifested by suicide bombing, nuclear, laser or chemical attack, Jewish settlements or the question of the Golan and the status of Jerusalem. Were there to be a nuclear attack, *and if the perpetrators were identifiable,* Israel would certainly respond in kind – known as the Samson option. This would, eschatologically speaking, likely be the last act before the second diaspora or, in Christian belief, the Second Coming, the Parousia, which follows the conversion of the Jews and precedes the end of the world. Such predictions in the past, however, have proved premature.

David Ben-Gurion once observed. "In order to be a realist in Israel, you must believe in miracles!" Perhaps only on this premise, a most worthy one, could there be rejoicing on earth and elsewhere. The Balfour celestial ensemble could perform a Te Deum, while Lloyd George's wraith could register two promissory notes upon his golden triangle. Indeed, as an old Welsh saying has it, *ar y diwedd y mae barnu*: it is at the end one passes judgement.

There appears, nevertheless, to be no real end to judge: a peace settlement negotiated by Yasser Arafat is regarded by many Palestinians as only the first step before the expunction of Israel, as if it were cosmetic surgery covering a suppurating wound. Suicide bombers are expendable, pustulating, when used, the peace process, itself constantly under intensive care, in an emotional situation which remains politically irreconcilable.

The Palestine Liberation Organization's charter still calls for the destruction of Israel, while Jewish encouragement of recent settlements on Arab land is undisputed: since Oslo, 40,000 acres have been confiscated. Israelis describe it as establishing facts on the ground. Jewish extremists consider this hallowed ground. Palestinian economic problems are exacerbated by the enforced reduction, following terrorist acts, of Arab employment in Israel: down 50% from 120,000.

"As things are," to quote David Grossman, the Israeli writer, "we are deprived of the future." The future of the twice-promised land is cast, opaquely, in half shadow, more penumbra than promise, more entropy than peace, and when Jewish *possession* is challenged physically or emotionally by the Arabs, the collective, dangerous corollary remains the disruptive and understandable Arab desire for *re-cession*.

Appendix One

EXTRACTS FROM *HANSARD* REPORTING THE PRIME MINISTER'S STATEMENT TO THE HOUSE OF COMMONS, ON 1 JULY 1946, CONCERNING PALESTINE; AND THE COLONIAL OFFICE'S *PALESTINE: STATEMENT OF INFORMATION RELATING TO ACTS OF VIOLENCE.* HMSO.

[Mr Clement Attlee was Prime Minister. Mr Arthur Creech-Jones was Colonial Secretary.]

PALESTINE (SITUATION)

The Prime Minister: The House has been informed from time to time of acts of sabotage and terrorism in Palestine. It has become increasingly clear in recent months that these incidents form part of a concerted plan prepared and executed by highly developed military organizations with widespread ramifications throughout the country.

The Anglo-American Committee called special attention to the development of illegal armed forces as a sinister feature of recent years in Palestine. The largest of these is Haganah, estimated to be about 70,000 strong, with a mobile striking force, the Palmach, some 5000 strong. This force has been developed on highly organized military lines and is armed with the most modern equipment. In addition there are two Jewish terrorist organizations – the Irgun Zvai Leumi, which is believed to have between 5000 and 6000 adherents trained in street fighting and sabotage, and the Stern Group which specializes in assassination. The Haganah have been responsible for many instances of destruction of property and armed resistance to the Government; the other two organizations have been responsible for numerous acts of violence and murder and for the recent kidnappings.

The Jewish Agency have been repeatedly warned, both by the High Commissioner and by His Majesty's Government, of the gravity of these developments and of the dangers to which they would lead. The Anglo-American Committee stated in their Report that such private armies constituted a danger to the peace of the world and that the Jewish Agency should at once resume active cooperation with the Mandatory Power. His Majesty's Government regarded it as essential that the Jewish Agency should take a positive part in the suppression of these illegal activities. In spite of these warnings the situation had not improved. On the contrary, there has recently been a recrudescence of terrorist activity. Within the past three weeks, sabotage of road and rail communications, including the blowing up of the principal bridges over the Jordan, has caused damage estimated at well over a quarter of a million pounds. On the night of 17th June the railway workshops at Haifa were seriously damaged by explosions and fire.

The climax came on 18th June, when six British officers were kidnapped, and two others were seriously wounded. Three of those kidnapped are still held captive. These are the culminating events in a campaign of violence which since December has caused the death of 16 British soldiers and five police (including the seven soldiers murdered in cold blood at Tel Aviv on 25th April) The material damage has exceeded £4,000,000. His Majesty's Government, as Mandatory, have an international duty to maintain law and order in Palestine and full authority to take all necessary steps to that end. It was clear we could no longer tolerate this direct challenge to our authority without abdicating this duty. I know what deep sympathy there is for the sufferings of the Jews in Europe and I appreciate the natural intensity of the feelings of those who experienced the atrocities of the Hitler regime, but this cannot condone the adoption by Jews in Palestine of some of the very worst of the methods of their oppressors in Europe.

His Majesty's Government (have) authorized the High Commissioner to take all necessary steps to restore order and to break up the illegal organizations, including the arrest of individuals believed to be responsible for the present campaign of violence. I am sorry to say that these included some of the leading members of the Jewish Agency, There is evidence of a close connection between the Agency and Haganah. A vast amount of arms, ammunition and explosives has already been found, the quantity of which has not yet been assessed.

These operations are not directed against the Jewish community as a whole, but solely against those who have taken an active part in the campaign of violence and those responsible for instigating and directing it. It is not our intention to close or proscribe the Agency as such [but] His Majesty's Government will not tolerate any attempts by any party to influence a decision in the Palestine question by force.

We have to face this position where there are two races in one small territory and we are charged with a Mandate in which we have to deal fairly with both these peoples. That is sometimes forgotten; and one might almost think from what was said by the hon. Member (Mr Sydney Silverman) that we were in Palestine as partners with the Jewish Agency for the creation of a Jewish State. That is not so. The Jewish Agency has a position to cooperate with the Government, but the Government of Palestine is the Government of the Mandatory power.

We have got to face the fact that there are strong forces in Palestine, and in the Jewish world, that have not accepted the idea only of a Jewish home, but are pressing for a Jewish State. It is no good blinking that fact. I quite agree that the Haganah started off by being an orderly and useful body of people, but there is no doubt whatever that, especially since the end of the war, it has to some extent changed, and we have evidence – I will produce the evidence in due course – of a very close link up between the Jewish Agency and Haganah. We also have evidence of the close connection between the Haganah and the Irgun.

We cannot get away from the fact that these are working together, and according to the information which we have, the only possible way of dealing with these widespread disturbances is to deal with the organization of the higher command. The last thing in the world we want to do is to destroy the Jewish Agency, but the Agency cannot be a cover for running an illegal army in illegal actions. All the evidence was that the Haganah has been closely connected with the Irgun and that the Haganah acts under the general direction of the Jewish Agency, certainly some members of the Executive of the Jewish Agency.

What we want is the greatest possible agreement between ourselves and the United States, and then try to get a policy which will be agreed and will bring peace. It is not our policy to enforce a policy on Palestine at the point of a bayonet, whether that policy is dictated by one side or the other in favour of one side or the other.

We are trying to deal fairly with the Jews and Arabs in Palestine. It is really no good suggesting that we have not an obligation to

Arabs as well as Jews. That is our Mandate. I notice in the Report it was said if British Forces were withdrawn, there would be immediate and prolonged bloodshed, the end of which it was impossible to predict.

I seriously ask what possible good does any hon. Member think can be done by wrecking trains, destroying bridges, shooting soldiers or kidnapping officers? No Government worthy of the name will yield to that kind of pressure, and certainly this Government is not going to do so. If we are suddenly going to admit something like a 20% addition (100,000 Jews) of the total population into a disturbed country with all kinds of economic difficulties, we have to contemplate that we may get disturbances, and may need more troops stationed there.

There is the closest possible connection between Members of the Executive of the Jewish Agency and the Haganah. That is not denied. There is evidence of a close connection and joint working between the Haganah and some of the terrorist organizations, and under these circumstances it was essential to deal with the whole network of this business. I think hon. Members have already agreed that the action of the troops in carrying out (their) duties has been exemplary. I assure the House, in conclusion, that as soon as possible the House shall be put in possession of all facts available, in order to try and get forward with the discussions on the (Anglo-American) Committee's report.

PALESTINE

STATEMENT OF INFORMATION

RELATING TO ACTS OF

VIOLENCE

Presented to Parliament by the Secretary of State

for the Colonies

By Command of His Majesty. July 1946.

Cmd. 6873. LONDON. HIS MAJESTY'S STATIONERY OFFICE.   Twopence Net.

Explanatory Notes

The following notes on the three Jewish illegal para-military organizations in Palestine are based on the Report of the Anglo-American Committee of Enquiry (pp.40–41). His Majesty's Government have reason to believe the figures given are on the conservative side.

The Haganah and Palmach: An illegal and well-armed military organization, organized under a central command with subsidiary territorial commands, in three branches, each of which includes women, a static force of settlers and townsfolk, with an estimated strength of 40,000;

a field army, based on the Jewish Settlement Police and trained in more mobile operations, with an estimated strength of 16,000;

a full-time force (Palmach), permanent, mobilized and provided with transport, with an estimated peace establishment of 2,000 and war establishment of some 6,000.

Something of the nature of conscription is in force: a year's service being obligatory for senior schoolchildren, male and female, between the ages of 17 and 18. The Jewish publication, *Haboker*, stated prior to 11th November 1945, "every Movement must submit to the Jewish Agency's Recruiting Department in Tel Aviv a roster of its members, male and female, who must enlist."

The Irgun Zvai Leumi (National Military Organization): formed in 1935 from dissident members of the Haganah. Operates under its secret command, with a strength estimated between 3,000 and 5,000.

The Stern Group originated as a dissident faction within the Irgun

177

Zvai Leumi when the latter decided temporarily to suspend activities in 1939. Its strength is said to be between 200 and 300 dangerous fanatics. They have been for some time fully cooperating with the Irgun Zvai Leumi, since both are equally committed to a policy of unrestrained extremism.

PALESTINE

Statement of Information relating to Acts of Violence

The information which was in the possession of His Majesty's Government when they undertook their recent action in Palestine [Operation "Agatha" 29 June 1946] led them to draw the following conclusions :–

(1) That Haganah and its associated force the Palmach (working under the political control of prominent members of the Jewish Agency) have been engaging in carefully planned movements of sabotage and violence under the guise of "the Jewish Resistance Movement";
(2) that the Irgun Zvai Leumi and the Stern Group have worked since last Autumn in co-operation with the Haganah High Command on certain of these operations; and
(3) that the broadcasting station "Kol Israel", which claims to be "the Voice of the Resistance Movement" and which was working under the general direction of the Jewish Agency has been supporting these organizations.

The evidence on which these conclusions are based is derived in the main from three sources –

(i) Information which has been obtained showing that between the 23rd September, 1945, and the 3rd November, 1945, seven telegrams passed between London and Jerusalem, and a further telegram on 12th May 1946. Copies of these have been interpreted and are here set out;

(ii) various broadcasts by "Kol Israel" between 31st October, 1945, and 23rd June, 1946, referring to specific acts of violence and sabotage; and

(iii) information on various dates derived from the pamphlet Hamas (the publication of the Stern group), from Herut (the publication of the Irgun Zvai Leumi) and from Eshnav (the publication of "the Jewish Resistance Movement"). Examples from these pamphlets are set out in this Paper.

This evidence relates to the three widespread sabotage operations of the 31st October/1st November, 1945; 20-25th February, 1946, and 16th-18th June, 1946. All three para-military organizations participated in these actions which not only caused very serious destruction but also loss of life.

I – ATTACK ON RAILWAYS, POLICE LAUNCHES AND HAIFA REFINERY – 31st OCTOBER – 1st NOVEMBER, 1945.

Note:– The Palmach carried out widespread attacks on the Palestine Railway system. The line was blown in 153 places, completely disrupting it. Other charges, though laid, did not explode. Three police launches were destroyed by explosives, two at Haifa and one at Jaffa. The same night, the Irgun Zvai Leumi attacked Lydda Station and Yards causing damage to three locomotives, the destruction of one signal box, and the burning of an engine shed. Several casualties were inflicted, including the death of one British soldier. A further attempt was made on the same night by the Stern Group to blow up the oil refinery at Haifa.

This incident was carefully planned in advance as part of a deliberate policy. It was intended as a warning to His Majesty's Government of the consequences that would follow if they did not comply with the wishes of the Yishuv (the Jewish Community in Palestine). The Jewish Agency Executive was not prepared to wait for a declaration of Government policy, but decided to cause "one serious incident" in order to influence that policy. These facts can plainly be seen from the following telegrams.

Telegram No. 1.
To London from (Moshe) Sneh in Jerusalem – 23rd September, 1945.

> "It is suggested that we do not wait for the official announcement but call upon all Jewry to warn the authorities and to raise the morale of the Yishuv. If you agree ask Zeev Sharif for statistical material about absorptive capacity and if you do not agree tell him that this material is not yet required. *It has also been suggested that we cause one serious incident.* We would then publish a declaration to the effect that it is *only a warning and an indication of much more serious incidents* that would threaten the safety of all British interests in the country, should the Government decide against us.
> "Wire your views with the reference as before but referring to statistical material about immigration during the war years.

The Stern Group have expressed their willingness to join us completely on the basis or our programme of activity. This time the intention seems serious. If there is such a union we may assume that we can prevent independent action even by IZL. Wire you views on the question of the union referring to statistical material about Jewish recruitment to the Army. Sneh."

N.B. (Moshe) Sneh is Security member of the Jewish Agency Executive. IZL is the Irgun Zvai Leumi.

That the Agency Executive agreed to the above action is clearly shown in the following telegrams:-

Telegram No 2.

To London from Bernard Joseph in Jerusalem – 10th October, 1945.

> "Eliezer Kaplan basing himself on a word from Hayyim via Nwbw says that we should undertake nothing before you give us instructions. He is opposed to any real action on our part until we hear from you.
> "Other members, however, are of the opinion that this is necessary to back your political effort with activities which do not bear the character of a general conflict.
> "It is essential that we should know at once whether such actions are likely to be useful or detrimental to your struggle.
> "Should you be opposed to any action whatever, wire that we should wait for the arrival of Wlsly.
> "Should you agree to isolated actions, wire you agree to sending a deputation to the dominions.
> "If Hayyim meant us only avoid a general conflict not isolated cases, send greetings to Chill for the birth of his daughter."

N.B. Bernard Joseph is legal adviser to the Jewish Agency and a member of its Executive. He acts in Shertok's absence as Head of the Political Department. Eliezer Kaplan is Head of the Agency's Financial Department and a member of its Executive.

Telegram No 3.

From Moshe Shertok in London to Bernard Joseph in Jerusalem – 12th October, 1945.

"David will not leave before fortnight. Meanwhile probably revisit Paris. Regarding Dobkin written. David himself favoured delegate dominions. Please congratulate Chill on birth of daughter. Signed Shertok."

N.B. – (1) Mosha Shertok is Head of the (Jewish) Agency's Political Department and a member of the Executive.

(2) A reference to telegram No. 2 will show that the phrases about "delegate dominions" and "greetings to Chill" meant that it was desired, whilst avoiding a general conflict, to indulge in isolated actions.

Telegram No 4.

To London from Jerusalem – 2nd November, 1945.

"The Executive refuses to give authority to the political department to act within the limits of Ben-Gurion's instructions. Gsbr argues he will oppose this as soon as Ben-Gurion and Shertok return. I declared I will act according to the instructions which I have received until an authoritative message is received which cancels Ben-Gurion's instructions. They did not dare to cancel the instructions but insisted we inform the Executive in advance of each action and that they should have the right of veto. *We received agreement for the police boats and for the railways.* All activities may thus be spoiled owing to pressure from the party on Bernard Joseph and on Eliahu."

N.B. – David Ben-Gurion is Chairman of the Jewish Agency Executive.
For the operations of the 31st October–1st November the Agency sought and obtained the co-operation of the "dissident organizations".

Telegram No 5.

To London from Jerusalem – 1st November, 1945.

"We have come to a working arrangement with the dissident organizations according to which we shall assign certain tasks to them under our command. They will act only according to our plan. Sneh, Shaul, Meiroff, and Bernard Joseph consider such an agreement as most desirable, but it is not being put into effect

because the (Mapai) Party is delaying it. Some of them are opposed to any sort of activity and especially to any agreement with the dissidents. Information on the operations follows:-

"The following activities were carried out on Wednesday night. Two boats were sunk in the Haifa harbour and a third at Jaffa. The boats had been used to chase immigrants. Railway lines were blown up in 50 centres, in all 500 explosions. Railway traffic was stopped from the Syrian frontier to Gaza, from Haifa to Samakh, from Lydda to Jerusalem. In all the activities no one was hurt, stopped or arrested.

"The same night, the IZL attacked the Lydda station causing serious damage and some casualties. During the same night the Stern Group caused serious sabotage at the refineries at Haifa and one man was killed. *The dissidents had previously informed us of this and we did not object to Lydda but were opposed to the refinery job.* Had the agreement come into effect we could have avoided victims at Lydda and prevented the refinery operation. I regard the fact the Party and the Executive are witholding their approval as a crime.

"The activities have made a great impression in the country. The authorities are bewildered and have proclaimed a curfew on the roads at night. They are waiting for instructions from London. We are apprehensive of a general attack against the Haganah. We have taken the necessary security measures and are prepared for sacrifices Confirm by telegram to Ada enquiries about the health of her children."

Hamaas, the publication of the Stern Group in referring to the above operation, stated:-

"The events of 1st November have given a striking expression to the firm resolution of the Jews to fight for the freedom of their homeland. The scope of the attack has proved the Jews are capable of acting under the most difficult conditions. However, the most significant achievement on that night was that for the first time the attack was coordinated and concentrated. The Jewish Resistance Movement has embraced all the Jewish resistance forces with a view to their being guided by a single authority which would control the common fight". ("Hamaas" Issue No. 2 of November, 1945.)

These operations were widely publicized by the Jewish illegal broadcasting station, Kol Israel, as follows :-

"The paralysing of the Railways all over the country through cutting the lines in 242 places serves as a warning to the Government of the White Paper. The nights of heroism since Athlit* are an expression of our strength and decision. We lament the British, Arab and Jewish victims who fell in the attacks on the railways and ports of Palestine. They are all victims of the White Paper. All our men returned safely with their equipment. None of our men is missing." (2nd November, 1945).

As proof of the fact that the Kol Israel station was working with the agreement of the Jewish Agency, reference may be made to the following telegrams. (See also telegram No 8):-

Telegram No 6.

To London from Sneh in Jerusalem – 12th October, 1945.

"With effect from 4/10 the broadcasts of the 'Voice of Israel' have been renewed. Two broadcasts were successful. Eliezer Kaplan and Bernard Joseph were invited to see the High Commissioner this morning.
"The agreement for the renewal of the broadcasts and the Athlit* undertakings have been obtained with difficulty. In future I shall not enquire but decide in conjunction with Shaul Meiroff and Kn'ny."

Telegram No 7.

To London from Jerusalem – 14th October, 1945.

"The Voice of Israel started to function as the broadcasting station of the Jewish Resistance Movement three days before we received your letter and your telegram. We also have had the same doubts and we voiced them before the broadcasts were started, but the expert says that there are no grounds for anxiety from the technical point of view."

N.B. – The phrase "grounds for anxiety from the technical point of view" probably refers to apprehension that the station, which is a mobile one, might be located.

* On 10 October the Palmach released over 200 illegal immigrants from Athlit Clearance Camp. A British police tender was ambushed during the subsequent search for the escaped persons and one British policeman and two Palestinians were wounded.

II – ATTACKS ON HAIFA RADAR STATION, PALESTINE MOBILE FORCE CAMPS, AND AIRFIELDS – 20th–25th FEBRUARY, 1946.

Note. – On 20th February, 1946, the Palmach attacked the RAF Radar Station, Haifa, blowing it up and seriously wounding two RAF NCOs and inflicting lesser injuries on six others. Two days later the Palmach carried out co-ordinated attacks on Palestine Mobile Force camps at Shaffa Amr, Kfar Vitkin and Sarona. At Shaffa Amr serious damage was caused. One police officer suffered head injuries. Three British women and one child suffered from shock. On 25th February, the Irgun Zvai Leumi and Stern group followed this up with attacks on airfields at Lydda, Petah Tikvah, and Qastina, destroying seven aircraft and damaging eight others.

These incidents seem to have been intended as a "second warning", as the "first warning" on 31st October/1st November had been "disregarded". These incidents were described in a Kol Israel broadcast of the 3rd March, 1946.

> "This last fortnight has seen a renewed intensity in the struggle of the Jewish people against the forces which aim to throttle them and their natural aspirations for normal nationhood in their National Home.
>
> "The attack on the Radar Station on Mount Carmel was aimed at destroying one of the principal agents of the Government in its hunt for Jewish refugees. The sabotage of the airfields (i.e. by Irgun Zvai Leumi and Stern Groups) was the sabotage of a weapon which has been degraded from its glorious fight against the evil forces of Nazism to the dishonourable task of fighting against the victims of Nazism.
>
> "Those three attacks are symptomatic of our struggle. In all cases the onslaught was made against the weapon used by the White Paper in its despicable battle to repudiate its undertaking to the Jewish people and the world, and not against the men who use this weapon. It is not our object to cause loss of life of any Briton in this country; we have nothing against them because we realise that they are but the instruments of a policy, and in many cases unwilling instruments."

In addition to the above broadcast, *Herut*, the publication of the Irgun Zvai Leumi, and *Eshnav*, the pamphlet published in the name of the Resistance Movement, made the following allusions to these extensive operations :-

Heavy tasks were imposed on all the Forces of the nation. The soldiers of the Haganah were ordered to attack the forces in their lairs (i.e. The Palestine Mobile Force). No less difficult was the task imposed on the members of the National Military Organization [IZL] who were sent to attack the military airfields at Qastina and the central airfield at Lydda; and on the members of the Fighters for Freedom of Israel (Stern Group) who were ordered to attack the aerodrome at Kfar Sirkin. The importance of this week's events lies in the fact that this was the first time that the military bases of the British rulers were shaken" (*Herut*, Issue No.55 of February, 1946)

"A Big Week: the actions of this glorious week have been carried out with the support of the entire, united Jewish youth. This is a political achievement. The Palestine Mobile Force has been attacked by the Haganah; at two camps considerable damage has been inflicted. At Sarona the fighters retired after a continuation of the attack had proved useless. Here four of them fell. Lydda and Qastina airfields have been attacked by Irgun Zvai Leumi whilst Lohomei Herut Israel (Stern) chose the airfield at Kfar Sirkin. (*Herut*. Issue No 56 of February 1946

The first warning on 1st November, 1945, by the Jewish Resistance was disregarded and the whole Yishuv was compelled to carry out a second warning during the last fortnight in the attacks on Palestine Mobile Force Stations and Airfields." (*Eshnav*, Issue No 116 of 4th March, 1946).

III ATTACKS ON ROAD AND RAIL BRIDGES, RAILWAY WORKSHOPS AND KIDNAPPING OF BRITISH OFFICERS – 16th to 18th JUNE, 1946.

Note During the evening of 16th June, 1946, Haganah carried out attacks on road and rail bridges on the frontier of Palestine causing damage estimated at £250,000. Four road and four rail bridges were destroyed or damaged during the night, and one road bridge across the Jordan was destroyed by a delayed action mine, while attempts were being made to remove the charges. One British officer of the Royal Engineers was killed by the explosion. The following evening the Stern Group carried out an attack on the Haifa Railway Workshops.

On 18th June, 1946, five British officers were kidnapped while lunching at an officers' club in Tel Aviv and a sixth British officer was kidnapped in a main street of Jerusalem.

Indication that a further series of incidents might be imminent was given on 12th May, 1946, when Kol Israel broadcast a warning which it considered "desirable" to "lay before His Majesty's Government". The text of this broadcast was as follows:

"The Jewish Resistance Movement thinks it *desirable to publish the warning it intends to lay before His Majesty's Government.* Present British policy is executing a dangerous manoeuvre and is based on an erroneous assumption: Britain, in evacuating Syria, Lebanon and Egypt intends to concentrate her military bases in Palestine and is therefore concerned to strengthen her hold over the mandate, and is using her responsibility to the Jewish people merely as a means to that end. But this double game will not work. Britain cannot hold both ends of the rope; she cannot exploit the tragic Jewish question for her own benefit as mandatory power, while attempting to wriggle out of the various responsibilities which that mandate confers.

From the Zionist point of view, the tepid conclusion of the (Anglo-American) *Commission bear no relation to the political claims of the Jewish people,* but even so, in the execution of these proposals, the British Government is displaying a vacillation at once disappointing and discreditable. We would therefore warn His Majesty's Government that if it does not fulfil its responsibilities under the mandate – above all with regard to the question of immigration – the Jewish people will feel obliged to lay before the nations of the world the request that the British leave Palestine. The Jewish Resistance Movement will make every effort to hinder the transfer of British Bases to Palestine and to prevent their establishment in the country."

This broadcast is of particular significance by reason of the fact that it was given at the express request of Moshe Shertok, Head of the Jewish Agency's Political Department and a member of its Executive Committee, and had also been passed to David Ben-Gurion, Chairman of the Executive Committee. This is made clear in the following telegram :-

Telegram No 8

To "Daniel" in London from Sneh in Jerusalem –

12th May 1946
"Please pass on to Ben-Gurion the text of the broadcast of Kol Israel
sent herewith; with a note that the broadcast was made at the
request of Shertok."

The telegram then repeats textually the broadcast message of the
same date.

There followed on the night of 16th June, 1946, the widespread
and carefully planned attacks on vital communications and on the
following night the attack on railway workshops. Kol Israel
accepted full responsibility on behalf of "the Resistance Movement
for the renewal of its activity as a result of the delaying policy of the
British Government."
Kol Israel Broadcast. 18th June, 1946.

"The action of blowing up the bridges expressed the high
morale and courage of the Jewish fighters who carried out the
attack. They had to pass long distances and to carry a large
quantity of material for that purpose. The withdrawal was
most difficult since all the police and army were on their feet
and aircraft were looking for the attackers; despite all this, the
operation was executed and all objectives were reached
according to plan without causing any loss of life to the
guards.

"There were some casualties among the attackers in the
North owing to an unfortunate accident which was caused by
the fall of a rocket directly onto a lorry loaded with explosives
and the whole load blew up and the persons there were killed.
Honour to their memory! The Army and Police became furious and started to discharge their wrath on the peaceful
people of the nearby settlements; many settlers of Beth
Haareva, Matzuva and Eilon were arrested and taken to
Acre.

"Many messages of heartfelt appreciation were sent by various personalities and journalists to the Resistance Movement
for *the renewal of its activity as a result of the delaying policy of*
the British Government, the recent Bevin speech and the known
announcement of Attlee. These objectives were chosen to dis-
turb British bases and communications, to prevent the Arabs
of the neighbouring countries who talked so much about com-

ing to fight the Jews in Palestine, and to mark the closing up of these frontiers before Jewish immigrants."

23rd June, 1946.

"This is the Voice of Israel, the voice of the Jewish Resistance. Last week we had to destroy the bridges – these bridges are just as much use to us as the authorities but they had to be destroyed to show our feelings."

Conclusion

The evidence contained in the foregoing pages is not, and is not intended to be, a complete statement of all the evidence in the possession of His Majesty's Government. Nor are the specific instances herein referred to by any means a complete list of all the incidents of violence and sabotage which have taken place in recent months. The fact is that in the first six months of 1946 there were nearly fifty separate incidents involving violence, and in many cases loss of life: material damage to a very great extent has been done to railway installations, police and RAF stations, and coastguard stations. Roads have ben mined and vehicles have been blown up.

The above operations were widespread in character and caused very extensive damage. When they were almost immediately followed by the kidnapping of British officers, it was no longer possible for His Majesty's Government to adopt a passive attitude. Unless the Government were prepared to yield to threats of violence and to abandon all hope of establishing law and order, they were bound to take active steps against any persons or organizations who had made themselves responsible for the planning and carrying out of the outrages which are dealt with in this Paper.

Appendix Two

THE AUTHOR'S LEAVE FROM PALESTINE IN ITALY AND CANADA

I spent two leaves while serving in Palestine, respectively in Italy and Canada. On 10 November, 1946, I flew to Cairo from Lydda, now known as Lod, but to the Crusaders Saint George, who suffered martyrdom at Nicomedia, where he was put to death by Diocletian on 23 April, 303, and buried at Lydda where his tomb, if it be his, may be seen. Gibbon, in his *Decline and Fall*, surprisingly confused him with an Arian Archbishop. The true George was a Roman officer of rank who refused to carry out a Christian persecution ordered by the emperor. The Bosphorus was long known as the Arm of Saint George. Such was his fame, the Moslems venerated him, and still do under the name of El Kedir, whose soul animated the saint.

Animated by the thought of eighteen days' leave, the ninety-minute flight to Cairo in a Dakota was the beginning of a rather roundabout trip via Tobruk, Malta and then Rome where we landed on a steel mesh runway, used in the War, which had ended eighteen months previously. First, I stayed at the Metropolitan Hotel in Cairo, where I met the bride, as I have mentioned, of an Irish Guards officer I knew, Giles Vandeleur, and saved her from a consolation course of dry martinis. I then left Cairo at the unholy hour of 0400.

In Rome General Eddie Goulburn, formerly commander of 1st Guards Brigade, kindly put me up and I dined with him and his Coldstream ADC, Tony Lake, at his residence in Via Asmara, 11.

The next day he lent me his car and driver to go to Perugia. I stayed ten days there, and in the country, with the Sorbellos. We went to Assisi which I saw for the first time. We visited the British War cemetery where Grenadier, Coldstream and ten Welsh Guardsmen were buried. Nearly all were killed at Perugia, including my signaller, Guardsman Jones 62, John Nicholl-Carne and "Fogg" Elliot. A school friend, Tony Bailes, DCLI, killed near Lake Traimeno, was also buried there.

We lunched with Molly Berkeley, whom I had met in London. Molly, or Mary, was a Bostonian, the widow of the last earl and an old friend of Gian di Sorbello's American mother. Tall and elegant, then around 63, she was a fair-haired beauty when younger, and had lost little of her allure in later life. Her villa, a converted chapel, dedicated to San Lorenzo, was built on the narrow ridge above the town, 1300 feet above sea level, with a remarkable view over the Tiber valley. Behind was a ravine, and beyond were hills which soon merged with the Apennines. The town's mineral water source also filled her pool. The converted chapel had excellent acoustics and was later much used by guests during the Spoleto Festival. Molly had bought the place before the War from a local gentleman indebted at bridge.

I was asked to stay with her on 10 August, 1975, the feast of San Lorenzo. She died the next day, fittingly the feast of Saint Clare of Assisi. The town had honoured her civically, recognizing her charities, her labour in restoration, her spirituality, like her age, well concealed. After the war she adopted six orphans, two from Cassino. One of them became the boy star in the film "Bicycle Thieves".

On 23 November I arose in Perugia at 0445 to catch the bus to Rome at 0600, which then took four and a half hours. I stayed with Gian di Sorbello's brother, Uguccione, a member of the Allied "A" Force during the War, and saw the film "Casablanca" with Kinka di Sorbello's mother, Marchesa di Cavriani. We had lunch the next day in her house. Her butler was then aged 85, born in 1861, in the Papal States, just before Italy was united. He had been in service, man and boy, for more than seventy years. Any idea of bringing this devoted *maggiordomo* into the 18th century, let alone the 20th, had long been abandoned. He had the rare grace of rejoicing in his hardly arduous daily grind.

The Marchesa's brother had been a Polish banker. He refused to leave Warsaw in 1939, even though a private train comprising five carriages had been sent to evacuate him, his wife and his belongings to Italy. He spent the War hidden in a convent, at great risk to all concerned. He lost all his possessions, first under Nazi

191

rule and then under the communists. Although Christian, he and his sister's parents were Jews.

That evening I dined with General Eddie and Tony Lake and lunched with them the following day. We went to the War Crimes Court, where Colonel General Eberhart von Mackensen and Lieutenant General Kurt Maeltzer were being tried in connection with the Ardeatine Caves Massacre. Field Marshal Albert Kesselring was in court as a witness. The case concerned the summary execution of 335 hostages on 24 March, 1944, in retaliation for the killing of 32 German soldiers the day before by Italian partisans as they marched through Rome.

Rome had been in Mackensen's 14th Army area, before he was sacked by Kesselring in 1944 for failing to make provisions against the Anzio breakout, and Maeltzer, at the time, was the military commander of the city. An earlier bomb had killed 30 German officers and men at the railway station. Maeltzer imposed a curfew. This time Hitler intervened through the SS/SD command, although Kesselring was commander-in-chief of the German armies in Italy. None claimed ignorance of the affair. The SS man on the spot was Colonel Herbert Kappler, then aged 36. His immediate superior was General Karl Wolff, and above him were Himmler and Hitler.

The trial lasted eleven days. It was a travesty. The British president was from the War Office. His complexion florid, his courtroom control was minimal: two Italian women screamed abuse from the back. The president failed to have them ejected; both he and the prosecutor were considered by General Eddie to be a disgrace. The interpreter was a German refugee whose translations were challenged. We left. Eddie telephoned London. The president was sacked and replaced.

Kesselring was tried separately, with the same lack of direction: "Tortuous, ill-informed and rambling" was how one of the witnesses, Lieutenant-Colonel A.P. Scotland, called it. All three were condemned to death. Mackensen requested not to be blindfolded – but after intervention by both Churchill and Field Marshal Alexander with the prime minister Clement Attlee, the sentences were commuted to twenty years. Maeltzer died in prison. Kesselring and Mackensen served six years, being released in 1952. The first died in 1960, the second in 1969. Kappler was given life – a legal technicality precluded the death sentence – and served thirty-two years. He escaped from a Rome prison hospital, but died the next year from cancer.

While in Perugia I had bought 2000 16-bore cartridges from Falconi's. I asked Tony Scarisbrick, Grenadiers, a Mons contemporary serving in Rome, for a chit stating that the cartridges were for Army use in Palestine. He demurred. On 25 November I dined once more with his superior, General Eddie, but for some reason I did not ask him. Once again on this trip I rose in the early hours, this time at 0335. I walked to the air booking centre and caught the bus to Ciampino aerodrome. After delays, we reached Al'Adhem, Tobruk, at 1745 and stayed the night.

On 27 November my diary records: *"Arrive Cairo. A little trouble about the 2000 cartridges."* Egyptian customs were not concerned with British servicemen until the war ended and the British Army withdrew to the Canal Zone, under the terms of the 1936 Anglo-Egyptian treaty. Consequently I was asked what I had to declare. My interrogator was a tall, fezzed, customs man, I think Sudanese – the Sudan being still Anglo-Egyptian, with an interchange of officials at that level – who told me I needed a chit for the cartridges. This was a situation I had foreseen. I said it was in my bag and retired round the corner, where I found a piece of paper and wrote out the necessary statement, and signed it per pro E.H. Goulburn, Major General, O.C. British Military Mission, Rome. Admittedly it lacked the all-important stamp. The customs man looked at it and turned it over. "Cairo Airport" was marked on the back. He laughed so much I thought he was going to collapse. He waved me through. He wished me luck. I reciprocated and dined with Jean Vandeleur.

Once again, on 28 November, I was up before dawn at 0430, having slept in an armchair, and left Cairo at 0600, arriving Lydda at 0830, at the same time as Field Marshal Montgomery, wearing his beret with two badges. I saluted the great man before telephoning Andrew Wemyss, Scots Guards, my mechanically minded No 2 at Brigade Headquarters, to send me a jeep and driver. My cartridges were largely shared with Bill Gore-Langton, the Brigade Major, who also had a 16-bore – and his one arm, the other, as mentioned, having been lost at Salerno in Italy.

Seven months later I left again from Lydda airport, this time bound for New York and Winnipeg, Canada. I was taking three months leave which came under such strange acronyms as LILOP and PYTHON. The first meant Leave in Lieu of Python, but the full wording of the second escapes me. I was entitled to end of War leave and possibly some local leave in addition. A return to the United Kingdom would have been free of cost. Middle East Land Forces, and for all I know the War Office, felt a trip with my mother to see her brother in the Dominion of Canada was on my account. This time the aeroplane was a Skymaster. We went via Cairo and arrived in Rome at 0600. I spent most of the night chatting to the French air hostess. She was called Malou Bonnet and, appropriately, tried on all the ladies' hats of which there were many in those days, and asked my opinion.

In Rome I had a bath and shave in Uguccione di Sorbello's flat, but he was unable to persuade the Italian authorities to give me a temporary visa and so enable me to accept TWA's offer of a passage the following week. So I returned to the plane. We arrived at Geneva in the afternoon, then Paris and Shannon. The dates in my diary show I left on 1 July, 1947, and was at Shannon the following day, after leaving at midnight for Iceland. Thereafter we flew to Gander in Newfoundland, and then on to Boston and New York. We touched down at 1400 local time – forty-eight hours after I had left Lydda.

The reader will have appreciated that jetlag was not a factor in this saga. On the contrary, passengers had time to meet one another. Two Americans were particularly kind: one gave me the names and addresses of friends in New York and Long Island. Another, Charles Coster, asked me to stay at his club as his guest. We were met by his day chauffeur in a Cadillac which seemed to stretch from La Guardia airport to the Knickerbocker Club on 62nd Street, New York.

Doris Marquette Palfi was the one who introduced me to her friends. She was a tragic figure who was dying of cancer and had said goodbye to her husband and young daughter in Rome. On Long island I stayed with her friends there at Sands Point and then Syosset, visited the Atlantic Beach Club and saw one or two games of polo at the Meadow Brook (now Meadowbrook) Club. In New York, culture vulturing did not feature: my diary carries such entries and exoticisms as the Savoy Plaza, El Morocco, St Regis Hotel, King Cole Bar, 21 Club, the Colony and the Copacabana. One thing I did discover, en route, were the taboos of Manhattan: colour, religion and gender barriers. I was not served at the St Regis Long Bar because my guest was a woman, although we went in the evening. She was a friend of friends in Tel Aviv.

On 9 July I was presented to the Empress Zita. She was then in her fifties and lived until well into her nineties. Also there were the Archduke and Archduchess Franz-Joseph, and the good lady who had taken me there, Marjorie de Jong. Cole Porter was at the piano. He was then around fifty-six and composing music for "Kiss me Kate". At my request he played "Night and Day" and "Begin the Beguine". I mentally did a double check that they were his creations and not Irving Berlin's.

On Sunday, 13 July I was lying beside my host's swimming pool on Long Island. The immensely dignified, grey-haired black butler brought drinks and nearly needed a second trolley to carry the Sunday newspaper, running to around a hundred pages. Therein I read the news of the kidnapped sergeants Clifford Martin and Mervyn Paice. My diary simply records the fact. Only later, as we know, was the full horror revealed. The revulsion in New York was symptomatic of world opinion. The act was no fight for freedom but a disgusting manifestation of evil.

On 21 July, my mother having arrived at New York, we left La Guardia airport and landed first at Detroit, then Minneapolis where we changed aeroplanes, and arrived in Winnipeg where my uncle, Robert Taylor, and his wife Kirsty met us. My mother and her brother had not seen one another for twenty-eight years, the last time being in 1919. My uncle had volunteered for the Royal Canadian Engineers in 1918 and then served in Europe.

Empire building in 1911, when Robert left home aged twenty-one, was a far-flung enterprise. Nearly two hundred miles west-north-west of Winnipeg, in the middle of the prairie, was a hamlet called St Lazare. He left the train and spent the first night in a culvert, presumably a dry one. He then joined the Hudson Bay Railway survey party. It moved north, planned the route and named lakes: so many that they ran out of names. Six years later, the survey completed, with the end of the line at Fort Churchill, Hudson Bay, he volunteered.

After the First World War Robert returned to the company which now formed part of the Canadian National Railway. He was a civil engineer. In 1937 he became Engineer of Buildings for the western region, 1700 miles of track from Lake Superior to Vancouver Island. His son, my first cousin Ted, was spending his vacation at Jasper Park in the Rockies. We stopped there, in the midst of these mountains with peaks reaching 12,000 feet, after crossing a thousand miles of prairie on our way to Vancouver Island.

We started again and went to the observation car at the rear. The track had many bends and, going through the mountains, where the tree line stopped well short of the peaks, we could see the 150-ton six-coupled wheel engine and the line ahead. We were getting up steam and passing through Yellowhead Pass, when towards us, on the single track, we saw a four-wheel, one-ton bogie approaching. The maintenance man aboard, winching his way home, had mistimed his return. He jumped.

The huge, snow-plough fenders of our engine hit the bogie. It shot into the air and crashed into the ravine on our left, where it lay, its wheels spinning and its steel frame twisted. Our driver

195

steamed on. Vancouver was reached without further incident: no train robbers, no Indians, certainly no Eskimos, just magnificent scenery and fresh river trout for dinner. It was a few thousand miles from Palestine and we had not yet crossed over to Vancouver Island, named after George Vancouver, companion of Cook.

My aunt Lillian, father's eldest sister, with whom we were going to stay, had left England on a cruise with her governess, in the early part of the new reign – Edward VII's – while in her twenties. The two events were unconnected. Aunt Lillian and her governess were in Boston to stay with friends where she met Lord Wilfred Hargreaves. A fundamental question in Edwardian England was: who was he? There was no dukedom or marquisate which bore the family name of Hargreaves, the younger sons in reserve being bestowed with the honorary prefix of lord before their Christian names.

It transpired that he was named after his mother who had been born Alice Lord. The mystery solved, the suitor approved by the governess acting in proxy for the parents, the marriage followed and the newly weds went to Pullman, Washington State, where my first cousin, also Lillian – known as Babs – was born in 1908. Her father, Wilfred, was an architect and co-creator of the plans for Washington State University.

Later, in Victoria, British Columbia, he had much to do with the Province's monolithic public buildings which made the most solid of medieval castles look frail. At this time, too, the Empress Hotel had just been built in Victoria, around 1910. There my grandfather, after whom I had been named, and his brother-in-law, Tom Forsyth-Forrest, took the train from San Francisco, stayed two days, left £100 and returned whence they had come. Tom had three grandsons, my cousins, in the Welsh Guards: Pip and Michael Bankier and Peter Hastings.

My aunt's house was in Cadboro Bay. I went swimming with Robert Taylor in Telegraph Bay on the Pacific Coast. It was freezing. We returned later by ferry and took the CPR track to Winnipeg, calling at Calgary, meeting Babs and her daughter Pamela, now a young grandmother, then aged eight. On 8 September I wandered round the back streets of Winnipeg and came across a brass plate which announced the presence of the Guards' Association of Canada. I climbed to the first floor. The young man who opened the door refused to speak. The mystery remained unresolved.

I had a warmer welcome in the evening from my friend and constant companion in Winnipeg (other than attractive private houses and gardens not a very interesting town in an architectural municipal sense and surrounded by prairie) who was a first cousin of Ted's, called Connie Cooper. We bicycled outside the town, braving the mosquito bites which wrought havoc with my mother. For physical reasons unclear to me new blood, that is to say blood of strangers to the region, is irresistible to any of the trillion trillion mosquitoes which zoom and zing their short lives around the innumerable lakes and rivers of Manitoba. Midgies in Scotland are a minuscule menace by comparison.

On 12 September there was dramatic display of Northern Lights, Aurora Borealis, swinging across the sky in brilliant beams of light in many colours. My uncle Robert told me "up north" they were at rooftop level. He had, as my mother was fond of saying, been ninety miles from the Eskimos. Certainly well inside trapper country, the basic *raison d'être* for the Hudson Bay Company, and many a wild mink was sent back to my mother and my grandmother.

Sadly, on 20 September I left Canada to begin my return to Palestine. After twelve hours I arrived at La Guardia New York on the day La Guardia, a former mayor of New York, died. I telephoned the Belgian manager of the Saint Regis Hotel, Pierre Boltinke, but the place was full, so I stayed at the Ritz Carlton. They were both too expensive to hang around for long. Luckily friends I had met earlier, Harry and Vee Morse-Meyers, put me up at 70 W. 45 Street.

23.9.47. My diary entry recorded a strange experience:*"Dining quietly with Harry, Vee and Kenneth Ballantyne, Harry's friend, a New Zealander, who shares his painter's studio in the same flat, when we are disturbed by their house ghost!"* I have never seen a ghost, although I have met those who have, but I have heard them. This one had gone west. The noise I heard was quite clear, that of two heavy footsteps on the wooden floor of the ballustraded gallery above us, which led to the studio. The cat raised its hackles, the dog growled, then ran up the staircase, circling around the apparition which only Vee – and the dog – could see.

Vee had been born a McNee and was the Canadian granddaughter of a Highlander who had been "cleared" from his croft and settled in Canada, Vee was Gaelic and had the sight. I had the fright. After a couple of minutes the dog returned, the cat relaxed and the ghost faded. "Was its visor open or closed?" asked Harry. "Open," said Vee. I was then told the background. In the corner was a suit of armour, made in Milan in the fifteenth century, probably for a condottiere, in this case, apparently, a Scot.

He had, it seemed, an attachment to his hatchment which his armour could be said to represent. My bed was next to the armour. I wondered if it were not good manners to leave a bottle of whisky

197

on the table. The dog growled once. Otherwise, the night passed quietly and in the end I slept.

30.9.47. "Go to Flushing Meadow and witness the admission of Pakistan and the Yemen to the United Nations." It was here, two months later, on 29 November, that the General Assembly voted for Palestine partition. I was free to wander wherever I wished, and did so, and remember the tiered, semi-oval-shaped chamber well, with a central aisle leading up to the dais where the president of the assembly sat. It was to him that the burnoosed delegates of the Yemen presented their credentials.

Two former Welsh Guards officers, with whom I had served in the 3rd Battalion in Italy, Francis Egerton and Elydir Williams, were attached to the British contingent at the UN. They kindly arranged my visit. A third Welsh Guardsman in New York at that time was Howell Moore-Gwyn, Regimental Adjutant. He and his wife, Ann, sister of Edward Montagu, Grenadier Motor Transport Officer in Palestine, were consulting specialists. Howell had cancer and died shortly afterwards. *"She and his ashes returned to London,"* I wrote to my mother, who had remained longer in Winnipeg.

A fourth Welsh Guardsman was Ronnie Furse, with whom I had served in Italy, where he had lost an eye. He was working in New York and was an excellent guide to the jazz dives of that era – Eddie Condon at 47 W 3rd Street; Mugsie Spanier (Nick's) 7th Avenue S. at 10th Street; Jimmy Ryan's; Famous Door with Jack Teagarden, 56 W. 52; there was also Downbeat, and we could hear Coleman Hawkins at the Three Deuces on 72 W 72.

We dined at the Colony or 21. Sadly, such places as the Metropolitan Museum of Art were entirely neglected. I was, however, twenty-two and loved jazz.

Pierre Boltinke and his wife Ursula kindly invited me to a cocktail party in their Saint Regis Hotel flat. A fellow guest was Lord Downe, a cousin of my brother officer, Lewis Dawnay. I wrote in my diary, rather uncharitably, he was *"rather an old bore"*. Lewis was pleased to hear, however, that I had met him, but a little shocked to learn he was in the wool trade: alpaca, no doubt, with a side line in ermine.

Yet the Archduke Franz-Joseph and his blonde wife, Martha, were passing themselves off as interior decorators. My friend, Dimitri of Russia, Grand Duke and formerly Ensign in His Imperial Majesty's Preobrazhenski Guards, had held the same job as Pierre Boltinke. The woof and weft of trade were, after all, how monarchs made their pile.

4.10.47. "Leave New York at 0130. Touch down at Boston and Gander in beautiful weather. Cross Atlantic also in good weather. Arrive

Shannon in the evening." I arrived in Paris during the early hours of Sunday morning, 5 October. The plane landed in Rome at Midday. The flight had taken some 28½ hours, allowing for time differences. I spent ten days with the Sorbellos in the country, lunched with Molly Berkeley, as before, and caught the flight from Rome to Lydda which was going via Athens and Cairo. On board was the wife of the Grenadier Commanding Officer, John Davies. She was bound for Cairo. Wives and families had been evacuated from Palestine nine months previously. In nine month's time we would also sail out of Haifa harbour, the last to leave.

The plane landed at Lydda on 16 October, near our camp at Petah Ticvah. I was glad to be back, after three and a half months' absence, safe in the insecurity of service in Palestine. The trip, now commonplace in jet aircraft, provided my mother and myself with a lifetime of recollections, not least relating to friends and family members we met, but the nine-month gestation period ahead for the definitively non-identical embryos conceived by the United Nations in Palestine preceded decades of struggle and destruction.

Appendix Three

PALESTINE

SUMMARY OF DATES AND DEEDS

7 February 1939.

Palestine Conference opens in London. Jews and Arabs reject proposition of jointly run country with independence in ten years. The British Parliament approves it – 30 Jews are MPs – and the following proposals were adopted: Jewish immigration to stop after five years, during which time 75,000 Jews would be admitted. This would give Jews one-third of the population. Land transfers from Arabs to Jews were to be regulated. Referred to as the 1939 White Paper.

3 September 1939.

Britain and France declare war against Germany. Mufti of Jerusalem reciprocates Hitler's offer of friendship.

11 April 1942.

Zionist conference at Biltmore Hotel, New York, demands Jewish State, covering the whole of Palestine.

30 June 1942.

German *Afrika Korps*, under Rommel, reaches el Alamein, 60 miles from Alexandria. German pincer movement from the north, after Ukraine advance, and from the south, via Egypt, becomes major threat to British position: the mandate and Jewish existence.

23 October 1942.

British Eighth Army, commanded by Montgomery, drives Rommel out of Egypt, at battle of el Alamein. By 12 November *Afrika Korps* is in full retreat.

8 May 1945.	V.E. Day.
13 August 1945.	President Truman requests immediate admission of 100,000 Jews to Palestine. The World Zionist Congress demands 1,000,000 displaced persons to be admitted. An estimated 6,000,000 Jews are considered to have been murdered by the Nazis.
20 August 1945.	Arab states warn : Jewish state means war.
15 April 1946.	British and French troops evacuate Lebanon.
29 April 1946.	Anglo-American Committee recommends independent State, with local and provincial autonomy. Rejected by Arabs and Jews.
25 May 1946.	Kingdom of Transjordan proclaimed. Emir Abdullah becomes King.
1 July 1946.	British Prime Minister, Clement Attlee, states in commons: "We have evidence of a very close link between the Jewish Agency and Haganah, and Haganah and Irgun."
22 July 1946.	Wing of King David Hotel, Jerusalem occupied by British Government, is blown up by Irgun terrorists. Many Jews among 91 killed.
September to December, 1946.	London Conference – Ernest Bevin, Foreign Secretary – is boycotted by Jews. Arabs propose Arab-dominated State. The Zionist Congress at Basel calls for a Jewish State.
7 February 1947.	Final British proposal: trustee administration over divided Arab and Jewish zones. This is rejected by Arabs and Jews.
2 April 1947.	Thirty-one years after accepting Sherif Hussein's terms for Palestine – independence as an Arab State – and thirty years after the Balfour declaration – "national home for the Jewish people" in Palestine – the British Government refers the problem to the United Nations.
29 November 1947.	United Nations General assembly votes for Palestine partition. Jerusalem to be under United Nations control. Approved by Jews. Rejected by Arabs.
17 December 1947.	Arab League states it will stop any division of Palestine by force.

January 1948.	Irgun and Stern terrorist activities, and inter-ethnic fighting between Arabs and Jews, both increase. This is followed by Arab flight, particularly from Haifa and Jaffa. Refugees enter Gaza strip, Lebanon, then Syria and Jordan. Jewish terrorism in North Africa and Middle East is carried out deliberately to antagonize local Arabs against Jews with whom, in many cases, they have co-existed for millenia, in order to enforce Jewish flight to Israel, and so increase the Jewish population.
14 May 1948.	British Mandate officially ends at midnight. State of Israel declared. Chaim Weizmann is president; David Ben-Gurion prime minister.
15 May 1948.	King Abdullah authorizes Jordanian Arab League to enter Palestine and Jerusalem Old City. The Arab League attacks Israel. This war lasts until July, 1949.
30 June 1948.	The last British troops – 1st Guards Brigade Group – leave Haifa.
17 September 1948.	United Nations mediator, Count Bernadotte assassinated by Jewish terrorists. Armistice lines upheld by France, Britain and United States.
14 December 1949.	Jerusalem internationalization ignored by Israel whose government moves to the New City.
24 April 1950.	Arab Jerusalem and Arab Palestine incorporated finally into Jordan.

Appendix Four

ORDER OF BATTLE: 1st GUARDS BRIGADE, OTHER FORMATIONS AND UNITS.

DATES.	FORMATION/REGIMENT	OFFICERS/W01s	LOCATION
17.10.45.	1st Guards Brigade arrives in Palestine.	Brigadier E.H. Goulburn Major M. Fitzalan-Howard Major W.S.I. Whitelaw Captain E. Imbert-Terry Captain M. Boyd Captain J.F. Lascelles	Nazareth (October 1945 – January 47)
17.10.45.	3rd Battalion Grenadier Guards.	O.C.: Lt. Col. P.T. Clifton. (Oct. 45–Jan. 47) O.C.: Lt.Col. H.R.H. Davies (Mar. 47–Apr. 48)* Adj: Capt. W.S. Dugdale (Oct. 45–Apr. 46) Adj: Capt. A.N. Breitmeyer (Apr. 46–Apr. 48)* RSM W.O.1. J. Baker (Oct. 45–Jul. 46) RSM W.O.1. R.E. Butler (Jul. 46–Sep. 46) RSM W.O.1. H.J. Wood (Sep. 46–Apr. 48)*	Hadera (October 1945 – January 47) Lydda (January 1947 – April 1948)
17.10.45.	3rd Battalion Coldstream Guards.	O.C.: Lt. Col. R.E.J.C. Coates (Oct. 45–Dec. 46) O.C.: Lt. Col. W.L. Steele (Dec. 46–Mar. 48)* Adj: Capt. J.T. Paget (Oct. 45–Mar. 48)* RSM W.O.1. H Joel (Oct. 45– Mar. 47) RSM W.O.1. C. Smy (Mar. 47–Mar. 48)*	Pardes Hanna: October 1945. Megiddo: December 1945 Acre: June 1946 Tel Aviv/Sarona/Petah Ticvah: January 1947 Nathanya: July 47 Sarafand: Sep 47 Zerqa: Oct 47 Nathanya: Nov 47 – March 1948.

*Dates relate only to Palestine.

17.10.45.	1st Battalion Welsh Guards.	O.C.: Lt. Col. R.B. Hodgkinson (Oct. 45–Feb. 47) Lt. Col. A.W.A. Malcolm (Feb. 47–Apr. 48)* Adj: Capt. J.M. Spencer-Smith (Oct. 45–Apr. 46) Adj: Capt. P.R. Leuchars (Apr. 46–Apr. 48)* RSM W.O.1. A. Rees (Oct. 45–Apr. 48)*	Pardes Hanna: October 1945 Tiberias: Nov 45–January 1947 Rosh Pinna: Oct 46 – January 47 Metullah: October 1945 – January 47. Sarafand: January 1947 Beit Lid: June 1947 Lydda: September 47 Beit Lid: November 47–April 1948.
April 46–May 48.	1st (Guards) Parachute Battalion.	O.C.: Lt. Col. E.J.B. Nelson Adj: Captain M.H. Jenkins	Various locations including Citrus House, Tel Aviv.
1.1.47.	1st Guards Brigade.	Brigadier J.N.R. Moore + Major I.W.Gore-Langton+ Major L. Dawnay Captain P.F.F. Brutton Capt. The Hon. D. Erskine+ Captain A.J. Gibson-Watt Captain S.C. Tilleard + + Succeeded by : Brigadier G.F. Johnson Major S. Bolitho Captain N.S. Kearsley Captain D. Marsh	Petah Ticvah: January 1947 – July 1947 Nathanya: July 1947 – September 1947 Petah Ticvah: Sep. 47 – Oct 47 Transjordan: Oct – Dec 1947 Nathanya: Dec. 1947 – April 1948 Haifa: April 1948 – June 1948.
12.3.47.	1st Battalion Irish Guards.	O.C.: Lt. Col. D. M.L. Gordon-Watson Adj: Major J.W. Berridge RSM: W.O.1. G. Howe	Athlet: March 1947 (Under 6th Airborne Div.) Khassa Camp, near Gaza: May 47 (61 Armd Bde. 1 Div.) Jerusalem: July 47 (8th Inf. Bde) Khassa Camp: Oct 1947 Rosh Pinna/Safad: Jan – May 48 Haifa: May – June 1948.
10.5.47.	The Life Guards.	O.C.: Lt. Col. F.F.B. St George Adj: Capt. D.L.S. Hodson RCM: W.O.1. J. Hyland	Khassa Camp: May 1947 (Under direct command 1st Division) – May 48.
10.2.48	1st Battalion Grenadier Guards.	O.C.: Lt. Col. C.M.F. Deakin Adj: Capt. J.F.D. Johnston RSM: W.O.L. AJ Spratley	Lydda and Haifa: Feb 48 – June 1948.
1.3.48.	1st Battalion Coldstream Guards.	O.C.: Lt. Col. J. Chandos-Pole Adj: Capt. R.J.D.E. Buckland RSM: W.O.1. R.W. Smith	Nathanya: March – April 1948 Haifa: April – June 1948.

Index

Williams, Major E.G. (Welsh Guards), 198
Windham, Judge R. (later Chief Justice), 80
Wolf, General Karl (S.S.), 192
Wolf, Peter, 136
Wood, A. (Air Ministry Works Department), 74, 87, 100
Wood, Regimental Sergeant Major (W.O.I) H.J. (Grenadier Guards), 203
Woodhead Commission, 25, 29
World Zionist Conference, 25

X-Command, 12, 13, 15, 23, 30, 34, 36, 37, 41, 46–48, 52, 65, 67, 73, 77, 78, 87, 89, 138

Yalta, 26
Yishuv, 12, 31, 35, 46, 49, 69, 82, 88, 94, 101, 102, 163, 179, 185
Yizernitzky, Yitzhak (Shamir), 20, 50, 160, 162, 170
Young, Lieutenant G.D. (Welsh Guards), 75

Zerqa, 59, 203
Zetler, Yehoshua, 160, 161
Zikhron Ya'aqov, 157, 158
Zita, Empress of Austria-Hungary, 194
Zwern the tailor, 93